Tom Slater is a graduate of the Burwood Teachers College and Monash University, Melbourne, Australia. Since 1969 he has been involved in the camps program of the Scripture Union Victoria and is currently the Schools' Work Co-ordinator. He was largely instrumental in developing the Coolamatong camp complex in Gippsland, eastern Victoria, an innovative centre of school camping and holiday camps.

His first book, *The Camping Book*, was published in 1976. He is married to June and they have two children.

To
June, Peter and Jocelyn
without whose help this book
would not have been written

The Temporary Community

ORGANIZED CAMPING FOR URBAN SOCIETY

Tom Slater

An Albatross Book

© Tom Slater 1984

Published in Australia by
Albatross Books
PO Box 320, Sutherland
NSW 2232, Australia

First edition 1984

National Library of Australia
Cataloguing-in-Publication data

   Slater, Tom, 1943–
   The temporary community.

   ISBN 0 86760 013 6

   1. Camps. 2. Camp counselors. Title.
796.54'22

Typeset by Rochester Photosetting Service, Sydney
Printed by Singapore National Printers

Contents

	Foreword	7
	Introduction	11
	Author's Note	13

Part One: The Philosophy of the Temporary Community

1.	**A Camping Philosophy:** Do we need it?	17
2.	**Popular Camping Theory:** Is it adequate for today?	27
3.	**Organized Camping:** What makes it tick?	41
4.	**The Key to Organized Camping:** Is the 'temporary community' crucial?	48
5.	**The Temporary Community:** What are its essential elements?	57

Part Two: The Practice of the Temporary Community

6.	**Planning a Camp:** What are the basic principles?	71
7.	**Programming with a Purpose:** What are the main elements?	79
8.	**The Art of Leadership:** How can we identify and develop it?	91
9.	**Authority, Discipline and Leadership Styles:** How do we maintain discipline in camp?	105
10.	**Values and the Temporary Community:** Are there some guidelines?	121

11.	**Camping and Education:**	
	How serious are we?	**137**
12.	**Family Camping:**	
	What does it offer?	**146**

Part Three: **'Coolamatong' —**
a Philosophy in Practice

13.	**Camp Coolamatong:**	
	How is it distinctive?	**159**
14.	**The Farm Camp Development:**	
	How did the design reflect the philosophy?	**168**
15.	**Relationships in the Community:**	
	How do they develop?	**177**

Part Four: **The Temporary Community**
and the Church

16.	**The Theory of Christian Camping:**	
	Is it relevant?	**191**
17.	**Camping and Christian Education:**	
	How can camping strengthen the church?	**203**
18.	**Camping and Christian Outreach:**	
	What are the benefits?	**212**
19.	**Leadership on Christian Camps:**	
	What are the practical challenges?	**226**

| **Appendix A:** | **Defining Camping** | **241** |

| **Appendix B:** | **The Management Structure** | |
| | **of Coolamatong** | **248** |

| **Appendix C:** | **Some Guidelines to Health** | |
| | **and Safety** | **250** |

| | **Index** | **254** |

Foreword

MY FIRST REACTION on reading this book was to feel sorry that I am now probably too old to be a camper at a camp run by Tom Slater. This is no armchair theorist speaking, but a seasoned practitioner. He's in touch with what is really happening.

But the book is considerably more than a collection of recollected experiences and rules of thumb. My second reaction was to feel sorry for myself (again!) because this book was unavailable when, many years ago, I was more heavily engaged in running camps and in training camp leaders and directors than I am now. How I struggled to achieve that important mix between encouraging the development of an integrated philosophy of camping on the one hand and giving help at the nuts and bolts level on the other. How I used to wish I had more time to explore larger trends and findings in the international camping scene, to avoid becoming unreflectively locked in to local traditions of camping.

Tom Slater has done this and kept the canvas broad. The result is that we are not only given realistic advice on many details such as safety and personal counselling, but we are also given critical principles which equip us to evaluate such trends as, for example, school camps. The promotion of school camps needs careful scrutiny, because it is so often predicated on the assumption that school teachers are naturally suited to running camps. It is part of that same professional arrogance which often prompts them to look down on youth workers trained by a different professional route.

What is not realized is that a person trained primarily for classroom teaching can easily become addicted to the paradigm of formal instruction and carry it with him wherever he goes. Many school camps are a formal timetable transposed into a residential setting, where the teachers staffing the camp are relatively unskilled or unconcerned with fostering relationships and maintaining social order in the expanded learning environment they have taken on.

This is criticism from the inside: *I* am teacher-trained and I train teachers. To the extent that I am aware of our professional failings at this point, it is because of a parallel involvement in voluntary youth work and camping. This has forced me to become more sensitive to the differences between various kinds of learning environment. In particular I have found that the different factors involved in voluntary, informal contexts as against compulsory, formal contexts need close study. Part of the genius of camping is its suitability for the voluntary investment of the self in rewarding experiences of nature, solitariness and community. These are not the kinds of learning which are readily picked up by school exams!

Nor are they inevitable outcomes of 'going on a camp'. As the author convincingly argues, simple relocation in an outdoor setting doesn't necessarily guarantee even 'outdoor education', let alone new discoveries of self or community. I think of the man I saw in a camping ground unloading his lawn mower to trim the site he had hired! Suburbia can have a very thick skin.

Slater's notion of camping as the creation of a 'temporary community' is seminal and plausible, especially when he couples it with the proper use of outdoor settings and educational opportunities. The adjective 'temporary' puts a realistic brake on the euphoria of some theorists who make extravagant claims for the value-changing potential of camps, whereas the noun 'community' sets a bracing agenda for styles of camping most likely to minister to the multiplying needs of youth and families in our vast and fractured societies.

This book will fill a serious gap in the abundance of manuals on camping because it starts asking questions at the right level. It does *not* assume the unchallengeable value of anything to which the camping label is attached. Nor does it allow a rather considerable range of questionable practices to go unchallenged. It is fashionable, for example, to talk about conservation and environmental concern, but Slater shows that camping may well fail to reflect these values, despite being for many an alleged return to nature. Similarly the opportunity for close relationships may be missed, or may be abused by unethical adult pressure. Slater has wise words to say about each of these issues.

To say much more about the book would be like telling the reader how the plot ends! I must not steal any more of its valuable thunder. But it needs saying that Slater is a Christian. He is honest about the fact that this has informed his analysis. But he doesn't parade the fact constantly, and I believe *anyone* involved in camping, whatever his persuasion, will identify with the sane illumination which Slater brings to the field. His vision is timely and up-to-date.

Brian Hill,
Murdoch University, Perth

Brian Hill is Professor of Education at Murdoch University in Western Australia. In 1983 he chaired a government Youth Task Force whose report is entitled *Co-ordination of Youth Affairs in Western Australia.*

Introduction

THIS BOOK IS WRITTEN with a wide audience in mind — outdoor educators, classroom teachers, community youth workers and others who run camping programs for young and old. This may be for only a week or two each year — there are still very few camping professionals. Most camp leaders are volunteers or 'amateurs' when it comes to organized camping. Yet all leaders, whatever their background and experience, confront a wide range of situations and issues which demand a controlled, considered response.

There is also the large number of people involved in camping programs sponsored by Christian organizations and churches. Those who have read *The Camping Book* (Anzea Publishers, 1976), now out of print, will no doubt be looking for specific principles of Christian camping. These are dealt with in the fourth section of this book.

In order not to distract or unnecessarily annoy readers who do not commence with any Christian assumptions, explicit Christian comment has been confined almost entirely to this last section. But as Dr Norman Currie, Director-General of Education in the State of Victoria, Australia, said in 1983: 'Talk about value-free education is arrant nonsense.' The same is true of camping theory.

It is simply not possible to offer any serious view about organized camping without expressing one's values: about ecology, lifestyle, leadership, safety, relationships and a host of other subjects. Inevitably, then, my own Christian presuppositions are reflected throughout the book. There is no question whether they should be there — it could not be otherwise. Whether they are valid or not is for the reader to decide.

There is another way in which the book is written for a wide audience. I have attempted to begin with principles that will stand the scrutiny and stimulate the thinking of planners and educationalists. At the same time I have sought to apply the arguments to real-life camping situations — to 'where the rubber meets the road', where voluntary camp leaders are devoting their holidays to the needs of others in the down-to-earth, day-and-night sharing of their lives with campers.

Perhaps this goal seems overly optimistic. But the aim throughout has been to inspire the reader to recognize and grasp the privilege of camp leadership. The measure of the book's success will not so much be seen in knowledgeable leaders as in satisfied campers who have been stretched, encouraged, taught, excited and challenged — and, above all, wholly cared for.

Author's Note

Throughout this book the personal pronoun 'he' is used where either gender is implied. The reason is simple and, I hope, acceptable to most readers.

Because the English language has no neutral third-person-singular personal pronoun, there are only two ways of giving balance. The first is to use expressions like 'his/hers' and 'his or hers'. This produces sentences like: 'He/she recognizes what others can offer him/her, as well as what he/she can give', and 'This enables the leader to be himself/herself without trying to change his/her personality or behaviour — to be something that he/she really isn't' (Chapter 8).

The second is to alternate the use of 'he' and 'she' throughout the book, giving the reader the problem of determining whether the choice in each case is significant or arbitrary.

The alternatives are either unbearably clumsy, disconcertingly specific or plain misleading. Since the whole style of the book depends heavily on examples, the decision was made to use 'his or her' from time to time, as in normal speech, but to opt for the traditional generic use of 'he' wherever stylistic reasons favoured it. Literary pedantry rather than male chauvinism is the root problem.

Part One:
The Philosophy of the Temporary Community

1
A Camping Philosophy:
Do we need it?

I SIT AT MY DESK and try to make sense of the column of figures in front of me. Typewriters rattle in the background. The intercom leaps into life in the adjoining office.

I reach for some paper to jot down a memo about some budget figures for a Council meeting. I'm conscious of a slight feeling of physical discomfort. Although I'm sitting in a comfortable enough swivel chair, it's not quite right for my angular frame. I lean on the arm-rests, straighten up, relocate myself and look around.

On the wall, a map: a bright patch of blue lakes and green forest areas. In an instant I'm four hours' drive away at a favourite camping place. My eyes travel to a photo on another wall: me in that old yellow slicker, with three kids hanging over the side of a boat, slicing through the chop in a stiff breeze. I can almost feel the wind on my face as I warm to the recollection of a good day's sailing.

Most offices have holiday photos on the wall: the postcard from last year's trip, a poster of a forest or seashore, a colour print of the family or of friends — reminders of good times in the other world 'out there'. It's strange how long we make these temporary experiences last. They might be brief, but they come to have a significance out of proportion to the time they take — points of personal stability and self-realization away from the workaday world where individual identity is so often submerged or lost.

Images of camping
Stock images of camping spring easily to mind:
* A crackling campfire, ringed by little tents, on the shore of a lake.

* A look of apprehension, combined with heart-stopping excitement, as a small girl comes slinging down the flying fox at high speed.
* The stillness of a forest, broken only by the approaching shouts of a group of children on a treasure hunt.
* A sing-along around a fireplace, snow on the ground outside.
* The plop of a stone in the water, flicked absent-mindedly by a camper as he sits with his back to a tree, thinking about the father he can't get on with back at home.

These are some of the common images of camping — images, I suggest, that come easily to all of us. For camping has an enviable record for providing the young, the bored, the lonely, the adventure-seeker and the individual family with valuable experiences not normally available at home.

There may be bad experiences, too, of course, but even an ordinary camping experience can become a highlight in the mind's eye. For the enthusiast, the 'simple joys of camping' are praised almost religiously. Past moments become invested with an air of enchantment and significance.

Perhaps such enthusiasm for camping exists *just because* camping has always been a holiday activity. Although nomadic people appear to 'go camping' as a permanent condition, camping in our society is a temporary experience outside our normal lifestyle. More people look forward to holidays to come than wait impatiently for them to end. Camping is seen as relief from work, a means of 'getting away from it all'.

Little can dampen the keen camper's enthusiasm, the worst misfortunes becoming the subject of fond reminiscing. It's a standing joke that rain follows our friends' camper-van wherever it goes. Drought-breaking deluges seem to follow its route from one part of the country to another. But each year the van is cheerfully hitched up again, and the family heads off for another fortnight of sleepless nights and wet days.

What the pundits say

If holiday campers think that camping is 'worth the trouble', camping books certainly support the idea. A rapid glance through the standard texts turns up some instructive expressions from a diverse group of camping writers. The most common thread is that camping is *fun*. But there is more to it than that, as these quotations show.

The first reflects enthusiasm and conviction:

> There is something to appeal to almost everyone in camping . . . a satisfying experience that finds no parallel in the sophisticated make-believe world of modern towns and cities.[1]

The next writer becomes almost poetic. The 'people of the little tents' are described in heroic terms as:

> those men and women who feel the call of the wilderness, who have struggled out of 'the cradle of custom' to follow that call to journey to a lonely land.[2]

This sort of wistfulness pales beside the positive euphoria of the following lines:

> There's something about being with people who give themselves to organized camping that is downright enchanting. No matter in which camp they are found, they'll be the same — happy, genial folks, those wonderful folks who make up camp staffs.[3]

Such extravagance is uncommon, but a settled conviction about the good things offered by camping still comes through most camping books. Compare this comment from a basic text on outdoor education:

> Camping may constitute a partial answer to some of the youth problems of today.[4]

And again:

> The camp is rich in opportunity for sensitizing the camper to the deep meanings and values of life in the group, in the camp community and in the universe of nature.[5]

These camping writers picture camping as an activity which yields deeply satisfying and enjoyable personal experiences to participants. But not all camping experiences are as good as each other. Being a leader on an organized camp can be very demanding. We could just as easily list some other camping images, like having a snake in your sleeping bag, putting up with the camper who steals other people's belongings, or finding a role for the leader who can't get on with anyone.

Recipe versus philosophy

Good camping experiences don't just happen automatically. A number of prior conditions must exist before we can expect success:

(a) *Good leaders*

This means being trained for the job, with the necessary leadership skills, knowing how to handle discipline, and command respect.

(b) *Good planning*

This means not relying on last minute brainstorms, but having sound advance planning, with time for detailed preparation.

(c) *Good relationships*

You may have all the facilities, skills and plans in the world and still have a camp which is marred by bad relationships.

(d) *Good weather*

Almost totally unpredictable, but keep hoping!

(e) *Good environment*

Important for most camps.

Perhaps this looks like a fairly simple 'recipe' for success. Camping offers obvious rewards for modern urbanized people. We know that the ingredients of success include good leadership, planning, environment and so on. The formula seems straightforward. Perhaps we should be able to move straight on to methodology — the 'how to' of leadership, planning and programming.

What is a camping philosophy anyway, and why do we need it?

Developing a camping philosophy

All that we have talked about so far is part of *camping theory*. It includes common perceptions about the content, value and conditions of effective camping. Camping theory encompasses all sorts of camping philosophies and methodologies. Camping theory is the sum total of what serious camping exponents have claimed about the why and how of camping.

The camping philosophy of an individual or an organization is a product of knowledge, experience and, hopefully, thoughtful reflection as well.

The development of an organization's philosophy is illustrated in Chapter 6. It is essential that people involved in organized camping — whether they are group leaders, camp directors or administrators — develop their own camping philosophy. We now consider why this is so.

Philosophy at the 'micro' level

A camping philosophy is individually applied by camp leaders and teams of leaders. It has quite specific and practical implications. Consider the case of the humble cassette player.

If you are involved in a camping program, you will know that some camper on every camp is sure to bring along a portable cassette and want to carry it around everywhere. But it won't be quietly playing in his or her ear — it will be turned up to full volume!

I once transported some Scouts by boat to a remote camping spot. This was to be 'a real camping experience', so the chosen place was far away from any town where diversion might be sought. To increase the sense of adventure, the campers had to wade out to the boat to get on board. Once at the point of arrival, there was no choice either: the campers had to jump into the water and swim (or wade) ashore.

I was dismayed when one seventeen-year-old clambered aboard clutching a cassette player as big as a briefcase. It was turned on as soon as he found a place to get out of the wind and was still going full strength when he leapt into the water at our destination. There may be no significance in the fact, but he appeared to derive little enjoyment from his piece of indispensable equipment.

What *is* the appropriate response to campers who clearly plan to attach their right ear to a radio or cassette for the length of their stay in camp? It is not good enough to simply act or react as a matter of instinct. Shouting at the wayward camper or confiscating the offending machine will only alienate him or her completely. Ignoring the problem, even *if* you don't mind the music being played, may ruin the camp for someone else. Indeed, in an important sense, it might ruin the camp for the camper as well. An adequate camping theory must be developed to assess such commonplace situations confronting the camp leader.

On the other hand we can be too simplistic about the issues. Camping theory is also *complex*. Again, take the example of the cassette player:

* How important is it to the total camping experience to cut ourselves off from the trappings of our materialistic, technological culture?

* How important are the rights of other campers to quietness? When does the individual have to conform to the group?
* What if the cassette player is the only security a particular camper has — the only thing between him or her and the 'terror of the wild'? When is it right to take away such emotional crutches?
* Would banning the use of the machine put our relationship with the camper at risk?

Such considerations must be weighed up against *other* relevant considerations. We therefore must decide on our *priorities* as well. One leader may decide that the natural environment is so important to the idea of camping that any electronic or 'packaged' entertainment should be banned. If campers don't agree to these terms, they needn't come. Another leader may believe that getting this particular camper away from home for a while is sufficiently paramount to compromise the purity of the natural setting for a while to include him or her in the total experience. These are valid alternatives that must be evaluated according to the particular circumstance. Camping philosophy is as specific and practical as that.

Philosophy at the 'macro' level

It is not enough for individual leaders to develop their own approach, however. Constant review of an organization's philosophy is always necessary for the continued relevance and quality of its program. Changes in social patterns and people's needs on one hand and an organization's personnel and resources on the other demand regular re-evaluation of objectives and programs.

At least seven features of the contemporary scene are a challenge to a review of camping philosophy on a broad scale:

1. The bias towards 'practical' questions

I suppose that many camping people are activists by nature — practical people who would rather 'do' than 'think'. Unfortunately, however, people occasionally even disparage the process of questioning fundamentals at all with an attitude of 'Let's get on with the real business of camping'. Many of these are successful camp operators. They know how to run a camp well and can organize programs at the drop of a hat on '300 ways to cut down on maintenance', 'keeping staff happy', 'pruning the catering budget', or even 'dealing with problem kids'.

The difficulty in getting camping people to evaluate their theory at all is confirmed by a survey of the literature of camping. Camping literature is long on skills, programs, facilities, activities, administration, buildings, site development and even counselling techniques, but short on books which seriously explore, at any real depth, the basis for organized camping.

Notice that the word 'practical' in the above heading is in inverted commas. It is an illusion to think that the 'real business of camping' is practical, while supposing that having a basic theory is an optional extra. The fact is that a sound camping philosophy is supremely practical: it provides the necessary basis for good practice. 'The French Revolution did not begin with the storming of the Bastille, but in the libraries of the philosophers'![6]

2. The growth of camping in education
While school camping programs have mushroomed in Australia in recent years, the case for school camping is rarely argued, except within a narrowly defined context of 'outdoor education'. This is a cause for concern at several levels:

(a) A residential activity
Schools are involved with children for a limited number of hours each day. The residential nature of camping raises a whole range of questions: Why *should* certain activities be run residentially at all? What are the ethical implications for teachers? How can values be best communicated in a residential situation?

Camping experiences are not merely extensions of classroom education. They are different in kind, involving value judgements about the way in which a living-together situation should be structured. Yet, while manuals on safety and activity leadership are written and pored over, these larger questions are rarely explored.

(b) Quality of school camps
There is a wide variation in the quality of school camping and in the level of experience of teachers required to run them. There *are* some excellent programs, but in other cases some school camps do little more than entertain students.

Teachers need to agree not only on the reasons for the camp, but on their specific objectives, their expectations of student behaviour on camp and on ways in which the camp may be enriched as a truly socializing experience.

(c) Cost of school camps
Parents are asked to pay considerable amounts of money to send their children away on school camps. Some parents cannot afford it at all, while no doubt many others part with the money without protest because they don't want to 'make a fuss' or have their children feeling left out of it. After all, 'all the other kids are going'. The question is not whether school camps are justified, but whether there is any real attempt to justify them to parents and on what grounds.

3. Economic and social changes
If it is cheaper for a boy from Toronto to fly to Europe for the summer than to go to summer camp in Ontario, there is a problem for the traditional camp. If a Victorian girl has been on a costly school tour of Central Australia in October, there is a problem for the church youth department who hope to have her on their holiday camp in January.

4. Questions of social conscience
Wherever camping takes the form of relatively high-cost activities, or of programs dependent on the investment of millions of dollars in real estate and sophisticated facilities, we must question the return on investment. Is that sort of camping really justified by its benefits? Where camping programs appear to take no account of the needs of the poor, the disabled, an ethnic minority or the unemployed, we must allow ourselves to be disturbed until we come to terms with these challenges.

5. Sociological changes affecting the family
One does not need a strong Judaeo-Christian framework of belief to recognize what almost any teacher can testify to: despite the claims of trendy moralists and the shift in social attitudes, the breakdown of traditional marriage and family patterns has produced emotional chaos in the lives of untold thousands of children. Many children are growing up not only with the traumatic effects of separation and divorce, but virtually without any concrete models of fatherhood or of a happy marriage.

Many single parents are struggling to survive, with fragile families under great pressure. This should caution us against an organizational pattern where we remove children from their families for camping experiences. Such practice has done little to help children integrate the camp experience with life at home. And it certainly hasn't actively built family life or given people exciting and memorable experiences as families.

6. Urbanization and technology
The alienation between urbanized people in a technological society and the world of nature, with which human beings are contiguous and on which they depend, is profound. Living in' and exploring the outdoors, being exposed to its immensity and danger and enjoying its serenity contributes greatly to the mental and physical wholeness of all of us.

We thus should question the relative value of camping experiences which fail to take advantage of the environment. There are camp-sites where campers have easy access to local shopping centres. There are bush locations where virtually all meals are cooked and eaten indoors. There are health authorities which insist on dish-washing machines in camp kitchens. There are school camping programs without any intentional outdoor education emphasis at all. We are obliged to ask whether much of organized camping 'measures up' to the needs of an urbanized population.

The increased mobility of today's society is another pressure. There are a number of varied and valid responses. One might be to offer camping programs which incorporate travel as a basic feature. Another might be to create a deliberate and quite self-conscious alternative — a 'back-to-nature, simpler lifestyle' camp program.

The geographical spread of cities puts pressure on old, established camp-sites which were formerly 'in the country'. Yet while these sites may no longer provide the sort of adventure and rural 'feel' that they once did, they may provide an ideal place for a first camping experience, or for localized weekend camping where distance is a deterrent. Again, many sites need up-grading to be really suitable for family camps. There are certainly economic implications for organizations which wish to remain relevant, as well as economic challenges to their viability.

7. Use of the environment
Growing consciousness of the environmental crisis brought about by unbridled exploitation brings with it a dual challenge. There is

the challenge to *educate* people *in* the natural environment about issues of ecological survival. With this goes the whole process of helping people to *value* the natural environment and to use it creatively for their personal health and wholeness — to become familiar with it and at home in it.

Ultimately we must face the question of whether there will be an environment to enjoy in the future at all. Responsible camping authorities will minimize as far as possible the impact of camping on the natural environment.

Making a beginning

There is a case for taking a deeper look at popular camping theory. Part of our case rests on an analysis of the status of camping in society at this particular time. However, we also need to periodically analyse and evaluate our fundamental reasons for doing everything we do. Unless we review our basic ideas about camping, new generations of leaders will simply continue to reiterate old methods regardless of their relevance to contemporary society.

Worse than irrelevance, however, is *abuse*. Organized group camping involves the intentional creation of quite deliberate social settings. These have the potential for good or bad, the capacity to produce first-rate or second-rate experiences. The bored, the lonely, the homesick, the ridiculed, the angry and the unsafe exist alongside the 'happy campers' of popular image.

A first step will be to analyse popular camping theory and to identify the key issues to be considered by anyone who wants a sound basis on which to build a proper camping program.

1   Jack Cox, *Modern Camping*, Stanley Paul, London 1968, p.17
2   Paddy Pallin, *Bushwalking and Camping*, Sydney 1959, p.6
3   Floyd and Pauline Todd, *Camping for Christian Youth*, Baker Book House, Grand Rapids 1980, p.130
4   Julian W. Smith, Reynold E. Carlson, Hugh B. Masters, George W. Donaldson, *Outdoor Education*, Prentice Hall, 2nd edition, p.129
5   Hedley S. Dimock (ed.), *Administration of the Modern Camp*, Association Press, New York 1969, p.37
6   J. Rinzema, *The Sexual Revolution*, Eerdmans, Grand Rapids 1972, p.23

2
Popular Camping Theory:
Is it adequate for today?

THE OTHER DAY I came across a letter from a seventeen-year-old camper. I remember Linda well, not just because she was full of vitality and something of an extrovert, but also because she was so forthright in her opinions. She banged a drum for a number of causes, in her letter describing herself as an idealistic radical who wished to change the world overnight.

Talking about the effect of coming away on camp, Linda wrote:

> The camp was worthwhile and the activities were fun, but something happens when you're living for a week with people you only usually see through the day. It's good — there's a sort of warmth and closeness that's difficult to explain. This was inspired mainly by the environment and the atmosphere of the camp.
> It cleared my head a little of what I'm not exactly sure, but being away from everything I'm so familiar with and secure in gave me a peculiar freedom to think. Being in the same surroundings and limiting your thinking hinders your brain's advancement somehow — if you know what I mean.

This statement, a personal expression of the effect of a camping experience on a girl, is evidence of the value of camping.

So far there seems little reason to question this. Certainly we need to be relevant to the needs of people. We need to train leaders. We even need to think about our aims once in a while. These things take time, but at least we know camping 'works'. Being outdoors is great, camping is basically fun and we can learn a lot in the process. We can assume all these things — or can we?

Unfortunately we cannot. When we look at the main elements of popular camping, we can't 'simply assume' anything. We can't even assume every camping experience will be fun — let alone valuable. We have to go back to basics.

Basic principles are always harder to think about than practical things. Making a model aeroplane is obviously more fun for most of us than studying aerodynamics. But if nobody had studied aerodynamics, home-made aeroplanes wouldn't fly.

'Well then', you may reply, 'basic principles are important, but only a few have to understand them. The hobbyist doesn't *have* to understand aerodynamics. I don't *have* to understand camping theory. I'm just a small group leader; I'm just a camp cook. As long as the camp organizers, administrators and directors do their homework on principles, I can just concentrate on the practical task before me.'

Unfortunately camping is about people, not balsa wood. It's about values, not designs. It's about relationships, not just cutting out and glueing. And the tent leader isn't like an aircraft modeller — he is actually a part of the thing that's being 'made'. What's more, the tent leader (or cook) can't escape from the problems. The modeller can turn off the light and shut the door, returning to the task when he's not so tired or frustrated. But the camp leader can't walk away from the problem camper.

Every camp leader must appreciate and share the working philosophy of the camp. An organized camp is a subtle network of relationships. It is a dynamic mix of leadership objectives and camper expectations. It is affected externally by weather and equipment, and internally by the currents of pleasure and frustration, jealousy and generosity which ebb and flow among the participants. The quality of any camp community depends on leaders working to a united purpose and not against each other.

Three common assumptions about camping are made by various camping writers:
* the ability of camping to provide good experiences for the participants
* the value-forming potential of camping
* the emphasis on the outdoors as the context for camping activities.

We must now examine each of these assumptions. In the process we will find that each of them raises a number of fundamental issues.

The provision of good experiences
Linda said in her letter that her camp was 'worthwhile' and the activities were 'fun'. Was this a foregone conclusion? Camping in

our society has traditionally been a purely voluntary activity — it has only survived because people keep wanting it. One might be forgiven, then, for assuming that to experience such deep satisfactions one needs merely to 'go camping' with the appropriate equipment, congenial company and a good map.

But when it comes to organized group camping on a larger scale, it is not so simple. All too easily we are apt to make assumptions about the probability of all our campers having good experiences. There are several reasons for caution about this:

1. We don't all enjoy the same things

Whether a person regards a particular experience as being worthwhile or enjoyable depends on a whole range of factors.

A group of teenage campers made a night trip on the Gippsland Lakes. For two-and-a-half hours they charted their course through narrow channels, past sandbars and islands and across large stretches of open lake with only the boat's compass, the navigational beacons around the lakes and the knowledge of the helmsman to guide them. A few were entranced by the beauty of the whole trip, which began as a magnificent sunset faded and ended in water so quiet and still you could see the stars reflected in it. Some, however, were oblivious to both those aspects and derived their enjoyment from flirting with each other under cover of darkness. This last group, it seems, could have enjoyed the experience equally in a pin-ball parlour.

All the campers enjoyed themselves, but for rather different reasons. What they thought was 'good' about the experience depended on their personal interests, dispositions at the time and level of maturity. Experience is subjective. If we are honest, we will admit that we cannot always please everyone.

ISSUES RAISED:
☐ Does it matter how people enjoy themselves, as long as they do enjoy themselves?
☐ Can planning take account of the differing needs and interests of campers? Should we cater for everyone?

2. We don't believe all experiences are as valuable as each other

In the case of the night cruise, some of the campers enjoyed themselves differently from the way in which the leaders would have hoped. For those leaders, the mere fact that 'they all enjoyed themselves' was less than a satisfactory result. Because they were conscious of the special enjoyment available (in the form of the beautiful surroundings and the excitement of night navigation), the leaders were disappointed with the preoccupation of some of the campers with each other. It robbed them of a genuine appreciation of their surroundings, an experience which they might well never have again.

Readers will undoubtedly feel very differently from one another about this particular example. What's wrong with a few teenagers flirting in the dark anyway? Who says they should be more interested in sunsets, or finding their way in the dark? What would you expect of normal kids?

However, we cannot altogether dodge the thrust of this issue. If we don't believe some experiences are 'better' than others, we should not be in the business of organizing camping programs. Why do we believe it is better for Billy to be canoeing than smashing windows? At a camp on a hot afternoon, we really need such personal conviction if we are to make Billy get up from his shady spot and go for a ten-kilometre paddle.

ISSUES RAISED:
☐ Do we have criteria for sorting out what we think are good, not-so-good or better experiences?
☐ Does it matter whether the camper thinks an experience is good or not? If so, how much?

3. We're not always sure what makes a group experience good
Some of the enjoyment of camping is due to intangible factors. This is one reason why it is so difficult to reproduce the 'group feeling' of a camp at a camp reunion. It may be exactly the same group of people, but the discontinuity between the reunion and the actual camping experience makes it impossible to reproduce the feeling which characterized the camp itself.

It cannot be assumed that what worked last year will necessarily work as well this year. We have not always developed adequate criteria for evaluating our activities and therefore we lack criteria by which to plan for further 'good' experiences or the elimination of 'bad' ones.

It is often difficult to say why a particular camp or camp event was good, or even whether it really was or not. Linda said in her letter: 'It's good — there's a sort of warmth and closeness that's difficult to explain.' We can affirm something as being worthwhile, yet find it impossible to fully interpret that personal feeling ourselves, let alone explain it to others. It's the sort of statement that is so often followed by 'you know what I mean'. The answer to that is 'yes' or 'no', according to whether one feels that one can identify a similar experience in one's past.

In the final analysis, we can't be sure why something 'clicked'. What is our response to this? To some extent we can reduce the mystery element by more thorough and perceptive analysis of the camp or experience in question. But too much introspection won't help. We kid ourselves if we think we are capable of manipulating people and events to reproduce the exact result we have achieved before.

ISSUES RAISED:
☐ Are we realistic about the possibilities of failure we can't account for? Leader morale depends on it.
☐ Have we developed adequate criteria for evaluating our camps? If not, we won't learn from our experiences, positive or negative.
☐ Do we assume that what 'worked' last year will work this year? Next time, we may be disappointed.

4. We can't guarantee good experiences
There is something unrepeatable about a really significant human experience. We have just established that we can't be sure of reproducing a special experience, simply because we're not exactly sure of what made it special. The uniqueness, the 'one-off' nature of a significant moment, is something extra. In a science experiment we can set up more or less identical situations and gain a predictable result. In life, circumstances are not so easily controlled and human responses not so predictable.

Our inability to guarantee good experiences, however, is not simply a result of our inability to precisely control circumstances and moods. The English scholar and writer C.S. Lewis talks in his autobiography about the elusiveness of joy whenever he consciously pursued it.[1] There is a mysterious element in human existence. When we seek to repeat an experience of special satisfaction for its own sake, it tends to escape us just when we thought we had it in our grasp.

Some leaders on organized camps endeavour to produce a high

level of emotional satisfaction in the group as a whole, and then are disappointed and soured by their failure to achieve an 'emotional high' which they have achieved previously. My own observation is that the kind of group feeling deliberately and consciously induced is generally inferior to that which emerges unselfconsciously in the course of a camp.

ISSUES RAISED:
□ What sort of satisfaction is it proper to seek, or to encourage campers to look for?
□ Are there any conditions which we can create which will predispose campers to the best experiences, even if we can't guarantee them?

5. Group living won't all be enjoyable
When we go camping together, we soon discover that there are problems inherent in the social nature of organized camping. Two people I knew always had a running battle on their camping trips because one, to the annoyance of his friend, spat out his toothpaste right next to the tent, while the other had the unfortunate habit of relieving himself in the vicinity of the tent during the night!

Paddy Pallin describes the scene when unprepared campers keep others awake at night, removing sticks and stones from under their sleeping bags which hadn't seemed worth bothering about when setting up camp! These are the kinds of conflicts which result from the individual idiosyncracies of campers.

On a more serious level, we have to be prepared to encounter behaviour and expectations which may not be merely idiosyncratic, but *anti-social*. Unless camping experiences are provided only for people whose co-operation can be guaranteed, this is a fact of life, not only warning us against utopian expectations, but requiring us to deal with anti-social tendencies which may unexpectedly emerge.

Odd behaviour. Anti-social behaviour. What about normal *human* behaviour? We're all a mixture of generosity and selfishness, good humour and anger. Human beings are by nature both social and independent creatures. When we structure a group camping experience, we have to take account not just of the more obvious anti-social tendencies which may emerge in particular campers, but also of the more subtle selfish instincts which are part of all of us.

This is of considerable significance at the leadership level. It is no good having campers waiting interminably for a turn at an activity while leaders are using the equipment. You can't have a communal experience when leaders adopt different behavioural standards or set different objectives. You won't communicate goodwill to campers while leaders are taking short-cuts, getting all the perks or ridiculing campers. Positive social experiences depend a lot more on 'who' and 'how', than on 'what' or 'when'.

ISSUES RAISED:
☐ To what extent do we aim to minimize conflict in our planning?
☐ Are we agreed on how to handle anti-social behaviour? Do we have a policy on discipline, for example?
☐ When can we ignore conflicts and when should we confront them?

All this should caution us against glibly assuming that camping experiences will necessarily be 'good'. That is not to say that the stock images we have of camping are altogether false. One striking feature of the images we began with — the campfire, the forest stillness and excited shouts, the magic moments of quietness and reflection — is that they are such typical images. They are, in a sense, 'perfectly ordinary' experiences in a camping context.

We have seen, nevertheless, that the ability of camping to provide good experiences for the camper is determined by a number of important and complex human factors. We cannot lightly assume that what works for one camp will work in another, or what is appropriate for one group of campers is appropriate to another.

Value-forming potential

We move on now to the second key element in popular camping theory. This is the idea that camping is an excellent context in which values can be taught. But this is not the kind of claim which can be noted, while we pass on to more practical questions. Once again, the proposition is deceptively simple.

It is one thing to say that we should teach values in camp; it is another thing to decide *what* values and *how* they should be taught. And someone is bound to ask whether we have a right to teach values at all. Let us look at each of these questions in turn:

1. Should we teach values at all?

In one sense, we don't have any choice. This is because our own values (whether we are conscious of them or not) are expressed implicitly in the way we do things and in the requirements we make (or don't make) of campers. Values are 'caught' as well as 'taught'.

While we insist on some standard of behaviour (e.g. 'everybody will help with washing up'), we often find ourselves teaching values explicitly — especially when we have to justify such a stand to a grumbling camper. On the other hand where we merely allow or condone some behaviour without explanation, we are teaching it implicitly. For example, if we allow people to use obscene language without restraint of any kind, it may be inferred that we do not regard this as offensive — or at least that we value lack of conflict between ourselves and the camper concerned more highly than the sensitivities of other campers.

Values inevitably shape programs, rules and organizations. If we are committed to those values, they will be implicitly taught to some degree: from 'care of the environment' to 'respect for persons'.

But we also have a choice about whether we will teach values consciously. If we say nothing about values, we turn our backs on opportunities which are really built-in to the camping experience. For example, we could emphasize the value of being an active contributor in the community by programming a community service project: planting some trees or painting a shed. We could clean up a beach or a stream, rather than merely use it for leisure.

On the other hand, the effectiveness of camping in imparting values can be easily exaggerated. I was visiting some high-rise Housing Commission flats to catch up with some former campers, when I came upon one of them engrossed in cutting down a young poplar tree with his pocket knife. I still remember the feeling of helplessness I had in trying to communicate that this was not a good idea. He just wasn't on my wave-length at all. To him it was a satisfying way to pass the time of day. As I looked down later from the twentieth floor, I could imagine his sense of achievement at seeing the tree lying horizontal on the ground.

My young friend simply didn't share my feelings about the value of trees in the concrete jungle — and perhaps I didn't share the feelings of frustration which prompted him to cut down the tree. Communicating a conservation ethic to him was more than I was capable of.

ISSUES RAISED:
☐ Do we devote time, in leadership training and camp planning, to clarifying the values we regard as most important?
☐ Do we take the value-forming potential of camping seriously, or are we merely content to give everyone 'a good time'?

2. What values will we teach and how will we teach them?

It is easy enough to talk about 'the deep meanings and values of life in the group, in the camp community and in the universe of nature', but what precisely does this mean? Do we mean the value of life in the community to the communist or to the democrat? Are we talking about the meaning of the universe according to the theologian or the scientist?

Before we can teach values, we must make value judgements. And there are value judgements galore to be made when we deliberately set up a community in microcosm for a few days.

In some camping circles it is an unwritten tradition that practical jokes, interference with property and general boorishness be regarded as normal and acceptable. Loading someone's food with pepper, putting salt in others' tea or getting 'seconds' or desserts before everyone is served, are tolerated as everyday enjoyments of community life.

Contrast this with the following statement about the learning possibilities of social living in a school camp:

> Eating together affords many situations for learning. Opportunity is presented for practising proper table etiquette and for engaging in social conversation. Staff members and guests are usually invited by student hosts and hostesses to sit at the various tables during each mealtime.
> There are additional learning activities at mealtime, such as decoration of the room and tables, after-dinner speeches and so forth. Meals should not be announced by gongs — campers should enter the dining room leisurely and visit in social groups until the meal is served. Such experiences are basic in developing a sensitivity to gracious living.[2]

No doubt this will sound quaint to some, if not totally irrelevant. Table cloths are a burden when you are bushwalking while table manners may seem a trifle remote to kids living largely on the streets.

But we mustn't dismiss too quickly the underlying vision of this account. It's not just a matter of making polite conversation or discouraging selfishness at mealtimes. What type of behaviour *is* appropriate for your campers — what are your overall objectives?

Meals are just one example where value judgements are relevant. We can add others. Should we allow kids to swear, smoke or put frogs in sleeping bags? Should we insist on a 'lights out' time? Should we allow campers to choose who they will sit with, do activities with or sleep with?

ISSUES RAISED:
☐ Do we have a consensus among leaders about our aims, objectives and standards?
☐ Have we satisfied ourselves that we have a valid basis for the value judgements we know we must make?
☐ Have we declared our general stance on values to campers and parents in advance?

An outdoor emphasis

The emphasis on the outdoors as a definitive feature of camping appears to be a straightforward aspect of popular camping theory. Camping is an outdoors pursuit — we all know that. Surely this is one assumption we can take for granted. Yet:

> Why are so many meals eaten in the brick-and-glass shelters we call dining rooms that keep the environment out? Why are there not more groups cooking pancakes for breakfast over open fires under trees, by rivers or on beaches? Why do so few groups spend time just lying on the grass looking at the stars?[3]

Apparently the outdoor element of camping is undervalued by camping practitioners. The outdoors is great in theory, provided we are reasonably warm and comfortable.

I remember a dawn service on a Sunday morning, followed by breakfast outdoors. The trouble was that the dawn was completely imperceptible because of thick fog, and we were almost carried away by mosquitoes at breakfast, being forced to retreat rapidly indoors! So, how serious are we about the outdoor environment really?

While historically camping is considered an outdoor activity, there is a considerable variation in the extent to which camping really occurs 'in the outdoors'. Even a tent is a concession to comfort, acknowledging our need for basic shelter. Today's super-equipped caravan can have all the luxuries of home.

While popular camping theory endorses the importance of the outdoor environment, there are at least three discernible facets of this emphasis.

1. A change of surroundings

Getting outdoors refreshes us in more ways than one. A brisk walk in the cold air blows away the mental cobwebs for the busy student. Outdoor activities offer the possibility of enjoying a real physical challenge, of becoming participants in active pursuits instead of mere spectators. Physical refreshment, a new mental perspective, a sense of achievement, the learning of survival skills and new ways to use leisure-time enjoyably, the opportunity to get fit and healthy — all these personal benefits are available in the outdoors.

These dimensions of camping philosophy have an honoured history. In an essay published in the *Camping Magazine* in 1936, W.H. Gibson offered this opinion:

> Our race began its career in the open. After a time it began to build houses. The houses were made closer and closer, tighter and tighter, until air was shut out. If a man were feeble, it was understood that the most dangerous thing he could do was to breathe air out-of-doors after sunset; night air was believed to be deadly though it was all that was available. The race was dying — dying of its own stupidity, dying from indoorness.[4]

Gibson goes on to quote the following verse:

> When ye houses were made of straw,
> Ye men were made of oak;
> When ye houses were made of oak,
> Ye men were made of straw.

According to some, 'the camping movement is a deliberate strategy to find that other world — our natural environment'.[5] For some it means 'leaving the cradle of custom',[6] leaving behind the 'make-believe of modern towns and cities'.[7] Camping means both getting away from and away to. It offers a change of surroundings.

ISSUES RAISED:
☐ Is the natural environment our natural environment?
☐ How can we help people take advantage of the change of surroundings to reflect on life?

2. Environmental education

For city children, camping affords an opportunity for understanding the sources and processes of securing those necessities on which their lives depend.[8]

To one who has run scores of camps for city children on the 'Coolamatong' farm property (see Part Three), this statement is not so much a vision as an everyday fact of life. Here one can observe the effect of the environment on children without much need for further scientific or sociological evidence.

I remember standing with an awe-struck group of primary school children, watching the birth of a calf. As the wet calf slid out in a mass of white membrane, one boy cried out, 'It even comes in a plastic bag!' I was reminded not simply of the capacity of nature to induce wonder, but the need sometimes to interpret its lessons to the urbanized young person.

Again I recall the day that some children watched me milking the cow, even having a squirt or two themselves. When they took the bucket of milk to the door, they asked my wife what she was going to do with it. She was considerably amused by the looks of incredulity and horror when she said that we would drink it!

In such ways city children begin to understand 'the sources and processes of securing the necessities on which their lives depend'. Even the vegetable garden is capable of unveiling mysteries hitherto concealed by the polystyrene and plastic packaging of the supermarket.

Observing children when they witness the slaughtering of a sheep is an education in itself. Children often indicate fewer inhibitions than adults, in whom society's 'refining' process is further advanced. Shearing, lambing, pasture management, natural regeneration after a bushfire, living with less water — all these facets have an important educative function.

Not every camping site offers such obvious indicators of our dependence on nature and the need for conservation of natural resources. We need to be responsible in utilizing the opportunities for raising campers' consciousness of the impact of mankind on the environment and our dependence on it.

ISSUES RAISED:

☐ Many camping programs operate in the outdoors at a purely recreational level. Do most of us need to take the environment more seriously?

☐ How can we foster a wise empathetic approach to the natural environment?

3. The spiritual dimension
Of all the characteristics of camping philosophy, this must be the one about which we can say almost nothing 'practical'. We use the word 'spiritual' in only the vaguest way, because we can't really put our finger on what it is we're exactly talking about. Even in our overwhelmingly secular society, people still find the need to talk about the value of certain experiences not capable of purely scientific or psychological analysis. The very fact we attach importance to this rather intangible dimension of camping should prompt us to question whether it is possible for us to predispose campers to this kind of experience.

One requirement often absent in organized camping is the deliberate provision of time for quietness, reflection and solitude. One is not likely to become attuned to the world of nature while listening to the Top Forty, or even when absorbed in a book — let alone being in the middle of an exciting group activity. One has to be able to hear the sounds, become conscious of the stillness or the zephyr stirring the leaves. It is difficult to get the 'switched on' generation to 'turn off' long enough to discover quietness and solitude. They feel insecure or bored when not being entertained.

But even when we are quiet, we products of modern technological society seem to lack the basic equipment of the Romantic poets for learning nature's lessons. Despite the arrogant claims of science (now heard less and less) to have the answers, confidence is hard to find. We really don't seem to know what life's all about.

ISSUES RAISED:
☐ Given that camping experts have consistently claimed a real spiritual value for the outdoor experience, do we take it seriously enough today? Are there any ways of predisposing ourselves to such experiences?
☐ What specifically do we mean by a 'spiritual dimension'? How is it distinct from pantheism?

We have completed our analysis of popular camping theory, noting various key features. In every case we have said 'yes, taken at face value, this theory sounds OK.' Camping *does* provide valuable experiences. Camping *does* have the potential to shape values. Camping as an out-of-doors experience *does* have importance for urbanized people. Camping provides a spiritual dimension to life in the twentieth century.

But in every case we have also said, 'This raises some important issues as well'. We cannot simply assume that an organized camp will yield these results.

1   C.S. Lewis, *Surprised by Joy*, Fontana Books, 1960. Of course 'joy' is used in a particular sense through the whole book.
2   *Outdoor Education*, op. cit., p.125
3   Mary-Ruth Marshall and David Merritt in *Challenges to Camping*, Rob Evans (ed.), Joint Board of Christian Education, Melbourne 1980, p.11
4   Quoted in D. and W. Hammerman, *Outdoor Education: A Book of Readings*, Burgess, Minneapolis 1973, p.63
5   Marshall and Merritt, op. cit., p.11
6   Paddy Pallin, op. cit., p.6
7   Jack Cox, op. cit., p.17
8   Hugh B. Masters in Hammerman, op. cit., p.22

3
Organized Camping:
What makes it tick?

I KNOW A MAN who owned a Mercedes Benz. He had an ostentatious streak and drove in an alarming way if he had an audience. He would drive quite fast at a wall and then stop suddenly a few centimetres short. He drove the car with pride for years, but had no understanding of mechanical things. I have it on good authority that one day his prized possession simply ground to a halt and wouldn't go again. The engine had seized. He had never put any oil in it.

We may draw a simple analogy here between organized camping and the Mercedes. It is not enough to drive a prestige car, capable of giving outstanding performance, and simply keep it going by putting in more petrol. Wonderful as the engine might be, it needs regular lubrication. Its performance needs to be monitored. Someone has to check it out, someone who can detect the signs of wear and malfunction. You can't assume it will continue to perform like a Mercedes just because everyone knows how good it is.

Camps roll on. We know they're a great thing. They attract people. (We are still putting the petrol in: money, effort, nights of planning, weekends and holidays.) But is the camp performing up to standard? We need two things to answer that. We need to understand what makes it tick — what is its 'genius'? And we need to monitor its performance, *our* performance.

The purpose of this chapter is to identify the fundamental attributes, the real heart of camping. But where should we look?

The essence of camping
What ingredients are commonly thought essential to the idea of camping? It is possible to represent them fairly with the following imaginary argument:

A.   Organized camping is *'living in the out-of-doors'*.

B.   That's a bit broad isn't it? Some people do that as a matter of course in their daily lives — like game wardens and drovers. I even knew a hermit who lived in a tent.

A.   Ah, that leads me on to the next point. Camping is a *'group living in the out-of-doors'*. We're talking about a social phenomenon.

B.   You mean, like an Eskimo community or a native village in New Guinea?

A.   No, we're not talking about normal living situations — we're talking about 'group living in the out-of-doors *for a special purpose.*

B.   Right, now I get it. You mean like a rock festival, where everyone goes to hear their favourite bands and let their hair down?

A.   Wrong again. It's not just an unco-ordinated thing where everyone does his own thing. Organized group camping has an *educational purpose,* under *experienced leadership.*

And so the debate goes on. People add bits and pieces to the definition until they are satisfied that they have all the ingredients considered essential. The trouble is you can take away one part or another and still maintain the original concept.

Camping can be individual — the jolly swagman camped by a billabong, even if he was alone and there was no waterskiing program. It can be indoors — like the camp a friend of mine ran at a permanent campsite where it rained continuously for the week! It can be done without experienced leadership — though the campsite won't be the same afterwards.

We might turn to the dictionary to settle the argument. But the best that the Concise Oxford can offer relevant to camping in our society is that 'camp' means the temporary quarters of nomads, gypsies and travellers; while 'to camp' means to encamp, lodge in a camp, lodge in a tent or in the open.

That doesn't help much, does it? In fact a dictionary definition can only include those features present whenever the word 'camping' is used.

This matter is of practical importance. It affects how camping is interpreted to government, defined by different camping exponents and understood by the general public. The detailed argument is not central to our purpose here. (Readers interested in these issues may follow them up in Appendix A, 'Defining Camping'.) We all probably have in mind a fairly well-developed idea of what camping is. But how should we understand camping? What are its real dynamics? When it works, what makes it successful?

We may study the contributions of other thoughtful and experienced exponents of camping. This may be called an inherited understanding. Three major attributes keep recurring in one way or another in the study of organized camping:

* Its outdoor context
* Its educational purpose
* Its community nature

At the risk of over-simplification, these three main emphases, and their relationship to each other, may be summarized as follows:

MODEL A

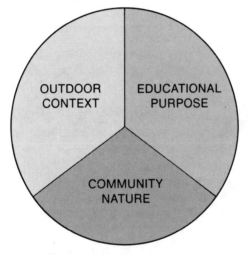

Here the three attributes are seen as being equally important, but as relatively independent of each other. This concept could be expressed in this way: 'Camping has always been an outdoor activity. However, while we enjoy the outdoors and gain spiritual strength from it, we shouldn't ignore the opportunities it offers for teaching. When we go into the outdoors in groups, we also have the chance to teach people about how to live together.'

The three attributes are seen as being independent of each other. The educational objectives exist alongside the others, but don't interlock or overlap with them. A badly eroded creek-bed would be utilized for an outdoor game or walk, but its significance for land conservation would go unnoticed. Yet a film on conservation might be shown back at camp at another time. A bushwalk might be conceived as an exciting outdoor activity, yet with no thought given to even minimal 'structures' (e.g. guided discussions around the campfire), which might develop mutual understanding and cohesion in the group.

Interestingly enough, this model could probably pass as a crude summary of the development of organized camping in North America: the recreational stage, the educational stage and the stage of social orientation and responsibility. These three stages overlap.[1]

Of course few people would admit to thinking this way. There is certainly a degree of artificiality about the model. But this kind of thinking is discernible nevertheless, not only in camping literature but in camping practice. Some camps are content with extreme variations of this model. For example, some school camping programs might be represented like this:

The educational dimensions of the program are conceived very narrowly (e.g. to teach the students how to ski). The outdoors is all-important. If there is no snow, students will have a bus tour instead. Virtually no attention is given to structuring the program so as to develop or reflect on the social dimensions of living together.

Alternatively some denominational camp programs might be represented like this:

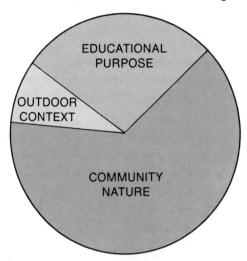

Here the primary aim is to really get to know each other at depth. Living together is considered the best way to do this. Campsites or conference centres offer sufficiently cheap accommodation and, besides, there are usually things to occupy campers there in free time. And of course it is also a good opportunity for some teaching sessions or discussion groups on one topic or another.

However applied, this concept has a fundamental weakness. The weakness of Model A is that it fails to take account of the ways in which the three facets of organized camping interact with each other. A fuller account of the implications of this will emerge in later chapters. Enough to note here that Model A impoverishes camping in two ways:

(a) It produces an unhealthy imbalance in total camp programs
There are of course perfectly valid variations of this approach, but the sorts of extreme variations illustrated are usually undesirable. For example, the school camp that treats the community dimension as incidental can produce unpleasant side-effects: bullying, campers not getting enough sleep, and unresolved tensions between groups of campers. In this way groups actually come into conflict with each other. A total absorption with outdoor 'activities' can result in negative group living experiences.

(b) It impoverishes every aspect of camp
The mental separation of the educational, social and recreational aspects means that the 'teachable·moments' in group relationships

will be lost. It means that leaders will be oblivious to the possibilities of mealtimes, activities or free time for the development of personal relationships. It means that opportunities for rewarding experiences in the outdoors will be lost because the educational aims are seen as distinct from the others in the same way as being 'at school' is distinct from being 'at home'.

MODEL B

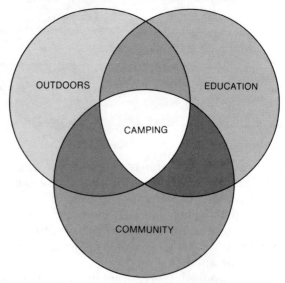

Here the three attributes are all seen as important, but they now interact. There is common ground. Camp is seen as communal, educational and outdoor-orientated at one and the same time. Each attitude enhances the other.

Instead of structuring a camp program proceeding from educational activities to community-developing activities, then to outdoor pursuits, each attribute is inter-related. Building a sense of community is seen as partly educational. Outdoor activities are seen as offering possibilities not just for recreation, but for building relationships and for teaching (whether science, maths or written language skills).

This model takes us to the heart of the matter. It affirms the three major values attributed to camping. It gives them all importance. Above all, it recognizes that the genius of camping is the way in which each dimension enhances the other.

Examples could be multiplied of how this process occurs. Three real-life illustrations come to mind readily:

* A group of fifteen- and sixteen-year-old boys are totally absorbed for an hour in identifying different species of birds (thirty-one species observed). Learning is accelerated by a stimulating environment (a National Park), high level of external interest (birds everywhere), peer approval (spontaneous element of competition induced, to our surprise, by the interest of peer group leader), and by a good teacher-pupil relationship (developed in the relaxed and informal atmosphere of the camp). Here education is enriched by the outdoor environment and the camp community.

* A camp of fifteen-year-olds is being made difficult by the unco-operative attitudes of a few rather rebellious boys. The complete transformation in their attitude and teachability comes when they are utterly involved in a lecture on explosives. The lecture is given by a leader who is an explosives expert, and illustrated by the blowing up of an old tree stump with dynamite. It is a turning point in their attitude and for the harmony of the whole camp. The community is enriched by a valuable educational use of the outdoor environment.

* A camp with a long tradition offers motor boat cruises, kayaking and sailing as regular options for morning activities. One year a leader decides to explain to each motor boat group the safety regulations, basic mechanics and rules for use of the boat. Some campers are really interested, sensing his concern to make the most of the experience. The outdoor recreation dimension is enriched by the educational emphasis and by the community dimension engendered by the leader, which makes it a conscious group activity.

Among writers who express a Model B philosophy of camping, there are of course considerable variations of emphasis. Again there is obvious artificiality in a model where each attribute is given equal importance. In any case it would be quite impossible to quantify with any precision the degree of emphasis which various practitioners would give to one attribute or the other.

Nevertheless these are differences of emphasis, having considerable practical importance. In the next chapter we will move from what has been broadly a critical analysis of popular camping theory to what could be called the construction of a particular camping philosophy.

1   Dimock, op. cit., Chapter 1

4

The Key to Organized Camping:
Is the 'temporary community' crucial?

MAKING CHOICES IS A BURDEN of adulthood. For some of us, even 'tea or coffee' is a difficult choice occurring with considerable regularity. Organizing a group camping activity involves a multitude of choices. Some are big (e.g. the choice of leaders). Some only seem big (e.g. changing two days' program around). Some are small (is there time for a swim before lunch?). Some only seem small (like whether to remind campers about sunburn).

Few, if any, of our choices are insignificant, but some have more profound consequences than others. Sometimes we do not recognize the consequences or we think we can avoid making choices altogether, just doing things the way we've done them before — though that, too, is a choice.

We have seen that the most fundamental, far-reaching choices we make are at the level of our basic presuppositions — our philosophy — and have demonstrated some of the connections between camping theory and practice. We now come to the most crucial part of our thesis: a fundamental choice of emphasis. We could be content with simply analysing common camping theory,[1] leaving the reader to the task of drawing his or her own conclusions. However while the three attributes mutually enrich one another, one particular choice may be more valid than the others.

We believe that of the three main attributes of camping already considered, the *community* aspect provides the best basis upon which to build the whole structure. While the educational and outdoors aspects are certainly regarded as important, the concept of camp as community is seen as worthy of even greater emphasis.

It will be obvious, of course, that other people espouse the primacy of different facets of camping. Some give the impression that the educational purpose of camping is the key focus. To do this, we must define 'education' so *broadly* that the term itself loses its distinctive thrust. Are we talking about education for leisure and recreation, education for living in the environment, or education for the very process of living itself? Whatever meaning we opt for, the educational purpose of camping is clearly primary. Unfortunately it is to say so much that we are not really saying much at all!

There are those who argue for the outdoor setting as camping's most distinctive characteristic. They are doing little more than stating the obvious.[2] Of course, from an historical or a contemporary perspective the images of camping tend to be solid and specific. Actual objects and places come to mind: brightly coloured tents, high mountains, green valleys and bubbling streams, ruck-sacks laden with the paraphernalia of outdoor living. But the outdoor emphasis should not become a dominating influence on our whole approach to organized camping, *just because* it is the most concrete feature presented to the mind by the word 'camping'. This is to confuse primary associations with primary meaning.

Camping as community

It is the contention of this book that 'the temporary community' should be the key feature of a sound camping philosophy. Why is an emphasis on camping as a 'temporary community' justified?

1. Community is the most distinctive attribute of camping

To start with, camping is only a small part of education. Indeed, it wouldn't even rate a mention by most people if they were asked to list twenty ways in which education takes place. Even educators would place relatively little importance on it. Camping is most commonly seen as one aspect of 'outdoor education'.

Similarly, organized camping is just one of many ways in which we can explore and enjoy the outdoors. Other methods range from the family picnic to the school excursion. Even amongst outdoor holiday activities, organized camping is just one of a whole range, from travelling in the family car to package tours.

But how many ways are available for modern urban people to experience community? Certainly there are examples of people who are attempting to do this. Some 'live in community' as a matter of convenience — such as sharing a house to save on rent.

Others have made courageous and far-reaching decisions as families to 'live communally' to seek a satisfying alternative to the deficiencies of a highly privatized and materialistic lifestyle. They have 'dropped out of the rat-race'. Yet only a tiny proportion of the population has felt that this is realistic for themselves and their families.

Organized group camping is an accessible way in which people can experience a degree of communal living. There are many ways of studying the environment, but few ways to experience living together. David Merritt has identified a number of reasons for 'the search for community' in camping:

> Because of its essential nature, camping offers unique opportunities for building community. It involves many aspects of life — working, relaxing, eating, preparing food, washing up, making decisions, carrying out those decisions . . . it is a residential experience with all that means for shared living.[3]

Aspects included in this community-building environment are 'time for experience to accumulate' and the new setting 'which makes possible the discovery of new dimensions to relationships with others'.[3]

There is no doubt that camping experiences are overwhelmingly evaluated by campers and leaders in terms of the *relationships* which characterized the camp. It is one thing to have great weather or be engaged in some exciting activities, educational or otherwise, but it is the *social* aspect of a particular camping experience which assumes key importance for all. In the final analysis, a camp is judged more on the relationships between campers than on any other factor.

2. Community is the most indispensable attribute of camping
This is hardly surprising. The communal or social structure of camping reflects closely the nature of human beings as social creatures:

> Men cannot survive in vacuo. Each of us needs human company if we are to mature as persons. It is doubtful, in fact, if we can speak of a person at all apart from his relationship and interaction with others.[4]

Many social commentators have emphasized the dehumanizing effects of our industrialized, technological society. We can live within a few metres of our neighbours without knowing their names. We squash into trains and buses, yet rarely engage in conversation with these strangers we touch. Many people only seem to relate to each other spontaneously when they are drunk or at a funeral.

Human communication is not an optional 'extra' like a backyard swimming pool. It isn't something we can afford to indulge in when there is nothing else to do. There are numerous indicators of the breakdown of human communication: drug addiction, the increase in suicide, rising divorce rates, family disintegration and so on. 'The total perspective that rises from all this data is one of deep distress in modern urban society.'[5]

If this is so, it must be a matter of profound importance to restore interpersonal communication. Camping is one small way in which individual sanity and health can be promoted. We can maintain physical existence in a concrete environment, impoverished though it may be. But to learn to share and love, to give *and* to receive, to converse, be honest and to become known — this is fundamental to human wholeness.

Thus we would rate the community dimension of camping above the outdoor, environmental aspects. We would attribute priority to the cultivation of community, and of the individual persons who make it up. This is hardly new. To quote the psychologist Carl Jung:

> It is becoming more and more obvious that it is not starvation, not microbes, not cancer but man himself who is mankind's greatest danger.[6]

But it isn't only psychologists and sociologists who promote the relative importance of this human dimension to the future of the race. Thoughtful environmentalists also agree. One writer says that the reason why man destroys his environment 'is because he doesn't understand how everything is related within the living world (ecology) or because he is reluctant to live accordingly'.[7]

Even an ecological understanding of the environment cannot stand alone. We must be willing to accept the necessary limitations on our free-wheeling lifestyle and profligate use of resources. Clearly we need something that will develop not just an awareness of environmental issues, but a desire to live accordingly. Camping, with its ability to create experiences of sharing and interdependence, surely has a role to play.

Writing on the subject of 'total environments for education', another writer comments:

> If we are to accomplish . . . the development of a 'conservation ethic', an attitude of responsibility for the environment, then our education must involve the <u>inner</u> environment of the child as well . . . The reasons why people 'conserve' are internal and we will fail if we do not develop in children a good inner environment. Why should the child who has not been conserved be concerned about wilderness, Californian condors or Antarctic penguins?[8]

You may remember my difficulty in communicating to a former camper my concern for the poplar tree he was cutting down. Here was a boy whose 'inner environment' had been greatly impoverished. Yet happily the experience of camp still had real significance for him at that level — a story too long to tell here.

An essay giving some historical perspectives on camping concludes this way:

> And now man has harnessed a force that, in one single flash, can destroy a whole city and most of the inhabitants in it. But the great question is not whether man can control this force, but rather whether he can control himself and whether he has the knowledge and skill to raise a generation of people who can live peacably together.[9]

It is the assertion of this book that positive experiences of community through organized camping can develop this knowledge and sharpen this skill. The camping movement has often majored on the less important aspects. It needs to major on the most important aspect of this role in society.

Why the 'temporary community' concept is crucial

All this constitutes a challenge to organized camping. The camping movement can sharpen its focus on the *educational possibilities* of camping, but it must do more than fill up a week of the school year. Camping must be recognized as far more than a technique for environmental studies or for teaching outdoor recreational skills. We must seriously address, in a continuing way, the implications of the residential nature of camping.

Organized camping can also sharpen its focus on its use of the *outdoor environment*, but we must do more than simply go to a campsite or walk in the mountains. We must become more aware of the environment and allow ourselves to spend 'quality time' in the natural world.

Camping as an experience of temporary community embraces both the educational and the outdoor emphases, with each mutually enriching the other. But the goal of temporary community goes further. The challenge is for organized camping to provide the following:

(a) *experiences* which give a taste of, and kindle a desire for, living in deeper harmony and relationship with others

(b) *models* of how relationships can be developed and difficulties dealt with in a community situation

(c) a *context* in which urban people can have an integrated experience of the natural environment — one that takes account of the inner, personal issues of human survival and growth, not merely of the external environment.

In case this all sounds too utopian or idealistic, we should note that this task is what organized camping has always set for itself. One quote will suffice:

> Group experience is a phase of program with unusual possibilities for education in social relations. Children change in their abilities to get along with others . . . campers may come to like those that formerly they had disliked. Tolerance develops. Skill in creating friendly feelings is acquired.[10]

There is solid evidence suggesting that parents see the socializing aspects of camp as the most valuable. A survey taken over two years showed that the vast majority of parents felt that knowledge, skills and appreciation of the outdoors was what children learnt most in school camps. The same parents, however, rated this *second* in importance to 'learning to live co-operatively', with the experiences of self-reliance and doing duties coming third and fourth respectively.[11]

The testimony of camp leaders accords with this as well. I recently asked a group of boys who had rafted down a river for a week how they had enjoyed themselves? The response was overwhelmingly positive. I asked the camp director how the same camp had gone. His response was reserved.

'The whole thing had gone well', he commented. 'But it wasn't until the last day or two that the boys really pulled their weight. Until then, they acted as though we leaders were just hired servants!' Co-operation in meal preparation and camp tasks had been only begrudging, the campers constantly rushing to be first in the queue for all the privileges. Like parents and past camp leaders, he placed considerable importance on the socializing aspects of camp.

It is one thing to talk about teaching people to love one another and live in peace, but doing it is another. The Manifesto of the Edinburgh Liberation Front said in 1972:

> Haste, waste, violence, loneliness, boredom, greed — this is the culture of modern Britain. . . The counter-culture must stress people,
> not property,
> not things,
> not politics,
> not psychiatry,
> not Gross National Product. . .[12]

But a critique of the counter-culture (and of the technological society) leaves this Manifesto looking rather hollow, too. The temporary community says, 'people, not property; people, not things; people, not programs...' Is this also too utopian and idealistic?

Personal presuppositions

It must be acknowledged that we are facing questions which cannot be answered without reference to our most fundamental beliefs about human nature. We've talked about teaching young people to live at peace with each other — about building caring relationships, about dealing with conflict and building friendships, about demonstrating models of community. What we are talking about is seeing camping as a significant tool for *social change*. The requirements of the temporary community are comprehensive yet stretching.

I've met some marvellous people in camping. As a Christian I am challenged by the compassion and commitment of others who don't share my beliefs. Yet, on balance, the rays of optimism are bright only by contrast with the overwhelming pessimism of the present time. The prevailing philosophy of our Western society is one of despair. Anyone proposing social solutions must not only answer the questions of economic viability and social justice. He must face the wall of apathy and cynicism which the sheer weight of human problems has created in our time and the seeming powerlessness of the individual or State to overcome global problems of gross inequality.

It is one thing to talk about love and quite another thing to practise it. In 1952 Bertrand Russell wrote of obstacles to human progress:

> What stands in the way? Not physical or technical obstacles, but only the evil passions in the human mind; suspicion, fear, lust for power, intolerance... The root of the matter is a very simple and old-fashioned thing, a thing so simple that I am almost ashamed to mention it, for fear of the derisive smile with which wise cynics will greet my words. The thing I mean — please forgive me for mentioning it — is love, Christian love or compassion.[13]

Yet Russell had already written in 1945:

> The Christian principle, 'Love your enemies', is good... there is nothing to be said against it except that it is too difficult for most of us to practise sincerely.[14]

We can't be choosey about which campers we are going to love or care about in the temporary community. It is the misfits, the rebels, the disturbed, the alienated and the depersonalized that the temporary community exists for. And we're *all* included — it's just a matter of degree.

I do not urge the 'temporary community' concept because of any confidence that we can 'pull it off'. Despite the exceptions, most of us camp leaders are as vulnerable, cantankerous, two-faced and given to 'self-preservation first' as most of the campers.

We can only make the temporary community work, ultimately, as we get love to work. According to the Christian faith this is possible — but we can't do it on our own. The Christian analysis sees mankind as made in the image of God — a basic stamp of dignity and potentiality which persists in all, despite the deficiencies to which human history and personal failure so amply testify. Yet more than ordinary goodwill is required to meet the human challenges of community living.

We believe that God's love is not only directed *towards* people, but that it can flow *through* them. Reconciliation with God leads not simply to inner peace, but to reconciliation with others. *This* is the real source of our confidence in the socializing possibilities of the temporary community. The way in which this peculiarly Christian perspective bears on camping is taken up in Part Four.

1   Of course we have not 'simply analyzed' at all, because the analysis has proceeded on the basis of our own chosen criteria.
2   For example, Dimock, op. cit., p.29: 'The most distinguishing criterion of camping'
3   D.R. Merritt, *Challenges to Camping*, op. cit., p.21
4   George Carey, *I Believe in Man*, Hodder and Stoughton, 1977, p.108.
5   See Rinzema, op. cit., p.107
6   C.G. Jung, 'Epilogue', *Modern Man in Search of a Soul*, Routledge Books, New York 1933
7   Ian Hore-Lacy, Teachers' Guide to *Living in a Food Web*, Thomas Nelson, 1975 (italics mine)
8   Matthew J. Brennan in Hammerman, op. cit., p.333
9   L.B. Sharp and E. De Alton Partridge in Hammerman, op. cit., p.62
10 Dimock, op. cit., pp.129-130
11 Hammerman, op. cit., pp. 383-387
12 See S. Barton Babbage, *Journal of Christian Education* paper 55, 1976, p.22
13 Quoted in *The Case for Christianity*, Lion Publishing, 1981, p.22
14 Quoted by Os Guiness in *Dust of Death*, InterVarsity Press, 1973, p.392

5

The Temporary Community:
What are its essential elements?

WE HAVE NOW MADE a fundamental choice of emphasis. This choice is reflected in the expression 'the temporary community'. While not necessarily invalidating other emphases, it does declare a position. Furthermore, this choice provides a key to the approach adopted in the rest of this book.

Part Two demonstrates how the temporary community concept works out practically. But before moving on, we will look at the major requirements for any camping program which has this fundamental emphasis.

1. An agreed basis
While the particular style and program of each camp will be different, it is essential that there is agreement about the basics. This agreement should not only exist between the leaders, but also in the group as a whole.

Agreement about objectives does not, of course, ensure a sense of community. Some marriages work like this and so do some camps. I can recall school cadet camps which still evoke memories of bullying, humiliation and loneliness. The only sense of community was the rather utilitarian comradeship experienced by a group of boys thrown together by the mutual need to survive.

There was an agreed basis, but it wasn't really shared by all the participants. And it didn't include the relational dimensions upon which any community worth the name must be built. What are the fundamental things that need to be agreed on to provide an adequate basis for the temporary community?

(a) Aims and objectives
Leaders must be agreed on the aims of the camp: what they want to achieve by the end of the camp, or as a result of it. They also

need to be agreed on the objectives: how they plan to go about achieving those aims. It is a temptation to take these things for granted, but a mistake to do so.

A camp director must be sure his leaders are agreed on their basic approach. Take, for example, a camp for school leavers which was run jointly by two organizations. Both had a similar basic philosophy, but one normally dealt with tertiary students, the other with secondary students.

The camp leadership team was comprised of representatives of each organization. The aim was clear enough: to orientate secondary students from one group to the tertiary programs of the other group. But nobody anticipated sufficiently the *differences* which might exist in leadership style. As a result there were areas of tension which threatened to significantly undermine the unity of the team itself.

The tertiary student leaders expected to talk well into the night with campers, while the secondary student leaders were used to getting campers off to bed around eleven o'clock. The first group were rather laissez-faire about program; the second were committed to a relatively organized structure. One group tended to treat matters of camper safety as though the campers were responsible adults, expected to look after themselves. This caused considerable anxiety to the other group, who were all too conscious of their *in loco parentis* responsibility for the campers.

It is necessary, therefore, to anticipate questions of basic approach on which leaders may differ and agree in advance on what the approach will be. However, two important qualifications should be made.

First, it is neither possible nor desirable to obtain total agreement on every issue amongst leaders. Total agreement on everything suggests boring conformity, lack of creativity, unhealthy subservience and a sense of unreality. The development of community is not achieved by excluding dissent, but by reconciling differences, achieving satisfactory compromises, or mutually submitting to a common goal.

Second, the campers themselves are members of the community. While campers may be only minimally involved in determining the camp's basic aims and approach, it is important that these be understood by the campers from the outset.

This has implications for the way the camp is advertised. Campers and/or parents should be able to select a camp which has aims and objectives within which the camper can live satisfactorily. There should be clear communication to campers about the program and basic expectations of behaviour right from the outset.

(b) Recognition of limitations
The limitations of the temporary community must be recognized. The most important limitation is embodied in the very term 'temporary'. The organized camping experience is, in practice, only short-term. But it is limited in other senses, also. One is the physical remoteness of the camping experience, its distance from ordinary life. There is often an air of unreality about it. Looking down from a towering ridge on to an unending landscape makes home, work or school seem far away. Doing interesting and adventurous activities is, by definition, 'extra-ordinary'.

Another limitation is the social remoteness of the camping experience. We often take children away from their families and then try to teach them how to live in families! We seek to teach ways of interrelating away from the primary group to which the campers must eventually relate.

There are inadequate responses to the recognition of the limitations of the temporary community. One is 'superintensity'. We may respond by making the most of our limited opportunities in an unhealthy way. We will then try to artificially accelerate the growth of relationships or the emotional rewards of the community. The result can be a real 'crash' when the camper returns to reality at home. The camper may also make emotional commitments or adopt forms of behaviour in the camp environment which cause embarrassment, even guilt, later on.

The other response is 'goal disorientation'. Here the leader is intimidated by the criticism that the camping environment is 'unreal', unrelated to the everyday experience of the urban young person, whether the deprived kid from the high-rise flats or the privileged student from the private school. As a result no real attempt is made to use the camping situation to teach ideas or behaviour patterns different from the norms of the campers.

A third inadequate response is simply not to recognize the limitations at all. This approach either discredits camping through exaggerated claims made for camping's capacity to be a real socializing influence, or isolates camping theory from other vital related areas of thought (such as education, sociology or, in the case of church camping, theology). This leads to failure to make adequate connections with the normal 'back home' situation of the camper.

The aims of a school camp, for example, may bear no relation to on-going relationships at school. School camps are sometimes aimed at providing the chance for teachers to get to know pupils better. Yet camps with just this aim have sometimes been held at the very end of the academic year, or been staffed by teachers who don't normally teach those campers. Because camps are treated in isolation from the total educational process, opportunities are often missed to teach in the field what has been dealt with only remotely in the classroom.

(c) Rules and standards

Some basic rules defining the limits of acceptable behaviour are necessary in any community, temporary or 'permanent'. This is obvious to most camp leaders and, as a principle, is not very controversial. However, its application is not so easy.

First, while we may agree on having rules in principle, we may disagree on what particular rules and standards should pertain to a particular camp. The temptation is to give up on the process of determining suitable rules altogether.

Second, when the crunch comes, the idea of actually enforcing agreed standards is often a source of tension for leaders. This opens up the whole area of discipline — the subject of Chapter 9.

Third, we need to recognize that clear 'boundaries' are required to carry out our most fundamental responsibility: the safety of campers.

Fourth, most campers — especially younger campers — have a psychological need to know what the boundaries of acceptable behaviour are. They need to know the limits if they are to feel secure within the camp community and to know how to contribute positively towards it.

Fifth, the development of a happy environment and good relationships requires us to look after the welfare of the community as a whole. Unless we have a hand-picked group of campers fully committed to our goals and values, we will almost always have some campers who want to act in ways which conflict with the interest of others in the group.

Finally, we have a moral as well as a legal obligation to control behaviour in the way a conscientious parent would when we have children as campers. This obligation is related to the residential nature of camping. The privilege of taking children and young people away on camp carries with it a special kind of responsibility. The issue of how we arrive at agreement about appropriate rules and standards is discussed in detail in Chapter 10.

2. Concern for individuals
At first sight this may seem a strange requirement, but it is utterly fundamental. We cannot achieve a sense of community while ignoring the needs of individuals. If individuals are angry, frustrated or hurt, they cannot be expected to care about co-operating, giving and caring for others. If a person is insecure and unwilling or unable to become known to others, communication cannot grow until others are prepared to 'become vulnerable' and make the first moves towards him.

> The plain fact is that a 'community', however temporary, cannot work without concern for persons. Where people are living together, for example, little things annoy. You become conscious of whether people snore, how they eat their food or whether they talk too much. You see people 'in the round' — not just when they have their respectable public mask on, but also when they are off-guard. In camp you can't keep up a front. You rub up against people day and night.
> This brings inevitable frictions. It is harder to accept people. You can't turn around and forget their annoying habits or idiosyncracies. Harmony has to be worked at. It requires us to care about people![1]

Professionalism is an enemy of community, if it means that programs become more important than individuals. Leaders may pressure or manipulate campers to make a program 'work'.

'Come on, you slacker, join in — you're spoiling it for everybody' may be a reflex response to an unco-operative camper. But what if the camper is really sick, or has withdrawn from the activity because he or she has been wounded inside by a thoughtless remark or action of someone else? You may very well get him or her involved in the activity under duress and keep the program going — but it will be at the expense of the camper, and of the community as well.

Caring for the individual *so that* the community will work is simply the same professionalism one step removed. This approach views community as an end and individual growth as a means to an end. But surely it is the other way around. Our fundamental concern is for *persons*; community is the means to help persons discover wholeness. What matters is the growth in the lives of individuals and the quality of their relationships. The camper is not primarily a client to be satisfied, a member of an activity group, or even an ingredient in a community we've decided to construct, but a person.

Dr Paul Tournier says:

> To become a person, to discover the world of persons, to acquire the sense of the person, to be more interested in people as persons than in their ideas, their party labels, their personage, means a complete revolution, changing the climate of our lives. Once adopted, it is an attitude which rapidly impregnates the whole of our lives.[2]

The challenge of all this is enormous. Tournier's book, chock full of case studies, will reward anyone concerned about authentic relationships. This is a subject which is paramount for camping people, because camping situations accelerate relationships between people — for better or worse.

3. Structures for community

It is implicit in the idea of organized camping that an organization and its leaders are assuming responsibility for the way in which things will be done. Much time is spent on timetables, programs and all the minutiae which make for the 'smooth running' of a camp. But the temporary community concept puts even these practical details in a new light. For example:

(a) Allocation of campers to groups

Do we simply allow campers to choose the groups they will live in and work with? Should they stay in the cliques that they may have arrived in? What about the risk of creating disgruntlement by splitting up such groups?

What principles govern these choices? Do we want to reinforce and enhance existing friendships? Do we want to maximize the challenge of camp life by placing campers in groups with which they may not readily 'gel'? Do we ignore such considerations and allocate campers according to their abilities and experience?

(b) Mealtimes

In site-based camping we usually consider various practical details: How many tables do we need? How many campers to each table? Is it easier to have waiters or queue for meals? Which leader will be in charge of maintaining law and order?

But we have already alluded to the possibilities of meals as a socializing activity. Should we have a leader at each table? (Some teachers on camps sit at tables by themselves and leave the kids to it. Others see meals as an opportunity to get to know the campers, and spread themselves around.) Should families sit together for meals?

Noisy and disruptive groups often develop at mealtimes, rushing in and grabbing the favoured table, 'saving seats' for their friends. Should we reduce the noise level, and therefore increase the potential for worthwhile conversation, by using place-cards?

(c) Basic program structure

Some camps still operate with the total camp as the basic unit for many activities. Others operate on a decentralized basis, with almost all facets of camp being experienced in a small group. Of course other factors than 'community' are also operating here. The objectives of an adventure camp, even the equipment available, may dictate that the small group is the basic unit in which almost everything happens.

It is easy to lose sight of the relationships potential of the small group, when whole group activities are easier to organize. I have observed two camps of about forty-five people using the same facilities for an overnight camp-out in totally different ways. One group went as a total group to the same camping spot and spent the night together under the stars. The other divided into five or six groups, each of which did something different.

In the latter case, the co-ordination of the whole exercise was complex, involving sharing and change-over of equipment between groups, e.g. kayaking down a river, sleeping under the stars, then cycling back to camp. The first camp was easier to organize, but the second had far greater potential for adventure and for fostering relationships in depth.

It is obviously important to evaluate various program options according to what sort of community experience you want to create. A family camp presents some obvious examples. If you feel it is important for families to grow in their ability to work together as families, activities involving family units in craft, sport, problem-solving, reflection and discussion will be important. If you want parents to relate together at some depth, sharing views on bringing up children, activities will be needed which provide a structure for that, while the children are occupied elsewhere. If you want whole families to interact with other whole families, this will need to be planned for.

(d) Decision-making

It is often in the decision-making process that conflicts arise and different expectations are encountered. Some teenage camps appear to make little provision for camper involvement in decision-making. This not only denies a great opportunity for learning to give and take, and 'wearing' responsibility for your own decisions, it also diminishes the possibility for campers to feel really involved in the process of determining the 'shape' of the camp.

Many years ago an incident occurred which alerted me to the way in which older teenagers want a say in shaping the type of community they live in: from nuclear bombs to the tidiness and layout of their own bedrooms.[3] I remember standing under a huge gum tree in the tent area one night, trying to persuade some older teenagers to go to bed. One particularly articulate girl wanted to know why they *should* go to bed; my answers clearly did not satisfy her.

I was struck with the idea of inviting her (and any other interested campers) to attend a leaders' meeting the next day. They jumped at the chance and contributed constructively. What surprised me was that their conclusions tended to be even more conservative than those of the leaders. The problem was not that the lights-out time, for example, was unreasonable; the rule had simply been dropped on them from above without reference to their opinions and feelings.

The idea of camper participation in planning has been seen by some as an almost definitive feature of *real* camping. The growth in camping in North America came by building larger camps rather than multiplying small-group camping. The sophistication of facilities and organization has been seen as an enemy of the real camping experience:

> In many cases the camp is simply an organized playground, with all of the equipment and devices used in the city simply moved out into the woods. Where this has happened, there has been a tendency for the camp program to revolve around equipment and facilities, and the youngsters have not had a chance to participate in the experience of living and planning their lives in small groups.[4]

By contrast a true camping program is one where 'youngsters are placed in a situation that requires of them a disposition to solve their own problems [and] co-operate with others'.[5]

This could be seen simply as a call for democracy in decision-making. The practice of democracy has certainly been a strong feature of North American camping theory, particularly because of the educative role of camping for future involvement in a democratic community. But there is a deeper dimension to camper participation. It highlights the need for decisions not merely to be handed down from above in an authoritarian fashion, but mediated to campers in a way which invites their response and acceptance.

Decision-making can be seen, therefore, as an important constituent in the temporary community. It can enable campers to participate deeply in fundamental community processes, it can be a model of humane but non-negotiable decision-making, and it can provide a vehicle for building relationships. Of course, the degree of camper involvement will depend on the age and composition of the campers, the specific aims of the camp and the nature of specific decisions. Some decisions (for example those pertaining to the moral and legal obligations of the leadership) will not be open to negotiation at all.

(e) A clear focus

We have already drawn attention in Chapter 2 to the elusiveness of 'the good experience'. If we are talking about quality camping, we are planning for the best experiences that we can offer the camper. This applies to the simple matter of enjoyment. The promise of enjoyment can mean anything from a straight spine-tingling sensation of excitement to moments when the spirit may be deeply moved.

In the experience of community the main ingredients — the relationships between participants — are varied and unpredictable. Yet we have already suggested that the best kind of group feeling is that which emerges unselfconsciously. The rewards of community tend to be given when we are least seeking them.

The bushfires in January 1983 in the State of Victoria are a good example. This common threat threw neighbours together. I asked one person if she knew her neighbours. The answer was 'Not before, but we do now'. Thousands of housewives and others were galvanized into action, sorting clothes and goods donated for the victims. In so doing they experienced 'community spirit' in a new way.

Yet these people were not looking for community. They discovered it as they worked together in a common (though traumatic) interest. This is consistent with the idea that 'personal relationships flower most naturally in joint effort in some social purpose'.[6] The best relationships are those based on the intention to love and serve the other person, not to get something from them.

Thus we need to provide suitably exciting, absorbing and worthwhile activities for campers — and program them at the right tempo. Campers need something to do and time to do it in. Both over-activity and idleness provide conditions which militate against community. In the former case, there is not enough time to get to know people: to converse, to find out what interests them. In the latter case, boredom and frustration can produce anti-social behaviour.

A sense of community can disintegrate when people form or stay in cliques, or boys and girls 'pair off' exclusively and shut other people out of their relationships. This is common where there is an inadequate focus on a common, absorbing activity in which campers are engaged. If good experiences tend to 'creep up on us' when we're not looking for them and elude us when we are too consciously seeking them, the *best* camping experiences may be expected to emerge where teenagers are absorbed in an activity, rather than sitting around trying to seek their own amusement.

Camping organizations should consider the value of 'service' camps. An example is a group of teenagers, with their own leaders, providing a holiday for some disadvantaged children. Such a camp may be expected to yield a deeper level of fulfilment than the traditional snow-skiing camp or whatever for those who can afford it. There is an inducement to evaluate our aims, the clientele we want to serve, the leaders we recruit and the leadership qualities we promote and nurture.

4. Quality leadership
The proposition is sometimes put forward in camping circles that it would be desirable to have a listing of camp leaders — a pool of people who could be called upon by anyone organizing a camping program. This idea has obvious appeal, both for would-be camp organizers and intending leaders.

Such a suggestion, however, if accepted uncritically, reflects a view of camping as certain kinds of outdoor activities, not as community. A person can have all the outdoor skills in the world and still be a liability in the temporary community.

Two young men came to a camp with good credentials for water-sport leadership. They couldn't fit in with the rest of the team. It was a real problem. The teacher who doesn't like students barely survives at school. Living with the same young people for five days is a misery if you can't get along with them.

There is no short-cut solution to finding the right leadership. You can't put a pin in a list, or even rely on an application form. An

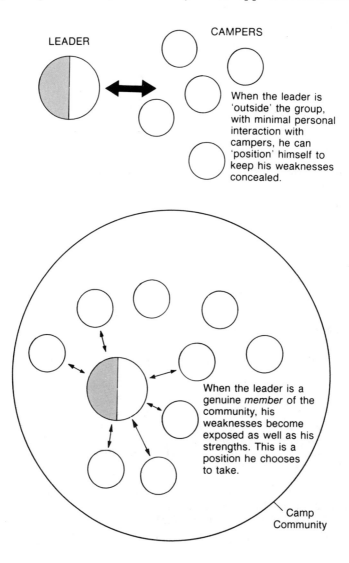

LEADER

CAMPERS

When the leader is 'outside' the group, with minimal personal interaction with campers, he can 'position' himself to keep his weaknesses concealed.

When the leader is a genuine *member* of the community, his weaknesses become exposed as well as his strengths. This is a position he chooses to take.

Camp Community

interview is necessary, but no guarantee. It does not accurately predict how a camp leader will function as a *member* of the community — where he will contribute his weaknesses as well as his strengths.

Most of us can hide our selfishness for a while. But in the cut-and-thrust of the temporary community, if we are serious about making real discoveries about conflict and reconciliation, we are vulnerable. To enter into other people's lives, to help and be helped, involves a two-way commitment.

Jim Punton of Frontier Youth Trust in the UK comments:

> What the kids demand of us opens up areas of our own personality that need healing, challenges bits of our own personality that have become too sterile and fixed and set. People who do frontier camping, in particular, are going to be younger and more enriched people as a result of it.[7]

There is much more to be said about leadership — the theme is developed in Chapters 8 and 9 — but one more remark is in order. The greatest demand on leadership arises out of the need for mutual trust. Speaking of the way in which relationships are developed within a group, David Merritt has said:

> One of the crucial concerns of planners and leaders in the early stage of a camp will be encouraging the development of a climate of trust and acceptance. Such developments take time. They require sensitive and patient working with people. They cannot be announced. Community does not result from a decision by leaders that there will be a community. It is the result of a group of people being with each other in particular ways that involve trust and acceptance.[8]

This can't happen without mature and unselfish leadership.

1   A point made in *The Camping Book*, Anzea Publishers, 1976, p.12
2   Paul Tournier, *The Meaning of Persons*, Harper & Row, 1973, pp.187-188
3   For example, the *Youth Say* Project, Sydney 1974
4   Hammerman, op. cit., p.60
5   Ibid.
6   Brian V. Hill, quoted in *The Camping Book*, op. cit., p.30
7   Jim Punton in *Gap* magazine, Issue 4:81, p.7
8   *Challenges to Camping*, op. cit., p.23

Part Two:
The Practice of the Temporary Community

6
Planning a Camp:
What are the basic principles?

AFTER DIRECTING DOZENS OF CAMPS over a period of twenty years, I still have trouble organizing and planning a camp. Sometimes this is due to a tired mental attitude, a 'here-we-go-again' sort of reaction. Sometimes it just reflects my own gifts: I'm not one of those who really enjoys detailed planning and organization. Whatever the cause, my colleagues are amused when I reach for a book to remind me what I have to do to organize the next camp.

The planning for any two camps will rarely be the same, if only because we may have a different group of leaders, with differing levels of understanding of our objectives and differing skills to contribute. Furthermore, if we are to take camping seriously, the planning of any camp should begin with basic aims as well as a thorough review and evaluation of how the last camp went. This task justifies the attempt at providing an overall scheme, a checklist for planning.

Organizations, directors and other camp leaders all have a role in planning. The organization should provide not only a basic philosophy, but also some organizational structures for leadership training, advertising, financial arrangements and facilities. Camp leaders, if they are to make their contribution adequately, must have some grasp of the overall picture as well, theoretical and organizational. Indeed, a director may well have outstanding leadership qualities, but still need the help of people with greater organizational gifts around him.

The functions of planning
In a team leadership situation, it is not enough simply for the *director* to know where he or she is going. Considerable anxiety

71

can be created in leaders who are not sure what is expected of them. Planning helps reduce anxiety. But there are three other broad functions of planning a camp which need to be understood:

1. We should ensure that the camp implements the philosophy and objectives of the sponsoring organization

Some organization (be it school, local church, scout group or whatever) is usually the parent agency for the camp program. The organization often is involved in more than just camping and therefore appoints a director for each camp, who is responsible for understanding the organization's objectives, interpreting them to other leaders and putting them into practice. This is a common structure; our approach here will assume this kind of structure.

THE PROCESS OF POLICY DEVELOPMENT IN AN ORGANIZATION

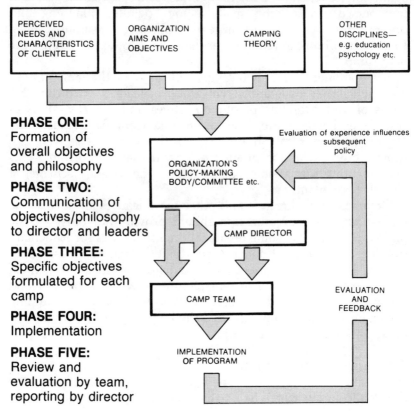

PERCEIVED NEEDS AND CHARACTERISTICS OF CLIENTELE

ORGANIZATION AIMS AND OBJECTIVES

CAMPING THEORY

OTHER DISCIPLINES— e.g. education psychology etc.

PHASE ONE: Formation of overall objectives and philosophy

PHASE TWO: Communication of objectives/philosophy to director and leaders

PHASE THREE: Specific objectives formulated for each camp

PHASE FOUR: Implementation

PHASE FIVE: Review and evaluation by team, reporting by director

Evaluation of experience influences subsequent policy

ORGANIZATION'S POLICY-MAKING BODY/COMMITTEE etc.

CAMP DIRECTOR

CAMP TEAM

EVALUATION AND FEEDBACK

IMPLEMENTATION OF PROGRAM

This diagram illustrates this facet of planning. It illustrates five phases in planning related to the implementation of basic objectives in the camp program:

Phase One: Determination of the organization's camping
                   objectives and philosophy
The organization's objectives are derived from four sources:
* the basic aims and philosophy of the organization
* camping theory
* its perception of who its clientele is and what their needs are
* other relevant areas of thought.

Phase Two: Communication of organizational objectives and
                   philosophy to the director
The extent to which this phase requires a structured program will depend on how familiar the candidate is with the organization already. The good director will of necessity have his own strong contact both with camping theory and with the clientele.

New directors should usually come from within the organization to ensure that they have assimilated the organization's basic philosophy. But the introduction of 'new blood' from outside the agency has the potential for renewing the vitality of the program.

Phase Three: Formation of specific objectives for each camp
This would normally be achieved by a combination of direct decision by the director, and discussion and planning among the leadership team.

Phase Four: Implementation
This occurs in the planning and execution of the camp program itself.

Phase Five: Review and evaluation
In a sense, this is where the planning process begins at the organizational level. Unless the camp program is adequately reviewed and evaluated by the camp leaders and, via reporting, by the organization, nothing will be learnt from the experience.

Experience and evaluation add to the pool of camping knowledge, reinforcing existing approaches or modifying them.

2. We should provide for the maximum utilization of opportunities

The aim of planning ahead is to ensure that we are able to make the most of the opportunities available. Good forward planning achieves the objectives of the camp in a number of ways:

(a) It facilitates adequate preparation

I have seen many great ideas fall flat because they simply didn't have the time to be implemented. For me, a game like 'storming the heights' is just a fun way to pass an hour with small boys. But with imagination and preparation, I have seen such an activity provide enjoyment for sixteen-year-olds for a whole afternoon. I observed the most lavish and intricate of preparations: diligent gathering of ammunition (including buckets of stirred-up water and horse manure), elaborate costuming, carefully drawn-up rules, earnest discussion of tactics, thoughtful attention to location — full attention to every detail.

(b) It communicates confidence to campers

I arrived at a residential conference the other day. As I approached the entrance to the building, the door swung open and I was greeted with a friendly smile by the organizer of the conference. That's good planning. He had prepared well enough to be free to do it; he had thought ahead in sufficient detail to know how he wanted the conference to begin.

When a family tumbles out of the car on arrival at the campsite, it is great if someone is there to greet them — to show them to their sleeping quarters or direct them to refreshments at the end of a long drive. It is great if someone can answer their questions (where it is safe for Johnny to play, where the toilet is, etc.) or to introduce them to other people that have arrived before them.

Detailed planning and preparation helps create a sense of caring and trust.

(c) It gives maximum adaptability in various circumstances

If you only plan ahead one day, what do you do when the weather thwarts your plans? The well-prepared leader can switch quickly to an alternative program prepared especially for such circumstances, or bring forward a suitable program segment from later-on in the camp. The un-planned camp grinds to an uncomfortable halt, while leaders desperately try to think of alternative activities.

3. We should minimize the unknown factors

Good planning includes forethought and investigation. There are always going to be things that we haven't counted on which will be awkward to handle. We should *anticipate* as many as possible. There is much that we can familiarize ourselves with in advance: the personal health and interests of the campers, the area we will be camping in, potential dangers, possible or likely weather conditions.

Take a walking trip for example. The good planner will minimize the unknown factor by careful checking of the route to be taken, consultation with local people and thorough preparation of food supplies. He will make some attempt to determine the fitness of the campers and check the suitability of their gear. He will find out everything he can and try to anticipate the possible difficulties which might arise. On the basis of this knowledge, he reduces the possibility of being caught unprepared and is more likely to arrive at his destination.

The poor planner knows what he'd like to do, but he doesn't take the trouble to 'minimize the unknown factor'. On the first day, Johnny is exhausted and George has to carry his pack as well as his own. They find that what appeared to be a substantial stream on the map has dried up and they have insufficient water. The leader pulls out his new tent and discovers it hasn't been supplied with any ropes. Good planning could have anticipated each of these problems and thus eliminated them.

Planning tasks

Once appointed, the director is involved in almost every part of the planning process. The following list outlines the various planning tasks and indicates where the main responsibilities lie. It can be seen that some tasks are carried out jointly by director, leaders, organization and even campers. The larger dots indicate major responsibility and the smaller ones indicate possible, but lesser involvement.

It is also easy to see how the tasks move across from one person to another, corresponding with the previous diagram. It is through this 'nuts and bolts' planning process, from major principles to fine detail, that objectives are achieved.

PLANNING TASKS	ORGANIZATION	DIRECTOR	LEADERS	CAMPERS
1. Establish overall aim and philosophy	*			
2. Appoint camp director	*			
3. (a) Major choice of type of camp	*	*		
(b) Make necessary site bookings	*	*		
4. Agree on organizational guidelines (e.g. deadlines, camp fee structure etc.)	*	*		
5. Prepare advertising, enrolment forms and promote	*	*		
6. Establish specific aims and objectives for this camp	*	*	*	
7. Recruit leaders, looking for balance of skills and personalities	*	*	*	
8. Identify training needs of leaders and plan to meet those		*	*	
9. Team preparation and planning				
★ investigation/familiarization/ information		*	*	
★ basic program structure		*	*	
★ timetable, specifics of program		*	*	
★ leadership roles, allocation of responsibilities		*	*	
★ appropriate training sessions	*	*	*	
10. Individual preparation by leaders in their own areas of responsibility			*	
11. Logistics: food, equipment, transport arrangements			*	
12. In-camp planning and evaluation				
— matters of principle		*	*	
— overall program		*	*	*
— group program		*	*	*
— camper's roles			*	*
13. Post-camp review, evaluation				
14. Reporting back to organization, suggestions for future action		*		
15. Follow-up of campers where appropriate			*	*

Camper participation in planning

The case for camper participation in decision-making was put forward in Chapter 5. But a few remarks are in order as to how that may take place.

(a) Size

A small group program structure will maximize the opportunities for participatory planning. It maximizes the opportunities for each group member to contribute and offers greater scope for people to pursue the different options they favour. Where there is no strong small group structure, possibilities still exist for campers to contribute to planning — such as a leader's meeting opened up to interested campers.

(b) Expectations

There need to be clear expectations about the extent of responsibility. Frustration will occur if campers expect the right to negotiate on non-negotiable issues, or regularly have their practical suggestions vetoed — however good the reasons may be.

(c) Appropriateness

The place and extent of participatory planning should be determined in advance by the leadership team in accordance with their objectives for the camp. It may sometimes be completely inappropriate. A 'stress' camping program can't work if campers can opt out of activities which frighten them.

Other factors affect this as well. For example, a well-planned *weekend* camp doesn't give much scope for in-camp planning. Some groups of campers may be incapable of serious participation in planning, or not want to be involved — though it is easy to make unwarranted assumptions about both.

(d) Cost

It needs to be recognized that a serious commitment to participatory planning includes a commitment to letting campers learn by their mistakes and living with what leaders see as poor choices. This is the 'price' of the true sharing of decisions.

(e) Limits

Participatory planning must not be allowed to squeeze out those vital meetings where leaders review, evaluate and adapt programs according to their judgement about how the camp's objectives are being met.

One word of caution is in order. It is vital not to fall into the trap of thinking that provision for in-camp planning with campers means less preparation beforehand. The opposite is true. Ways of shaping the community, when imposed by leaders, both define and close off options. Where options remain open, leaders need to be sufficiently prepared so that they can adapt.

7
Programming with a Purpose:
What are the main elements?

AN ENORMOUS VARIETY OF CAMPING is evident today, both in society at large and within particular organizations. It is possible to climb mountains, paddle canoes, fly aeroplanes, make pottery, develop your own photos, swing on flying foxes, watch movies, study electronics, ride waves, fly kites, cook damper, go bike touring, play guitars — and engage in many other activities within the camping program of one established organization. It might be tempting to conclude, therefore, that it really doesn't matter at all what sort of program you have, so long as it is fun!

There is an element of truth in this. But it could also be true that many activities that pass for camping may not contribute very much to our basic aims. Mere activity, however exciting, does not guarantee the achievement of deliberate goals. It is not enough to say that campers are being entertained or have plenty to do.

It is a sad fact that many parents see camps as little more than an expanded child-minding centre, a real-life TV which serves meals as well. A camp run purely on a commercial basis could probably survive by doing very little more than minding children, but what a miserable caricature of 'quality' camping that would be. We are talking about meshing certain social and educational ideals with the needs, aspirations and fears of real people — people with rich potential yet sometimes impoverished environments — and building them up, moulding them together, through the experience of a temporary community.

The basic choice: camping style
The first step to achieving our purpose is the form of camp we choose. The following table represents the main variables in organized camping:

MAJOR VARIABLES	MOST COMMON ALTERNATIVES		
	A	B	C
1. Age Grouping	YOUTH	FAMILY	OTHER (e.g. elderly, father and son, etc.)
2. Time Available	WEEKEND	4–5 DAYS (e.g. school camps)	7–10 DAYS (e.g. holiday camps)
3. Main Activity	ADVENTURE— including stress camping	RECREATION	SPECIAL INTEREST (e.g. service, arts, study camps)
4. Location	FIXED SITE	MOBILE (e.g. bushwalking, touring)	BASE CAMP PLUS OUT-TRIPS
5. Group Structure	SMALL GROUPS as basic units of community and program	WHOLE GROUP as basic unit of community and program	WHOLE GROUP for community SMALL GROUPS for activities

This scheme is not included merely as a descriptive device. Classification of camping styles is not our purpose. What is important is that we make conscious choices and satisfy ourselves that the style of program we come up with is the best way we know to achieve our basic objectives. What are the choices and how do we make them?

1. The camp director's choices
First, we should distinguish between the choices of the organization and those of the individual director.[1] The organization, be it school, church, society or even government

agency, has a breadth of resources which make choices more real. The individual camp director is limited by his own gifts and experiences.

Suppose I am a teacher, with water-sports experience. I am asked to take thirty Year 8 students to the school's campsite for a 'getting-to-know-you' camp at the start of the year. There are some canoes available, but the other teachers have no water-sports experience apart from a life-saving qualification. My camping style will look like this:

MAJOR VARIABLES	MOST COMMON ALTERNATIVES		
	A	B	C
1. Age Grouping	YOUTH	FAMILY	OTHER (e.g. elderly, father and son, etc.)
2. Time Available	WEEKEND	4-5 DAYS (e.g. school camps)	7-10 DAYS (e.g. holiday camps)
3. Main Activity	ADVENTURE— including stress camping	RECREATION	SPECIAL INTEREST (e.g. service, arts, study camps)
4. Location	FIXED SITE	MOBILE (e.g. bushwalking, touring)	BASE CAMP PLUS OUT-TRIPS
5. Group Structure	SMALL GROUPS as basic units of community and program	WHOLE GROUP as basic unit of community and program	WHOLE GROUP for community SMALL GROUPS for activities

Because of the limited skills of the staff available, the only real choice is probably 5B or 5C; option 5A would work against the aim of maximizing interaction between all teachers and students.

So the director's choices are relatively limited. He should really be doing what he likes doing and what he can do best. But this should not prevent him facing up to the challenge, which might come from the organization, to tackle something new that he doesn't feel so confident about. The most important thing is that he really believes in what he's doing.

2. The organization's choices

For an organization, however, there are many real choices available. The challenge for them is not to be content simply to maintain a varied program, but to really spend time asking what forms of camping will best fulfil the aims of the agency. Questions which might be asked at each level could be:

(a) Age grouping

A welfare agency might ask: Are these children best removed from their family setting for camp, or would it be possible to repair their relationships with their parents by taking the whole family away?

(b) Time available

A holiday camping organization might ask: Could this camp achieve its aims in less time, thus reducing the cost significantly and enabling more campers to come?

(c) Main activity

A youth organization might ask: Should we be running a 'stress' camping program, to develop our promising young leaders who have already tried other options?

(d) Location

A scout leader might ask: Given that this new group of scouts are raw beginners, would a site-based camp majoring on badge work be more suitable this time than our usual bushwalk?

(e) Group structure

A school might ask: Can we build in some significant group leadership by students which will help us identify the effective leaders and accelerate interaction between students without detracting from the marine biology program?

These are just a few examples of the sort of analysis which we need to apply regularly to our programs. Of course there are limitations to what we might like to do. For example:

* Cost

   It is no good running a program that campers cannot afford.
* Leadership

   We can't run an adventure program if we don't have leaders with the necessary skills.

3. Tools for making our choices

(a) Who are we planning for?

I remember running a special interest camp for adolescents. The basic format was an exploration by boat of the Gippsland Lakes.

We had visions of developing crews and watches, teaching navigation, ropes, knots and seamanship, and even examining the campers' knowledge at the end of the camp.

On reflection we selected the wrong style of camp for that particular group. The camp would have worked better with a single-sex group of younger or older kids! We adapted the daily program and approach accordingly. Next time round, the target group would be different.

But this question of who we are planning for has deeper significance than that. It isn't just a question of running a program that suits whoever comes on camp. Chapter 1 raised larger issues: changes in our society which create various human needs.

If the camping styles we choose are expensive, they will also tend to be exclusive. If our camping styles are suited only to young, active, athletic kids, how will we help families who really need a positive experience of community living? These are questions of strategy, even questions of conscience.

One agency aimed at two new target groups one year: kids who needed some money (rather than paying out camp fees) and kids who were not used to the structures of its regular programs. The two new camps attempted were, respectively, a 'pumpkin picking camp' (in which campers and leaders lived together on a large property and worked for wages) and a mobile surfing camp (which moved from beach to beach following the surf).

(b) What are our objectives?

This question requires not just a look at some list of aims enshrined in a filing cabinet, but sorting out priorities. There are books which give lists of 'camping objectives'. These are so detailed and comprehensive that they can be a recipe for insanity, unless realistically evaluated for each camp.

Short of dropping campers from an aeroplane without parachutes, stress camping (with its objective of stretching people to the limits of their perceived abilities) can hardly be achieved in a weekend.

'Education for constructive use of leisure' can hardly be achieved in a snow-skiing camp, if the campers belong to a socio-economic group where they are unlikely ever to repeat the experience. The development of the ability to take responsibility for one's decisions is not likely to be achieved in a camp where a total group of forty is the basis for all activities. The learning of 'survival skills in the outdoors' is not likely to be greatly advanced in a fixed-site program, but 'the ability to function effectively in a democratic society' might be enhanced.

Creating a camp program

It is impossible to be specific about the way in which programs should develop. Uniformity would be disastrous. Programs would not only be repetitive and boring, but irrelevant to the needs of different campers.

But if we can't produce a detailed road map of how to arrive at an appropriate program, we can provide a compass to show the general direction. The following suggestions apply to a seven-day camp, simply because it is helpful to have a reasonably common, concrete example. The ingredients of the program set out below are listed in the order suggested by a developmental understanding of how the temporary community works. This has two features:

(a) Chronological stages

These are stages in the growth of the program and relationships. They are represented by the vertical division on the diagram below.

(b) Phases of intensity

These are represented by the top line. Moving across from the left, we see represented a gradual build-up, then a tapering off in intensity in the consciousness of the group about its identity as a community.

PHASES IN A CAMP PROGRAM

a developmental approach to programming, each phase having a distinctive purpose

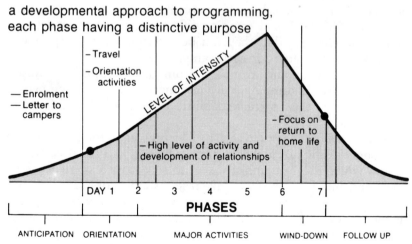

1. Anticipation stage

Camp really begins when the leaders and campers first assemble to go on a bus or train. But in a sense the anticipation, the excitement — even the fear — prior to camp is really part of the total camp experience.

The following activities may affect positively the expectations campers bring:

* A comprehensive and friendly letter to campers several weeks prior to camp.
* A meeting with campers and parents before camp to clarify requirements and build bridges.
* A warm welcome at the meeting point, with early arrival by leaders and name tags or other form of identification.
* Low-key, non-threatening games or projects prepared to entertain campers on a long journey, or facilitate the learning of others' names.

Obviously, some of these suggestions may be irrelevant to particular camps or circumstances, e.g. weekend camps operating with an existing, known group of people. The expectation and orientation phases of camp will either be very brief or covered over a period of time in the 'back home' situation.

2. Orientation stage

In some cases leaders who have gone ahead to set up camp may not have met the campers at all before they arrive. Some campers may have travelled independently as well. In either case, the main process of orientation will normally happen in the first day or two of camp. The sorts of activities which will be required in the first couple of days are those which:

* Help all campers and leaders to get acquainted. These range from arranging places at meals with place-cards, to particular games.
* Promote the development of trust and acceptance. These should be low-key and non-threatening, e.g. a discussion in which we discuss reactions to something 'out there', rather than introspection about personal matters.
* Develop the leaders' knowledge and understanding of the individual campers. This applies particularly to small group activities where group leaders will work with their own groups.
* Give campers a clear idea of what the leaders' expectations are. This will obviously cover aspects of safety, as well as the broad

purposes of the camp. Any up-front presentation will vary according to the group of campers. Rules, for example, may best be presented in a walk around the area, simply restated crisply to the whole group in a more formal setting for re-inforcement.

* Introduce the main activities and give basic training in the main skills that may be required later in the camp and on expeditions. A swimming test, for instance, may be important, or a thorough check of a camper's pack before he or she sets out on a five-day climb.

3. Major activities stage

During this stage the major activities of the camp are in full swing, the level of excitement peaking at the end of these few days. That peak might represent the climbing of a mountain, a competition, a 'highlight' small-group experience, a corroboree or whatever. But at best it will be a culmination of the activities of the preceding days, rather than an isolated event.

The planning of major ingredients of the program should take the following considerations into account:

* A balance between the strenuous and the restful, the tailoring of activities to the capabilities and needs of the campers.
* A balance between the desire to build strong relationships and the need for campers to have time to themselves. Some camps are now building the 'solo' experience into their program. Here campers spend several hours or a whole night in the bush by themselves, with leaders providing a periodic check on their safety.
* A balance between activity and reflection. Few camps make adequate provision for campers to reflect on their experiences and for leaders to draw out the lessons to be learned. Periods of excitement are great, but quieter times are just as important.
* Exploration and appreciation of the environment. Star-gazing is enhanced when the city smog is left behind; even a pair of binoculars increases what one can see — especially if someone knowledgeable is around to point out various features of the night sky.
* A contribution by the campers to the area. Some camps have organized a bush cricket match or concert for others in the camping ground of a national park. Some camps have a tradition of doing some work for a couple of hours to improve the site they are using.

* A little imagination can see potential for fun and community-building in dish-washing and cleaning duties, as well as in campfires and mealtimes.
* It is better to have more things planned than you have time for, than to have too little for campers to do. It is exciting to see a well-planned camp which can cater for the busy as well as the tired. Free time is very necessary. Some campers will look forward to it, but for others it will drag. A range of casual fill-in activities, from tree-climbing to rock-painting, will enrich the camp experience.
* People are the main program resource: the able camp director will be able to identify the skills and interests of leaders. Short talks by leaders on a favourite subject can add sparkle to a mealtime or campfire. The most interesting hobbies and experiences can be unearthed among the campers and demonstrated or told to the group.

4. Winding-down stage

If the temporary community has really 'gelled', it will continue to gather momentum until the end of the camp. Indeed, some leaders unthinkingly promote this, aiming to bring the camp to a climax on the last night. This can create difficulties for campers for whom the whole experience has been a 'highlight' anyway.

But the temporary community *is* temporary. It is not only misleading, but possibly harmful to create expectations and experiences which cannot be fulfilled or continued in the mainstream of the camper's life 'back home'.

This is a risk for the successful camp, particularly if leaders are not sufficiently mature to recognize the limited, 'unreal' nature of that community. Youth camps in particular are susceptible to this danger. Sometimes with great sincerity leaders identify with the problems that teenagers have with their parents, but they do it in such a way as to reinforce the camper's sense of frustration, even sense of self-righteousness concerning their relationships with their parents.

This sort of approach is inadequate. If the temporary community is to be considered valid, it must always point to the camper's home situation, equipping young people to live there. There has to be a genuine attempt to enable campers to transfer the lessons of community to home.

It is good for a teenager to find understanding and acceptance in camp. He or she may even make significant steps towards learning to share honestly with others, but this learning needs to be deliberately and consciously focussed on the home context. The ultimate aim must be to enable him or her to be honest, open, giving and receiving, seeking reconciliation with his or her mum and dad, family and friends.

During the last day or so, therefore, a conscious effort has to be made to help campers 'wind down' emotionally and to direct their attention to returning to their normal life. We have to think further ahead than the moment we wave goodbye. It is not fair to the parent if a child goes home emotionally overwrought or exhausted because we haven't programmed for a 'winding down' phase.

Programming for this phase of camp should include:
* a well-organized scaling-down of activities and preparations for cleaning of site, storage and equipment
* a gradual promotion of thoughtful attitudes to parents and others on returning home and discussions of problems likely to be encountered
* group photos (perhaps on the last full day, not at the last minute) and exchange of addresses
* a good last-night activity with a well-planned program to lead into a reasonable night's sleep.

5. Follow-up stage

Camp leaders have too often thought of their responsibilities as concluding when the camper disappears in a crowd of commuters after being dropped off at the end of camp. The way in which we actually 'deliver' campers back home is important, especially if they are children.

The way we part from campers is more than mere geography or transportation. Many will leave the temporary community with heavy hearts, dreading the return to the house they know, their brothers and sisters, the 'uncle' who hangs around mum or the teacher who 'picks' on them.

If we have developed close bonds with these campers, we may have the opportunity to be a continuing friend and helper. Not all will need us. Even those from 'tough' backgrounds have more resilience than we have. But a letter in the mail — or a phone call — a few weeks later may mean a lot to a child. The mature leader may be able to help a mum at her wits' end get on better with a son or daughter.

An extension of the program might include:
* a reunion with a barbecue meal at a leader's home
* a weekend camp, which could take the campers further in an area of study or skills already undertaken at camp
* phone calls, letter-writing and details of another camp in twelve months' time.

Making it happen
The daily timetable is not a strait-jacket, but a necessary tool to enable us to achieve what we've set out to do. Here again examples are limiting, but experience suggests that there are some useful pointers to help each director and team of leaders work out what is best for their campers:

1. Advance notice
The timetable needn't be the same every day, but uniformity is helpful. Advance knowledge of when campers need to be where helps give:
(a) young campers a sense of security
(b) older campers the freedom to plan for their own free time
(c) the cook time to make adjustments for any changes of plan.

2. Allocated time
We don't just need time for activities. There are as many facets of life in camp as there are at home. People want to clean their teeth and have time to get to where they are going, as well as eat, sleep and engage in exciting activities. Time must be allowed every day for:
* adequate sleep
* movement between places of eating, sleeping, activities and showers
* daily routines, such as dressing, washing, cooking and other duties
* eating meals — neither rushed, nor dragged out with endless announcements
* free time for talking and relaxing
* time for leaders to get together and review/discuss/share problems/ evaluate/make decisions
* time for activities — having too little time for the major activities is as frustrating as having no free time.

Programs for community?

I am conscious that I have said very little about programs specifically set up to create a sense of community. There are particular techniques, including relationship-building games and exercises, which can accelerate the development of honest interaction and understanding between people. There are plenty of books on the subject and training courses are generally accessible as well.

There are activities which can be used to 'develop community'. Some we have mentioned: decision-making, discussion in small groups, reflection on the camp experience, thoughtful use of meals to introduce new people to one another, activities which teach cooperation and so on. But beyond this we do not propose to go — and this is a conscious decision. The idea of 'building a temporary community' can have too mechanistic a ring. You can't build community like you can build a house — merely by assembling the required ingredients. The temporary community, as we see it, is about the quality of relationships between people.

Understood in this way, 'community' is a gift which we receive when relationships of interdependence, loving and forgiving occur between persons who are unique. This view of persons means that while we want such relationships to develop, we can't ultimately make them happen. We must respect the camper's right and need to participate in his own choice in his own time. Programming is aimed at creating the conditions which we hope will predispose campers to worthwhile experiences.

1   The term 'camp director' in this book refers to the person in charge of a particular camp program, not a campsite. This is very different from common American usage.

8

The Art of Leadership:
How can we identify and develop it?

WE HAVE ALREADY ESTABLISHED that quality leadership is an essential requirement of the temporary community. The temporary community depends on having leaders who can create a climate of trust and acceptance, and exercise practical care for campers without discrimination.

The demands of leadership

1. Nowhere to hide
The most pressing demands on camp leaders flow partly from their very membership of the community, with all their strengths and weaknesses. When you are living 'in the round' with people twenty-four hours a day, you can't hide much. Normally you can go home to your castle and lick your wounds. At camp you can't go anywhere.

2. Fatigue
Many camp activities are strenuous enough, but in addition leaders have heavy responsibilities, work harder and get less sleep. The personal pressure of relating to campers, especially those who need special help, is emotionally draining. Yet the leader is required to encourage weary campers, keep spirits up when it rains and, if successful court actions are any indication, probably not go to sleep either lest a camper sneak outside and put his foot in a disused rabbit trap.

3. The exercise of authority
Just as some people are physically stronger than others, so some carry the burden of leadership more lightly. Some groups are also easier to lead than others. But leadership and authority go very

much together. Authority doesn't have to be a nasty word. In the case of a children's camp, a leader has authority given to him by the parents. They expect him to exercise it in the interests of the safety and education of their child. In an adult camp, authority is given by the participants — an unwritten contract which recognizes that someone must accept responsibility. But the privilege has to be earned as well, if authority is to be sustained in difficult situations or crises.

Many leaders experience a conflict between the desire to build and maintain friendships, and the need to exercise authority. This needs to be resolved. There have been some classic examples in top-grade football of popular players, who, having become coaches, have rapidly found out that they can no longer be 'one of the boys' and obtain the desired results. The exercise of authority can be difficult.

4. Legal responsibility
Leaders have a legal responsibility to exercise a proper duty of care towards children. While the responsibility is the same for everyone, those leaders with an anxious temperament can find the tensions involved in supervising children very burdensome. I have sat next to parents who were totally relaxed about four-year-olds hanging by one foot from the top of some playground equipment and have been scarcely able to prevent myself from interfering!

5. Self-imposed demands
The leader who has high standards for his own performance places demands upon himself. Other people can shrug off poor performances, disappointing experiences and inadequate planning. But the leader who really believes in the objectives of the camp senses a responsibility to the campers and to the sponsoring organization for achieving high standards of program and relationships in the whole camp.

The implications of these demands of leadership are obvious in the recruitment and training of suitable leaders. There are important qualities which we must look for, and there are skills which in many cases can be brought out by suitable training.

Leadership qualities
It is consistent with the whole concept of organized camping as 'temporary community' that the all-important question is the sort

of person the leader is. This is a more important consideration than personality or abilities. There are some common characteristics of the quality leader. Here are just a few which could provide a starting point for self-evaluation or for leader recruitment.

1. Self-acceptance

This is a very basic virtue, yet we need to be cautious. None of us is perfect and most of us have areas of our personality or memories of failure which undermine our confidence. Our perception of what sort of person we are is coloured by these. It is a salutary experience as a father, for example, to realize that you may be reacting angrily to the behaviour of your child at least partly because it reminds you of a weakness of your own.

What we are talking about here is not self-satisfaction or supreme self-confidence, nor is it the opposite extreme of carelessness or disregard. It is that maturity which enables the leader to 'be himself' without trying to change his personality or behaviour — to be something that he really isn't, even trying to fulfil his image of the perfect leader!

If campers sense that leaders are putting on a 'pose', that sense of mutual respect, trust and confidence will not develop.

2. Commitment

The leader needs to be willing to become committed to the aims and objectives of the camp. He needs to be committed to the camp director and the other leaders, and he must be committed to the welfare of the campers.

We have all seen leaders who are committed to the camp program, but whose contribution is limited to their abilities as a skill instructor. A key feature of the sort of commitment required is unselfishness — in essence, commitment to someone else's interest rather than our own. This sort of leader will tend to be at the end of the queue, scrubbing that burnt porridge pot, or helping his campers settle down for the night while others are enjoying a mug of tea around the campfire or in the warmth of the kitchen.

Another feature of commitment is willingness to learn. Training is a negative word to some people, but it yields real rewards and can be thoroughly enjoyable. To be more useful in the camping program in which I was first involved I joined the university archery club, congratulating myself on choosing such a dull sport for the sake of camping. It was, in fact, a lot of fun and very rewarding.

I also joined a sailing club for the same reason, though I didn't think I could afford it. The first five Saturdays the weather was too bad to sail. I made a home-made canvas trapeze harness, which broke more than once to the great annoyance of the skipper. Furthermore, the owner had spent his last cent on the boat and couldn't afford a spinnaker. Eighteen years later I'm still learning how to put one up without getting it — or me — in a tangle. But I learnt much, enjoying every minute.

Willingness to learn is an on-going attitude and its most important feature includes willingness to accept advice, to do the unglamorous job and to have a go at something new.

3. Humility

This is another quality which may seem a strange choice. Yet humility is closely related to the understanding of camping as fundamentally a 'people' thing. As a matter of fact it is hard to think of any activity, if done in the interests of campers, which doesn't require humility.

I was about to say you don't need humility to drive a ski-boat, but to drive a ski-boat properly could involve just that. For example, driving it slowly for safety (or moderately for economy) could be hard when the situation lent itself to speed or showing off. To drive cheerfully hour after hour with beginners who fall off their skis can also require a special kind of humility.

Humility is the key to putting others first, the key to real service, the key to building relationships with people who may admire you just because you're a leader. The humble leader is the one who will seek out the reject, the isolate. He's the one who will let kids 'hang around' when they need to. He's the one who is able to listen rather than talk, and is therefore aware of how people are feeling and able to recognize weaknesses in the camp program and his own performance.

The humble person is a community person, because he recognizes what others can offer him, as well as what he can give. And he is prepared to conciliate — to back down when he is wrong, or apologize when he has hurt someone with a clumsy response or a sharp 'put-down'.

A key test of whether someone is a suitable leader is whether that person can be led — can work under someone else. A person who can't do that is unlikely to be able to command the loyalty and respect of others.

4. Sense of humour

A good sense of humour can contribute enormously to a camp. It's not just a matter of making people laugh — though that helps. The person who is quick-witted can do more than entertain. Humour can deflate tension and enable people to back down from an aggressive position or see the other point of view.

Humour is certainly a bridge between people of all ages. It can also put apparent conflicts into perspective. A favourite example of mine is from *Three Men in a Boat*, Jerome K. Jerome's tale of the adventures of three friends who took to the Thames in a boat for what was effectively a 'camping trip'. The extraordinary resilience and good humour of the three companions as they bungled their way up the Thames is epitomized in Harris' toast after supper. Having abandoned the fortnight's boating two days earlier because of rain, they sneak away to a favourite restaurant.

> 'Well,' said Harris, reaching his hand out for a glass, 'we had a pleasant trip, and my hearty thanks for it to old Father Thames — but I think we did well to chuck it in when we did. Here's to three men **out** of a boat!'[1]

5. Courage

A glance at the demands of leadership already mentioned should be enough to satisfy anyone that courage is a necessary attribute for a leader. Sometimes people are described as tireless workers or fearless leaders. But the leader hasn't been born yet who never got tired or never feared anything.

The able leader is someone who keeps going when tired, or who faces fear and overcomes it. Courage is only required when there is fear to be overcome. There is no virtue in a mere lack of fear — this may well reflect ignorance of the true nature of the task. The commitment to 'go somewhere', to take campers into new experiences of real value, almost inevitably involves courage.

We do not gauge this sort of courage by putting a prospective leader in a boxing ring with the world heavyweight champion and timing how long he stays in there. We are looking for people who have the courage of their convictions — people who are not mere followers, but who can take the course of action they believe to be right, whether popular or not. That sort of decision is part-and-parcel of the leadership task, just as it is part-and-parcel of responsible parenting or responsible government.

Structures for camp leadership: the team concept

In most organized camping, there is not one leader but several. In small mobile camps and family camps, the leaders may be relatively few and take a low profile. Even so, the concept of a leadership team which is almost a mini-community within the camp is well worth considering. In the larger temporary community, it is often essential.

In some organizations a camp director is appointed, that person being expected to run the camp, drawing in other people where necessary to assist. Sometimes the people who are actually running the program have had little or no involvement with the development of the actual aims of the camp. This reduces their status and function to that of 'helpers'. They carry out a program which really belongs to someone else.

With the team concept of leadership, the person given the responsibility for the camp recruits a team of leaders who will share the planning, organizing and execution of the camp from the beginning. This approach provides an effective structure for leadership.[2]

(a) Communication
From the outset communication breakdowns can be avoided amongst leaders through regular meetings. All leaders understand the aims, program and one another — not just the decisions, but the way they were arrived at.

(b) Planning
Team planning utilizes the available resources and insights of all leaders. The ideas and objectives arrived at by team planning will be the genuine fruit of discussion. Such plans are much more likely to be suited to the leaders themselves. Team planning puts people in the picture from the start.

(c) Motivation
Leaders will be much more highly motivated to perform well, if they have participated in planning and therefore believe in what they are doing. Besides, 'team life' is perhaps the richest reward for many leaders and often more than compensates for the sacrifices made in group leadership. Indeed 'team life' often provides the

source of strength to sustain group leaders in their sometimes lonely task, 'on their own' during an expedition or in a tent at night.

(d) Evaluation
Regular team meetings during camp and after enable the fullest evaluation to take place. Situations are examined in the light of all the leaders' observations, rather than from the limited viewpoint of one or two who may, by virtue of their roles, be simply unable to gain a true perspective.

(e) Organization
While organization is often best done by one or two people, the co-ordination (letting each leader know where he/she fits in and ironing out problems that occur) is best achieved in a team meeting. Organizers often overlook very small, seemingly irrelevant problems which emerge when plans are shared. It is often group leader Janette who points out that camper Susan won't be able to do the dishes because she's allergic to soap, or some such thing. . .

This view of the leaders as a 'team' has been called the 'concept of staff as an organic unit'. Speaking of the large site-based camp, Hedley Dimock says:

> The camp staff should be viewed as a functioning organism within the larger camp community, rather than as a combination of individuals filling various positions.[3]

This view is based on the belief that the leadership team corporately sets the tone and atmosphere (the camp spirit), embodies the values that the camp stands for, creates the conditions for the achievement of camp objectives and influences the quality of relationships in the camp as a whole.

Leadership ratios

If camping is conceived as community and not simply as outdoor activity, then the ratio of leaders to campers must be sufficiently high to enable the establishment of significant relationships between people. Leaders are 'guides to processes for people interacting with people as well as for people participating in program activities'. More leaders will be required than are needed simply to run activities or to keep law and order.

Another important factor is the way in which the structure of the program reflects the emphasis on the development of leader-camper relationships. I take it as a basic axiom of camping with children and young people that there should be a leader attached to each sleeping group. These groups should probably be no greater than seven or eight — and often less — and should be the basic unit of camp.

A third factor is the total size of the camp. It is important to decide in advance what the ceiling on the number of campers should be. If, for example, all the campers and leaders are to know each others' names, then a total of forty to forty-five is probably about the maximum for a week-long camp. Even then a real effort at learning names will be needed. Experience suggests that the feeling of a camp changes significantly when numbers rise above thirty campers. At that point you have a significantly less intimate unit.

There is no ideal number for a camp or a group. We need to decide in advance what the best ratios are for us, taking into account our aims, previous knowledge of the campers and the availability of good leaders for the program we have in mind.

Leadership roles

The precise roles which leaders are required to fulfil will vary according to the size of the total group. In small camps some leaders will perform more than one function. The director may also be a group leader, a group leader may be an instructor as well, and so on.

1. The camp director

We refer here to the person who is finally 'in charge' — ultimately responsible for all that happens in the camp. This task has five main aspects:

(a) Aims and objectives

The camp director is responsible for the formulation of the camp aims and objectives, within the framework of the organization's aims and objectives. His responsibility therefore includes familiarizing himself with what the organization's requirements are. Then, partly by his own planning and partly with the participation of his team, he must translate those broad aims into the specific aims of his own camp.

(b) Overall control

The director is responsible, in the final analysis, for everything that happens in camp. Since he obviously can't do everything, he has to develop the art of delegation. He will:

* choose the team of leaders to work with
* delegate tasks to facilitate all aspects of camp organization
* decide on the best way to involve each leader in tasks that he believes they can do
* continue his oversight, evaluating success with leaders to ensure that delegated tasks are accomplished and that leaders are coping.

(c) Morale

Morale is not just something on the surface, like laughter. People laugh nervously sometimes, or to cover up feelings of despondency or hurt. Good morale is a product of a sense of well-being, or knowing where you're going. People have gone to the stake with their heads held high and in good spirits, but not because it was fun.

Morale is a measure of how different people react under the same circumstances. There are bound to be difficulties, whether external (like the weather) or internal (like personality clashes). The director has a key role in keeping people focussed on essentials and in good spirit.

(d) Standards

High standards are an expression of our concern for the welfare of the camper at every level. A genuine concern for Ken or Anne will show itself in the way we look after his or her needs in every aspect of camp life. The camp director will see that the highest standards practicable are maintained in the areas of:

* safety in activities
* hygienic conditions for eating and ablutions
* preparation and organization of program
* care of personal and camp property
* conduct of leaders
* standards of teaching and instruction.

To do all this the director must be 'standards conscious'. The experienced leader who has been asked to accept director responsibility will be that sort of person. Nevertheless, he will also be prepared to insist on the maintenance of high standards by his team. As some of them are usually friends, this may require some courage and tact.

(e) Training

In an organization the director is a key link in the leadership

training process. First, he is a known person who has the respect
and friendship of grass-roots leaders. This makes him a key person
in motivation. The demands of the organization may seem
bureaucratic and remote. Most people need personal invitation
and encouragement to get them into training programs.

Second, the director is in a key position to do some of the most
significant training of all — training 'on the job'. He models
leadership. He gives opportunities to exercise it, through the
delegation of tasks. And he can conduct formal and informal
teaching sessions about leadership in the course of team planning
and the camp itself.

2. The group leader

Campers may be grouped in various ways, but the two most
common groupings are sleeping groups and activity groups. In
some cases the two may be different, but in many camps they are
the same. Either way, the leader who has the main responsibility
for looking after the welfare of each camper is the one who belongs
to a sleeping/living group.

The group leader's role is quite crucial in the temporary
community. The group leader variously performs the functions of
parent, brother or sister, teacher, nurse, counsellor, coach,
steward, magistrate, supervisor, secretary and, above all, friend.
This is where the care, encouragement, instruction, welfare,
advice, supervision, discipline, example — in short, the total care
for the camper — really happens. It is in the relationships between
all leaders and campers, but especially through the group leader.

This pivotal role is essentially practical. It is the group leader
who should know the camper's name first and start to gain a
personal understanding of the camper. It is the group leader who
will make sure each camper understands what is required, feels at
home and copes with the minor crises, whether flat torch batteries
or a headache.

The group leader's responsiblity is not only for the individual
campers in his group. He is also responsible for the functioning of
the group as a unit — the way they relate to one another, as well
as the way they contribute to the total life of the camp. One group
can have a large influence on the whole camp community —
positive or otherwise — in the way they make their presence felt,
undertake their duties or co-operate in 'whole group' activities.

This involves the group leader in helping the group work

together and in mediating camp policy to the group. He will not take sides with his own group. He may take up their cause in certain events, but he will maintain:

(a) Loyalty to the director
This does not mean blind obedience. The good leader will be open and honest with his opinions, but will accept the ruling of the camp director, keeping the director informed of how things are going in his own group.

(b) Commitment to the whole camp
The keen group leader can occasionally forget that the temporary community is larger than his own little group, important though that may be. He must have a real commitment to the camp community as a whole. This will express itself in the enthusiasm with which his group performs its washing-up duties, or in his preparedness to look out for the interests of other campers and leaders.

3. The specialist leader

Not all people who are willing and able to assist in camps have the gifts, temperament or inclination to be a director or a group leader. But they do have other skills and gifts which equip them for a diversity of specialist tasks which are of the utmost importance.

Common specialist tasks include:
* 'skill' instructors for activities
* cooks
* quartermaster (food and equipment supplies, fuel etc.)
* camp parents
* medical officer.

It is, of course, easy to overload a camp with leaders; a proper balance must be found. Too many leaders and their families can really detract from a camp for some age-groups. Campers start to wonder whether camp is really for them, or for the leaders to have a good holiday. But the specialists can contribute much more than their particular skills, whether it is driving a bus or teaching abseiling. Remember two things:

(a) Their part on the team
A real attempt should be made to organize team meetings so that specialists can take part — not only so that the team will benefit from their fellowship, but so that they will feel a part of the team and able to contribute to it.

In some cases this may be impossible during the actual camp, since team meetings often take place in the slack pre-meal time, when cooks are very busy and maintenance personnel will be patching up breakages that have occurred during activities.

(b) Their non-specialist contribution

Camp cooks, (especially motherly ones!) have an important contribution to make to the life of a camp. The kitchen is a homely sort of atmosphere; lonely people tend to gravitate towards the kitchen for warmth and friendship. An eggbeater can be put in the hand to take the mind off personal problems. The kindness of a cook who has time for people has, on countless occasions, restored the morale of a hurt or lonely camper — and sometimes of a leader as well.

Growing camp leadership

Almost by definition, camping involves us in activities and ways of relating to people which are outside the everyday experience of most of us. It is beyond our scope here to describe in detail the processes of growing adequate leadership, but a few key ideas deserve consideration:

1. Recruitment

The demands of the temporary community are so great that instructional or programming skills are not sufficient. What matters is the personal qualities of candidates and these must be carefully evaluated. Recruitment from among former campers helps, but new blood is also important. A carefully constructed application form for screening the potential leader can help, but usually an interview is necessary as well.

Problems often arise when the leader 'recruits' a friend and the camp director is placed in the awkward position of declining him if the new recruit is not suitable. There is always the temptation to take people along on the leadership team for their sake; we sometimes need to be more tough-minded about this. If the director is distracted and his energies are dissipated by resolving conflicts in the leadership team, or between a poor leader and campers, he is at a disadvantage.

Candidates for leadership should be informed accurately about the organization's requirements and policies, and about the particular role which they may be required to fulfil. In this way an unsuitable candidate will be given every opportunity to determine whether he wishes to proceed with his application. It will save embarrassment for the director and hard feelings for the person concerned if he chooses not to go, rather than needing to be told he is not suitable.

2. Training

There are many areas where training is required and innumerable ways in which it can be carried out. The following is a quick check-list of key areas which may be useful for those who need a starting-point to plan more adequate training schemes.

(a) Theory

Directors: camping philosophy — general policy of the organization principles of leadership

All leaders: objectives of the particular camp broad understanding of organization policy sound grasp of their own roles

(b) Practical skills

Directors: general competence in the area of the main camp activity — need not be expert up-front leadership skills teaching/training techniques management skills — especially the art of delegation understanding of group processes

Leaders: practical skills related to individual roles, whether activity leadership, group leadership or ancillary tasks like transport, provisions, medical, cooking

(c) Personal skills

Directors: understanding of campers — broad characteristics, and as individuals ability to win confidence and give a lead confidence in relating to parents and other groups perceptiveness — ability to identify problems and act on them, especially relationship problems ability to take the long view, maintain a balanced perspective

Leaders: ability to relate to campers on the basis of campers' needs (corporate and individual) — not their own needs

ability to work harmoniously with other leaders and contribute to group processes

tolerance and positive outlook

ability to gain the confidence of campers and maintain control where necessary

Some training is best done by the director himself during team meetings or in camp itself. The advantages of on-site training are:

* The situation is real, so the way of dealing with it is real.
* You can stand alongside and support the trainee as he learns.
* There is immediate facility for evaluation and relearning.
* The reality and immediacy of the live situation motivates the trainee to learn. He wants to know how to cope, and he can also have an immediate sense of achievement.
* The needs of the individual trainee become much more obvious in the actual camping situation.
* Skills can be demonstrated daily by accomplished leaders.

But the director has other things to do as well. Many aspects of training can be better achieved in other ways. Some aspects are the responsibility of the sponsoring organization. Some can be achieved through courses run by specialist groups in the community. Some can be done by guided reading. Training in many skills can be gained in sporting clubs, night classes, adult education courses or regular college courses.

However the training occurs, it won't happen without three pre-requisites:[4]

i. A conscious plan to develop leaders
ii. An inventory of leadership positions
iii. An inventory of potential leaders.

The spirit of the age is such that we cannot even assume that there is real consensus about the need for strong leadership at all. Indeed, some see the temporary community as requiring a fundamentally low-key shared leadership in which the exercise of authority in any traditional way is wrong in principle. The next chapter takes up this vital issue.

1 Jerome K. Jerome, *Three Men in a Boat*, Penguin, 1970, p.184
2 This outline first appeared in *The Camping Book*, op. cit., pp.51-52
3 Dimock, op. cit., p.93
4 R. Wolff, *Man at the Top*, Tyndale House, 1969, p.123

9
Authority, Discipline and Leadership Styles:
How do we maintain discipline in camp?

IT'S FUNNY HOW CAMPERS don't like going to bed. We have already recalled one warm January night when 'lights out' was the key point in a learning experience about decision-making. I vividly remember another — this time a cold May night in the late 1960s.

I was assisting in the running of a leadership conference for students in Years Eleven and Twelve of high school. It had been agreed by the conference staff that 11.00 pm was a reasonable 'lights out' time. On this night it was about eleven o'clock or a little after, when I was 'doing the rounds' of the cabins to get the lights turned off. It had been some time since supper, and ample time had been allowed to 'wind down' and get to bed.

Most groups were ready for sleeping, but one group showed no inclination to prepare for bed at all. When I poked my head in and made the usual noises about moving things along a bit, I was ignored and decided it was appropriate to make a polite but unambiguous statement about the need to get to bed.

To my great annoyance one prominent youth, with the support of others, proceeded to express the view that I should find something better to do and leave them to go to bed in their own good time.

I managed to suppress my school-teacher instincts sufficiently to discuss for a whole hour the pros and cons of a mandatory 'lights out' time. When the director of the conference complimented me for my patience, I felt proud, since she was a person whose excellent relationships with the students I much admired.

My initial response had been to justify the 'lights out' rule on the grounds that not to have one at all involved a considerable infringement on the rights of others. They needed a reasonable amount of sleep — an argument amply demonstrated by the thumps on the wall and the 'shut ups' from next door. But what really stunned me at the time was that it soon became abundantly clear that the root disagreement was not about the wisdom of lights out time, but whether I had any right to insist on it at all.

This struck me with sledgehammer force. I could remember myself as a camper less than ten years earlier sneaking out for a late-night stroll with a friend at the same conference. We had chosen to ignore the lights out rule, just as these kids were doing now. But when found by some vigilant staff-member, it did not enter our heads to question his right to send us packing. We were suitably mortified, especially because we were treated so kindly, and went back to camp.

In this way I became acutely aware of the extent to which attitudes to authority had changed. Later-on this was to be reinforced many times. I remember reading one day:

> In the modern world notions of supreme authority are not involved in the connotation of fatherhood. There is now something faintly ridiculous about the idea of a father trying to assert binding authority in the home . . . the comic strips in the cheap press have reduced the father to the stature of a genial and clumsy butt. He is a friendly but rather awkward bear about the house. He fills up the armchair, he has to be kept in good humour; but he must not be taken too seriously. . .!

> This image of the father is reproduced here in order to indicate the extent to which, in current thinking, the lovable has become the very antithesis of the powerful, the loving of the authoritative.

It seemed to be only the next day when I came across a comic strip which had precisely that image. In the first frame, the teenage boy was saying on the phone, 'Righto, I'll be right over!' In the second frame he says to father (sitting behind his newspaper in an armchair), 'I'm going to borrow the wheels, Pop!' In the third a voice floats up from behind the paper saying 'What are your two feet for?' In the fourth the teenager replies, 'One for the brake and one for the accelerator!' as he heads out of the door. Father is left in his chair with a big exclamation mark above the newspaper.

Clearly in these times some justification is required for the assertion that the exercise of authority is a necessary function of leadership.

Foundations of authoritative leadership
The exercise of authority is related to five assumptions about the temporary community.

1. A commitment to objectives
The idea of discipline and authority has immediate relevance if we wish to achieve our objectives. If it doesn't matter whether we teach something or reach something, it doesn't then matter whether the attitudes or actions of some members of the group make these objectives unachievable.

2. A commitment to particular values
Most, if not all, camping organizations and leaders have a commitment to certain values, expressed in the rules and standards of behaviour which give shape to the particular camp community. If, for example, conservation is highly valued, leaders have to decide how to deal with the campers who persistently play football in an ecologically fragile area or throw their rubbish in the bush.

The values concerned need not necessarily be the personal values of the leader, but may be values which parents of campers may assume would be upheld in camp. Any responsible leader has a commitment to uphold those values. If, for instance, a camper wanted to sleep with his girlfriend, it would pose a discipline problem for leaders in most situations.

It should be noted that we are not referring simply to middle-class values, or merely to certain moral viewpoints. 'Values' is to be understood as 'those aspects of our lives on which we place the greatest importance'. This could mean that a particular social value we prize may take second place to the importance of maintaining a trusting relationship — more of this in Chapter 10.

3. Legal responsibilities
The duty of care imposed on the camp leader inevitably involves him in restricting and controlling the behaviour of campers to ensure their safety. There are obviously many situations that arise where the camp leader has no choice but to insist on rules and commands being observed by campers.

4. Difficult campers
We established earlier that group living won't be all good. As long as campers reflect the diversity of the community at large, there

will be campers who are consistently difficult to manage. Others, in the excitement and perhaps freedom of the camp environment, will break out in uncharacteristic behaviour which will need to be checked before someone gets hurt.

5. A particular understanding of leadership
Sir William Slim, a great soldier and former governor-general of Australia, described leadership as that combination of persuasion, compulsion and example which enables you to get men to do what you want them to do.

Probably everyone is happy with 'example'. It is difficult to conceive of a serious argument against leadership by example. For one thing, it means that you won't ask anyone to do what you won't do yourself. And it is an invitation to follow, rather than a command.

Most people are probably happy with 'persuasion' as well, providing that it doesn't involve manipulation or blackmail. If legitimate means can be found to change people's minds, then they may follow willingly, even though they initially hesitate or refuse.

But compulsion? It is not immediately obvious to many people that compulsion has any place in the leadership of the temporary community. Even in the community as a whole, those of a libertarian persuasion would see compulsion as an *ultimate* weapon, to be used only as a last resort to prevent actions which are indisputably harmful to others.

But an element of compulsion has a legitimate and necessary place in camp leadership, albeit one which would rarely need to be used. If we are to take seriously our objectives, values and legal responsibilities and cope adequately with campers whose behaviour is destructive of the community and its objectives, we must come to terms with this. We need to take seriously the need for the leader to have the right to insist. The question is not whether he should have authority but how he should use it.

A positive concept of discipline
There are several ways in which the authority of a leader is recognized. For example, his judgement will be respected when he makes a decision on a matter of disagreement. His advice will be sought on a matter of importance. Our concern here is with authority as it applies to discipline.

To some people discipline is a dirty word. It has to do with rules and regulations and punishments. There is some truth, of course, in this concept. Discipline is a word like 'law'. It has to do with the limitation of behaviour.[2] It would be nice if laws were not necessary, but they are. And just as laws provide the framework to make society possible, so discipline helps people subordinate selfish interests to the welfare of the whole group.

Lack of discipline in a camp may result in injuries and damage to property. But, more subtly, it will result in unhappy experiences of all kinds, as the antisocial elements have their way. They will jump the queue and refuse to help with camp duties. They will monopolize the equipment and take someone else's piece of cake. They will 'pick on' the camper who is different in manners, dress or skin colour and keep other people awake at night.

If discipline is the means by which those sorts of behaviour are controlled, there must be something positive about it. Clearly, discipline involves some constraints on the behaviour of campers. They know what they are allowed to do and what they are not and, on the whole, they conform to the rules.

But good discipline is more than simply securing obedience. A sergeant-major can impose that sort of discipline by shouting and threatening. The sort of discipline we're talking about is not like that. We're talking about the tone, the total atmosphere of the camp — about camps in which a desired behaviour is achieved without damaging relationships and hurting people. Good discipline is characterized more by co-operation than by meek submission or rebellion. It is based on a clear understanding and acceptance of what behaviour is or isn't approved. Its results are obvious: good fun, co-operation, care of facilities, care for one another. But the way it is achieved is not quite so obvious.

Good discipline doesn't 'just happen'. Nor is it achieved by the rigid application of rules and punishments. Its achievement depends on the ability of camp leaders to create conditions in which common objectives are more attractive than the pursuit of selfish or destructive inclinations.

The sort of temporary community we have in mind is the sort in which these conditions prevail. But there are some quite specific skills which are required to make the theory work in the real-life camp situation:

(a) Anticipation
The discipline of your camp is not only the product of your total attitude to the camp and the campers; it is also being prepared in

advance for the sorts of problems that may arise. The first night of camp is too late to decide what time lights out should be, or how you will deal with the inevitable desire to talk all night. Insistence on immediate silence is quite unreal and asking for trouble. The whole team must be agreed as to what their approach will be.

(b) Communication

Having decided in advance on your general approach, you must then clearly explain what the 'boundaries' of behaviour are. If you don't want to allow campers to leave the campsite without permission, then you have to tell them before they have the opportunity to do so. It is unfair and unrealistic to expect campers to observe rules and standards which you have not clearly spelt out. In regard to important requirements, there may well be a case for a clear explanation of what is expected on the advertising material and/or the information sent to campers before camp.

We were reminded of 'persuasion' as a key element in Sir William Slim's definition of leadership. If we can effectively communicate our standards and objectives so that they become the standards and objectives of the campers, we are half-way there!

(c) Example

There is no question that the positive example of an effective leader 'rubs off' onto campers. If the leader fools about on his horse, so will the campers on theirs. If the leader throws himself into duties, so will the campers. This is quite obvious to an observer, yet many leaders seem to act selfishly or recklessly without any thought as to the effect on the campers. Unfortunately, their example is still effective and often produces poor discipline as readily as a good example produces good discipline.

(d) Supervision

The camp where leaders spend too much time with each other, 'hanging around' the kitchen after supper, is open to discipline problems. When you walk into a camp of thirteen-year-old boys at 10.00 pm you can tell in a moment whether they are being supervised adequately. If there are lots of shouts, banging, running footsteps, torchlights darting about among the cabins and threats like 'You wait, I'll get you later', it's a fair bet that the leaders are enjoying the warm glow of the kitchen after the evening program.

So many discipline problems are avoidable. Some arise from boredom; some because campers think no one will notice if they are not there. Sometimes it is the persecution of some 'small-fry' by a bully; at other times just a spontaneous but reckless response to circumstances. The mere presence of a good leader will minimize all these problems. This is a good reason for a high leader-camper ratio. Certainly, if leaders are going to take time off here and there, there must be others ensuring that the campers are adequately supervised. This also means choosing times for team meetings when campers are less likely to get up to mischief. Half-an-hour before rising time in the morning is one such time!

When all else fails

We must return now to the crunch question: What do you do when all else fails? The fact is that, despite our best efforts, occasions arise when there is a need to *insist* on certain behaviour because a camper is determined to do otherwise. The ability to exercise authority effectively depends on three inner attitudes:

1. Conviction about authority

Fundamental to effective action is the conviction that you have a *right* to insist.[3] Here we should focus more directly (though not exclusively) on the camp director. This is because the question of dealing with the 'ultimate' sort of defiance must come back to him or her.

There are times, of course, when a group leader must deal with these issues, too. We have a camp rule that no camper may swim in the surf at the Ninety Mile Beach. This is because of the danger of sharks and of campers being swept out to sea. If a small group has an overnight expedition in the area, perhaps sleeping in the dunes, the leader in charge sometimes faces the problem of campers who want to break this rule on a hot day. In this case, it is right and proper that the leader is able to say, 'Look, it's not my rule; I'm just not able to let you swim even if I wanted to.'

The camp director, then, needs to believe in his authority. He should be sure that the organization has invested its trust in him to uphold its policies and expects him to act accordingly. He should realize that parents (in the case of minors) expect him to maintain discipline. It is interesting that a 1982 survey showed that despite the apparent loss of certainty about discipline in education, lack of discipline is one of the main causes of community dissatisfaction with schools.[4]

In the case of preventing physical injury, there is no question that the director has not just a right but a legal responsibility to act with authority. Similarly, we believe that a camp director has a right and responsibility to the sponsoring organization, parents and campers to act with authority to uphold the objectives and standards of the camp.

2. Conviction about viewpoint

Alongside the conviction about authority is the conviction that you are right in the particular stand you are taking. Of course you won't be right about everything. Indeed you may have to be content that your chosen course is 'to the best of your understanding', the best one to take here and now, even though you are aware that later events may prove you wrong!

But the more convinced you are the better. That is why it is vital to anticipate potential difficulties. Experience is a great help here. This is one reason why it is better to have a mature person as director, even if he lacks great experience in the feature activities, rather than a less mature person who is an expert activity leader.

3. Care for the camper

The degree of willingness with which campers accept your requirements will be largely determined by what they think you feel about them. If you really have their best interests in mind and let this show, campers will not only accept your discipline more readily but also in a better spirit. I am not talking about anything soppy, of course. It hasn't got much to do with you telling them you care, nor with how readily you capitulate to their demands. Far from it. The measure of your care for them is shown by your determination to do what you believe is best for them. You may, in fact, demonstrate caring concern by refusing to let them do something that is dangerous or has 'fun' at the expense of somebody else.

There is no contradiction at all between care and absolute insistence on conformity to required behaviour. The notion of a loving insistence is very necessary if we are not to fall into the trap of mistaking *authoritarian* for *authoritative* leadership. Authoritarian leadership is a certain style of leadership, summed up in the phrase 'Because I said so!' It is often characterized by a heavy-handed style, where the conviction that we have the right to insist is not balanced by the recognition that authority is a gift to us for the benefit of the campers, not for our own survival or amusement.

Appropriate leadership styles

There are innumerable ways of classifying leadership styles in general. Styles of decision-making have been variously classified. One writer identifies three main styles — dictatorial, consensus or participative-delegation;[5] another five — democratic, autocratic, paternalistic, partisan or laissez-faire.[6] Our own personal leadership style will depend partly on our personality and partly on the models of leadership we have worked under and observed. But our attitudes should be informed by thoughtful reflection on a variety of human and theoretical models.

Decision-making is an important part of camp leadership, primarily for the director but also for the group leader, particularly when group participation in decision-making is called for. However our concern here is with leadership styles as it applies to the maintenance of good discipline.

Although an authoritarian style of leadership is an inappropriate one for the temporary community, authority must still be exercised by the camp leader. There are at least two factors which should determine the style of leadership we adopt:

(a) The background of the campers

The kinds of cultural differences which mark campers from different backgrounds are well illustrated by Jim Punton of the Frontier Youth Trust in the UK:

> Kids that FYT would work with most of the time have a particular way of handling conflict. They've had to stand firm and handle it in a way that uses their body. Some people on the other side would call that violence. However, these kids actually experience violence in verbal terms from teachers at school. They would experience sarcasm as violence because they don't know how to handle it. They would also experience being put down and made to feel small as violence. In middle-class circles, that wouldn't be violence. That would be a quite appropriate way for an adult to discipline a child. So there are two different patterns of handling conflict — and that's one of the challenges. If you've been brought up one way, chances are you'll have real problems when you come across kids handling their conflict in a quite different way, especially if the conflict is between you and the kid.[7]

It is interesting to note that a survey by the Irish Association for Curriculum Development revealed that 'more than half the school population preferred [corporal punishment] to sarcasm and other punishments, with 66% favouring it over lines'.[8] Clearly, it is not enough to say that any old approach to discipline will do.

There are two issues here. One is that different camper groups react differently to the same treatment. The other is that leaders and campers may have equally different ideas of what reasonable disciplinary measures are. This would not matter so much if the object of discipline was simply to secure a desired obedience, but it isn't. Discipline as a positive, total environment must be achieved by methods which don't unnecessarily alienate the camper. The leadership style we adopt should foster a spirit of mutual acceptance, with campers recognizing the limitations placed on them as necessary and reasonable.

Suppose that you have agreed that campers should not be allowed to smoke. With academic achievers who enjoy school, a 'school-teacherish' lecture on the penalties of smoking may be acceptable. For 'non-achievers', for whom anything to do with school is instinctively disliked, the confiscation of a packet of cigarettes may have all the connotations of 'police brutality'. A low key side-on approach — 'Make sure I don't see you with them' — will be far more effective than an aggressive, front-on approach.

This applies to the actual physical approach as well. It is far less threatening to ask someone a personal question when both are sitting with their backs to a tree, than if they are sitting opposite each other at a table. Yet a 'front-on' approach can sometimes be more effective than an oblique one. Some people would rather you 'came out with it' than beat around the bush.

(b) The age of the campers

The leadership style needs to be appropriate to the age of the campers. There will obviously be different approaches if the campers are primary school children, older teenagers or adults. Not only will the actual requirements be different, but the way in which they are communicated will be different. Here are three ways of communicating a particular rule.

* To eleven-year-olds:

    'One thing you must remember is that YOU ARE NOT ALLOWED TO LEAVE THE PROPERTY without permission.'

* To older teenagers:

    'You must appreciate that for your own safety and for our own protection, we have to insist that you do not leave the property without checking it out with a leader.'

* To adults:

    'Although it may seem a little restrictive, we do need to know where everyone is at any time. I need to ask you therefore to let me know if you intend to leave the property at any time.'

Readers may respond to these remarks about leadership in one of two ways. Some may feel overawed. To such I would say that an appropriate leadership style can be learnt. You can learn it by getting to know people and being perceptive of their differing responses. Don't be discouraged. Watch the way experienced leaders deal with particular problems and learn from their example. Your willingness to learn is the key; if you are willing you will learn fast.

Others may be tempted to dismiss all this as an unnecessary complication. That response is an indication either that they only work in one group with which they feel secure (which may be OK!), or that they probably unknowingly cause as many discipline problems as they solve.

The last resort
What do you do when all else fails? Here's a quick summary:

Sometimes the positive environment will fail to deter the disruptive camper. The leader needs conviction about his authority to deal with the situation. This does not mean that he has to act like a little Hitler. The style he adopts needs to be based on respect for the campers and the need not to alienate them unnecessarily.

Despite our best efforts, however, we will occasionally be put in a position where the camper has defied us. Our credibility will be at stake in his or her eyes, and in the eyes of the group, unless we act decisively. If we fail at this point, it will become impossible to maintain other rules and therefore impossible to carry out our responsibilities effectively. What then?

(a) Maintain the initiative
I used to think that there was a strong element of bluff involved in discipline, but always felt a bit awkward about this theory until I found noted educator Dr Anna Hogg saying just that:

> Every teacher knows that even when he is 'in full command' . . . any control he has over the class is in a sense a matter of bluff. In the event of a showdown his physical strength would be insufficient to meet an attack of forty, thirty or even fifteen pupils.[9]

Good discipline involves an element of willingness to submit on the part of the camper. Where the leader is not really in a position to enforce his rules, the camper's co-operation, even grudgingly given, is not just desirable but necessary. The leader must persuade the camper that in the final analysis it is better to 'conform', however much it goes against the inclination of the moment.

Short of sending a camper home, what can a leader do if someone really sets out to defy him? And even sending someone home is not always practicable, especially if you're a couple of days away from the nearest transport. The camper should feel that the leader can always 'go one better' — that he really could enforce if needed to.

There should be something about the leader's demeanour which makes the idea of a camper really defying him simply inconceivable. The campers can love him, respect him, even like him, but they're never completely sure that they've got his measure. The manner in which the effective leader deals with difficult campers or spells out a rule will itself say that 'he really means it'.

Suppose we have a disruptive group of fourteen-year-old boys. A broad warning hinting at a possible course of action ('We already have plans for anyone who doesn't co-operate') is better than a specific threat ('If you do that again I will send you home'). There are four reasons:

* The child's imagination will conjure up a far more fearsome punishment than you can suggest!
* The specific threat commits you to carry out the threat or back down.
* The specific threat may even be attractive to the child, or at least challenge him or her to try you out.
* Most importantly, the general warning reinforces the idea that you have the trump card and that acquiescence is going to be better than defiance.

(b) If possible, give a 'way out'

George Burton, who ran an open youth club in the tough inner London suburb of Canning Town, made it a policy to get to know the toughest members and leaders of each group. He wrote:

> We should give them particular time and attention, and never show them up or embarrass them in front of their mates. They must never be in the wrong, so we have to give them a let-out.
> Once I was told that Johnny had deliberately kicked a glass-paned door in the club entrance, breaking one of the panes. At the time I did

not want to force a confession out of him. He had caused me a tremendous amount of trouble in the club and I had had to bar him temporarily more than once. I felt he had begun to show some improvement and I wanted him to know that I had noticed the change for the better. Denying all knowledge of the offence he insisted, 'It was my brother. He looks like me, you know.'
'It could have been your brother,' I acknowledged. That was his let-out — and mine.[10]

By the grace of God, George Burton was an extraordinary person, yet he was prepared to call the police if he thought it was 'absolutely necessary'. On at least five occasions boys spat in his face on the way out. Instead of retaliating, he said, 'Good night, see you tomorrow night'. His example illustrates that there are ways of asserting one's authority without actually having to administer punishment on the one hand, or lose the initiative on the other.

It is a temptation to allow a camper to get under your skin in such a way that the issue of his or her behaviour becomes an emotional contest between you. This has happened to me many times. Our judgement of the importance of the issue can be clouded and the desire to preserve our own dignity (or ego) takes over. George Burton's example is not a demonstration of weakness, but of his consistent ability to apply his principle that 'people matter more than things'.

(c) Involve the campers in the process
Sometimes there will be no way of side-stepping the issue, especially with the persistent kind of difficulty. The skilful leader can involve the camper in the process of evaluating unacceptable behaviour.

I heard of a recent example where four boys had ganged up on another group of inoffensive campers, giving them a hard time for the first few days of camp. The camp director took them aside one morning. For half-an-hour she made them analyse their behaviour and its effect on the particular victims and on the camp community as a whole.

The director said very little. She asked questions; she set the agenda. But the campers went through the process of facing up to their actions. There were no threats and no punishments, but as a result the behaviour of those campers changed so dramatically that they contributed positively to the camp from then on.

This is a success story. There are hundreds of others to match that one. This approach is probably best suited to more mature campers, but not exclusively. It may be that an imposed punishment may be the quicker, simpler and better way of dealing with a discipline problem.

(d) Measure any punishment

The place of punishment in a camp is very complex, obviously varying with the nature of the group. In general we can say that, although we all have a natural sense of justice, we are not in the business of administering justice as camp leaders. Here are some general guidelines for consideration:

* Is punishment the best option for the particular camper?
* Is punishment necessary to deter a repetition of the behaviour?
* Is the punishment plainly fair? Does it 'fit the crime'?
  (For example, if someone has spoiled another camper's dessert with pepper, making him go without dessert himself is obviously a fair response. Making him wash all the cook's dishes is not so obviously fair.)
* Has this behaviour seriously threatened the safety and well-being of campers, or the possibility of achieving the objectives of the camp?
* Is punishment necessary to preserve the spirit of the camp community? If nasty or persistently anti-social behaviour were to pass without some appropriate action, would other campers live with a sense of outrage, even fear that they might be the next victim?
* How might the camper's parents feel about the punishment you are contemplating?

Fair warning should be given of what campers can expect if they cause trouble. Much depends on the attitude of the leader. He should be able to rebuke a camper in such a way that he really does 'get the message', but in a way which doesn't humiliate him in front of the others.

On the other hand, if the camper has proved something of a 'hero' in the eyes of the others and is openly parading his defiance, there is a case for making clear to the whole group, after dealing with him in private, what you have done about it. This may help dampen his ardour for showing off and discourage others from following suit.

The group leader should generally not be involved in handing out punishments. It should be the duty of the camp director to finally decide on and carry out any serious punishment that is considered absolutely necessary.

(e) As a last resort . . .

If the camp director feels that a punishment is required, but is unable to satisfy himself that an adequate punishment can be found which satisfies these criteria, the camper should be sent home.

This is no light decision. The camping experience is a superb opportunity for many difficult or deprived children to come into contact with nature, recreation and people who care. It is a sad thing indeed if someone for whom camp could mean so much is unable to fit in, to the point where he must be sent home. Such an impasse may well reflect badly on the camp itself (its philosophy, structures, leadership or advertising), but not necessarily so. In any case every precaution must be taken to ensure that the camper does in fact get home safely and every effort made to maintain some sort of friendly contact with the camper and his parents. It may be possible to provide a small-group camping experience at another time, or locate an agency running a more suitable kind of program. But the decision itself should not be avoided because of its difficulty.

(f) Look for causes

Avoiding difficult situations is much better than having to deal with them once they arise. We should ask ourselves whether the situation could have been avoided if we had done our job better.

Campers with too much energy can get into mischief. On the other hand over-tired campers are prone to react badly to provocation. A little gang of troublemakers may be split up. Some campers 'play up' to get attention — someone may need to give them extra time to listen to them. Some stupid acts occur because the first silly antics weren't nipped in the bud.

There may even have been a negative flavour to the camp rules — too many 'don'ts'. Plenty of praise for good performance is far better than constant criticism for bad behaviour. Sometimes campers 'get on top' of leaders who are too keen to win acceptance right from the start — another temptation for young leaders. The more senior leaders need to shoulder greater responsibility for discipline to help the younger ones. It is harder to try and gain control after a too-soft beginning — as every teacher knows.

1   Harry Blamires, *The Christian Mind*, SPCK, 1966, pp.137-138
2   See Dr Anna Hogg, 'School Discipline and a Christian Interpretation' in *Journal of Christian Education*, Vol.2, No.3, p.127
3   Ibid., p.124
4   Morgan Gallup Poll, quoted in Victorian Newsletter of the Australian College of Education, 1982
5   e.g. John W. Alexander, *Managing Our Work*, InterVarsity Press, p.84. Alexander favours the third option, where there is an adequate balance of confident decision-making, delegation and discussion.
6   e.g. Wolff, op. cit., pp.17-23
7   Punton, op. cit., p.6
8   A.C.E. Newsletter, op. cit., p.4
9   Hogg, op. cit., p.129
10 George Burton, *People Matter More Than Things*, Hodder and Stoughton, 1965, p.65

10

Values and the Temporary Community:

Are there some guidelines?

ST PAUL'S DISCOVERY CENTRE IS a campsite with a difference. It used to be a 'reformatory for boys' in fact and then an orphanage — and a real institution it was. Situated on a large island in Westernport Bay about 100 kms from the city of Melbourne, it still serves a vital social purpose, but there's a new agenda. Here, under the direction of Digby Hannah, the centre provides camping programs for the disadvantaged people from the big city under the auspices of its parent body, a welfare organization called the Mission of St James and St John.

St Paul's handbook for voluntary camp leaders describes the camping programs as 'seeking to create opportunities which would not otherwise exist, including opportunities to be outdoors and enjoy nature'. The handbook continues:

> About 5% of Australians are reported to have never had a holiday and one-third not for two years. In the 'Land of the Long Weekend' these statistics highlight the gap between those who have and those who have not. Many children and adults respond with delight to the unfamiliar freedom of the sea, sand, dunes, birds, forest, sun, wind and rain. It is our hope that lessons learned about the beauty of sights, sounds, sensations and life cycles will not be lost when people return to their urban environment.'[1]

This is a statement about some values of camping. Hundreds of value statements about camping have been written, but they are not always as carefully expressed as this one. Many claims made for the values of camping or of particular programs sound exaggerated and hollow. We have already seen that popular camping philosophy includes both the idea that camping is great (it has value) and that it has value-forming potential (it can teach values).

An example of the second kind of statement (i.e. the value-*forming* claim) is this view of Scout camping:

> It is still the Scout Master's golden opportunity to get his young people together over a period of time... and teach them to look after themselves. That really is the whole basis of scout camping — looking after yourself in the bush and looking after your mates.[2]

Here is a quite deliberate emphasis on camping as a means of teaching not just skills, but values: self-reliance and care for your friends.

Why values cannot be ignored
If we are serious about a commitment to organized camping, we cannot avoid considering our basic values.

1. Values determine organizational policies
Sometimes questions of social conscience demand a regular reappraisal of our priorities as organizations. The St Paul's Discovery Centre is an example of a camping program set up quite specifically for people who need to have a break from their normal environment: lone parent families who rarely have holidays; children from families whose parent or parents are sick or otherwise unable to cope; children and teenagers who are in institutional care; unemployed teenagers; handicapped children and others.

The aims of the camps (and by implication the values of the mission) clearly reflect the needs of this clientele. They include an emphasis on providing friendship and some opportunities to succeed in small ways which can give some self-esteem and confidence to people used to criticism and defeat.

2. Values shape the camp community
The values that we hold determine the major emphases of the camp program and the standards by which the camp community will be guided and controlled. One example will illustrate the implications of our decision about values for the 'shape' of our community.

I recently observed two camps run by the same organization. At Camp A, a couple of campers carried their large portable cassette players with them almost everywhere they went. A bagful of favourite cassettes assured them of the availability of their favourite music at peak volume at all times. The noise was impossible for other campers to escape from. Camp B issued the usual list of 'what to bring to camp' to its campers, but specifically excluded portable radios and cassette players.

The leaders of Camp A obviously had made a conscious decision to allow these campers to play their cassettes. They knew the campers before they came; they all came from a housing commission area. These were campers to whom the bush was totally unfamiliar and frightening. They were also kids who were suspicious of authority.

The leaders of Camp B had also made a conscious decision — to ban what the others had permitted. Their campers were more independent, from backgrounds richer in camping experiences and more used to being away from home and familiar surroundings. These campers would have expected the leaders to make this sort of rule. The fact that these quite different approaches were taken by two groups of camp leaders who shared the same basic aims and philosophy simply demonstrates how specific our value judgements must be.

Values also shape the community because personal values determine the way leaders perform. Negatively, the community cannot be positive and harmonious if the values of leaders major on self-gratification and self-preservation, or if the leaders are intolerant or insensitive to the values of the campers. Jim Punton, whose work with Frontier Youth Trust in the UK has already been mentioned, says:

> We are working cross-culturally. We must be in touch with the fact that we don't belong to the culture of the kids. If we're working with them, it's their culture that matters, not ours. A sensitivity, an openness and a caring for them in their cultural setting is absolutely paramount. We have to affirm the kids within their own culture and not negate it, because they're returning to it. We relate to them in terms of their codes as far as we can, recognizing that these kids have a whole series of other priorities to deal with, way before they come to the things we may not like.[3]

Clearly, values shape the community in a quite profound way, extending to the way in which we apply discipline, not simply to our definition of what is acceptable in terms of behaviour.

3. Some values have a clear ethical dimension

Some values simply represent a choice about preferred emphases. The lightweight camper may value mobility above comfort. The base camp enthusiast may value the predictability of a base-camp situation by comparison with the unpredictability of a mobile camp. It's not a question of right or wrong, but of what style is better than another for a particular purpose.

Similarly, the question of whether or not to allow campers to carry their cassette players around is not a moral one — it's a question of what will best achieve our specific aims.

But other value judgements involve ethical questions. Have we a right to punish campers? If so what are the practical limitations of such actions? What limitations on sexual relations between campers are morally *required*, as opposed to 'preferred'? Is there a moral obligation to ban the use of drugs or prevent violence among campers? Some would say that sound ecological practices are an ethical obligation. Some would say we have a 'moral obligation to open our camp program or training courses to everyone'[4] (i.e. regardless of their physical aptitude, for example).

4. Values cannot be assumed in our society

The attitudes to values in any cross-section of our society are very diverse. There are three characteristics of this diversity:

(a) Subjectivism

Some people would claim certain values, but would not be able to offer any objective justification for them. They would be content to say 'I would not let my daughter go to an R-rated movie' or 'I reckon premarital sex is OK providing you're careful', but not be able to justify that position by reference to any objective code of ethics.

(b) Relativism

A number of people would claim a commitment to certain values, but reject the idea that they necessarily applied to others in the group. They might even accept that at another time and in different circumstances these values might not be right for themselves either. They would feel that no one had a right to impose their values on other people: 'What's true for you isn't necessarily true for me'.

(c) Pluralism

A number would hold strongly to certain values, claiming an objective, even universal validity for them. Some of these would hold differing views from each other, but would hold firmly to their own position as being always right for them. This diversity of views, however strongly or weakly held, is pluralism.

One response to this diversity of values might be to say that, since everyone will never agree anyway, it doesn't much matter what position you take. Alternatively one might take the perceived lowest common denominator of values and be content with that. Perhaps no one would consciously adopt this stance, but in fact many of us are influenced by this in the way we respond to conflict.

The kinds of practical ethical considerations faced in camping require us to take values seriously. The diversity of values in the wider community requires confidence in our own ethical position and honesty in making it clear to the public.

5. Values are implicit in popular camping philosophy

In Chapter 2, we saw that proponents of camping claim quite explicit values for it. We looked at an example of how some leaders were disappointed at the way in which campers enjoyed a particular experience. Why? A clear answer is given in an essay entitled 'Education and Ecstasy':

> According to Timothy Leary, you can find ecstasy by the simple expedient of popping a pill, by turning on, tuning in and dropping out. But it isn't as simple as that. What matters is the quality of the alleged experience, its nature and its consequences.[5]

Most of us would find that analysis relatively uncontroversial. The pill-popping generation and the heavy drug scene have given incontrovertible proof of the inability of chemicals to provide meaning and strength for overcoming personal pain from societal pressures. But when it comes to finding alternative values, it is a different story. Some pursue environmental ideals with an almost evangelistic zeal, but have no strategy to help people solve problems in their own interior 'environment'. Others teach people about the importance of love, then drop lolly papers all over the place. If we claim certain values, let's make sure they are balanced and well-considered.

6. Values are needed by campers

In an article entitled 'The Suicide Plague' (*Australian Society*, November 1982), an analysis was given of why suicide is now the second most common cause of death amongst young Australians, second only to road accidents. Reasons suggested for severe teenage depression leading to suicide included: violence in society; the commercialization of sex and its relegation to a casual bodily function; a pervasive pessimism about life; membership of broken or chronically argumentative families; and 'the tendency for schools, parents and society in general to value intelligence and academic success above social skills and emotional development'.

The stakes are high. If camping is able to give experiences which build up young people, let's plan for this.

7. School camping raises special issues

The emergence of school camping on a broad scale in government schools has introduced a new element into the camping scene: the choice about whether to attend a camp or not is considerably reduced. The typical holiday camp is basically patronized by people who have come entirely on their own initiative. Furthermore, they have selected the sort of camp that they prefer from a range of options. Finally they have camped in the past with organizations that have a history of taking a clear, if generalized, values position.

But school camps are significantly different. First, while there may be no explicit requirement set down by the school, there is often an implicit suggestion that the student is 'expected' to go. Parents must provide a 'sound' reason for their child not going. In addition there will very often be a strong, though sometimes subtle peer group pressure on the child to go on a school camp.

Second, there is often no choice of camping style. This may be of little significance for the child, but it may well affect the way the family's camping dollar is spent. Parents are now faced with a real dilemma: Should they spend a substantial amount of money on sending a child to a school camp, the value of which may be dubious to them? Or should they save the money for a family holiday, or for sending their children on a holiday camp of their own choice and of recognizable value?

Third, parents may sometimes have reason to wonder what sort of values will determine the nature of the camp experience. My own observation is that one cannot assume that the same rules and standards which apply at school will be applied in the school camping situation. Many teachers (by no means all) seem to operate on the assumption that it is inappropriate that they do.

Smoking, bad language, disrespect, insolent behaviour towards teachers and (in co-ed camps) a much greater degree of physical intimacy in relationships are sometimes tolerated in the school camp situation. One is obliged to ask on what grounds this is so. What values support this different treatment, and should there not be an explicit statement to parents explaining this policy? In many cases the reasons amount to little more than a simple failure of nerve, plus lack of conviction, brought about by the absence of familiar authority structures within which teachers operate.

In summary, the significant lack of choices involved in school camps suggests that greater responsibility must be taken for explaining and justifying the rules and standards which will be applied at a school camp. If manuals on safety and organization and skills instruction are necessary, a commensurate amount of attention should be given to values.

8. Camping values affect the status of camping in the community

Park rangers are as good an indicator as any of the general community's perception of organized camping. Unfortunately one becomes painfully aware, at times, that the wider community is not always able to distinguish between organizations when it comes to criticizing the examples of bad management, slack safety standards and destructive behaviour which they encounter.

Because the values of an organization influence the kind of program it conducts, they inevitably affect the status of camping in the community. Bad news always travels further and faster than good news. The camping fraternity as a whole, therefore, needs to find ways of promoting the best values and standards in camping, bringing peer influence to bear on reluctant members to ensure that there is community confidence in camping generally.

Some starting points for determining values

It is not possible to lay down an agreed set of values for camping programs in general, but we will attempt to provide some starting points: a framework or checklist which may provide a tool for identifying and determining the basic values upon which the leaders of any camp need to be agreed.

(a) Rules

Rules are required for various reasons. Some are required for safety (value: camper protection) — the reader is referred to Appendix C on health and safety. Some are there for smooth functioning (value: achievement and efficiency). Some are there purely as an agreed means of structuring the community (value: group consensus).

'The fewer rules the better' is probably a good principle, but even those who work in a relatively informal and unstructured way with youth recognize that campers need rules, so that they know where they stand. 'Clear discipline, with a minimum number of rules but clear boundaries, is important for kids.'[6]

The word 'boundaries' is significant. It is a word that says 'Do whatever you like, but don't go further than this', rather than 'Don't do anything unless you have specific permission'.

> Campers need structure and boundaries, but freedom within the boundaries. They need external controls to protect them against themselves. They are grateful for fences, but they must test the limits — and there must be opportunities to discuss why this is so.[7]

(b) People first

The temporary community should attempt to express in its rules and whole mode of operation a combination of justice and mercy. Our approach should reflect a concern for people as they come to us, not as we would like them to be.

Some rules are organizational, designed to promote the smooth running of camp; other rules are behavioural, affecting or limiting campers' personal patterns of living. An example of the first kind of rule would be 'lights out' time. Suppose that campers don't seem willing to go to bed by the prescribed time. There may be good reasons for this. The person who puts people before rules will not be content to treat the matter simply as a discipline problem. He or she will question why there is opposition, perhaps recognizing that the expected time is unrealistic, that campers go to bed late at home, or that they have not had time to 'wind down' after an exciting evening. On the other hand, it may be that a troublemaker is just determined to keep everyone else awake. Only the discerning leader who has 'people' in mind will recognize the difference.

An example of the second kind would be rules concerning smoking and swearing. Jim Punton again expresses the importance of a 'people first' approach:

At camp, of all things the kids have got to work through, smoking is way down that list for me. I get a kick out of seeing a kid who is able to lose his hardness and begin to relate to another kid — to see a kid beginning to care for another kid, beginning to take responsibility. Those kinds of things are way up the list for me. If a kid can begin to make relationships, begin to show trust and not have that trust cause him to fall flat on his face, but actually find that when he trusts it works — those kinds of tentative steps in human relationships are way up for me. If the price that we've got to pay is to cough a little bit in the presence of smoke, then I'm prepared to do that.

I know it's important to help kids to see that some people are offended by certain words. We have a duty to the kids to help them understand that, if they don't want to hurt and offend, there are certain words they don't use in certain places with certain people. That's important. But, I think it's a strange thing if they can only have our friendship and our love on those kinds of terms.[8]

(c) Excellence
In the same way that a prime concern for people is a corrective to an overzealous emphasis on rules, so a concern for excellence is a corrective to an unthinking accommodation of the expectations or standards of the campers.

It is possible to affirm that conformity to certain standards must not be a condition of our care for campers, but still to encourage and, where appropriate, to insist upon the observance of standards of behaviour which may not come easily to the camper. Mere capitulation to the low standards set by a dominant group is a betrayal of the educative process as well as of the ideals of the community.

I remember a group of sixteen- to seventeen-year-olds in a school camp at Camp Coolamatong. They were from a working class area and the tone of the camp was set by a group of kids who constituted the rougher element of the class. After a couple of days obscene language loudly dominated all group activities, but the teachers did not comment or attempt to curtail the trend. We were about to go into the shearing shed and I said to the group something like this:

Shearing sheds are often pretty rough places, but language and stories always moderate when women are around. I have frankly been disgusted with the language of some of you blokes so far and I'm sure others in the group find it offensive too. (Heads nodded in agreement.) Now, if you can't control the four-letter words while we're in the shed — stay out!

As you can imagine this was a somewhat awkward moment, but everyone went in to the shed and I don't think I heard so much as a 'bloody' for a couple of days! But the important point is that I don't believe that action detracted from my relationship with the group, including the particular people I had rebuked.

On the contrary, I believe that our relationship, if it was affected at all, was enhanced, a possibility which I think will make sense in the context of the Coolamatong experience as described later on. Indeed a group of boys hung back later as I was cleaning the shed, pummelling me with questions about why I worked here and expressing their appreciation of the assertion of some positive values.

(d) Individual and group needs

If one holds the value of the freedom of the individual camper to choose as he pleases a consistent application of this value could result in near chaos organizationally: the destruction of property and facilities or environment, and a total lack of a real community spirit. On the other hand, a dedicated commitment to the supreme importance of creating a community spirit could result in a poor level of one-to-one relationships, frustration for many campers who didn't share the enjoyment of the activities chosen by or imposed on the group, and a real tameness about the whole camp for the rugged individualists in the group.

This is, of course, an exaggerated contrast. It is possible to value freedom of choice *and* the engendering of a spirit of co-operation and community. But there are bound to be some conflicts of interest. We have to make rules which are suited to the needs of as many campers as possible, accepting that not all will suit all campers equally well. This requires a degree of flexibility and adaptability — and courage to restrict what may seem a fairly innocuous freedom for a few for the sake of the whole.

For example, smoking in eating areas or bedrooms will cause significant discomfort to others. In some places (e.g. hike tents, petrol storages and haystacks), there is a significant safety factor as well. There are sound reasons for banning smoking in many camps, but there are other situations where a ban on smoking might simply reflect the personal preference of a leader, rather than respect for the individual camper.

It is often possible to create ways in which minority interests can be catered for, as well as the majority. The designation of places where campers can smoke might be one example. Such action need not imply approval of the activity. It is simply an interpretation of how care for *all* the campers can best be expressed in that particular temporary community.

(e) In loco parentis

Not all aspects of behaviour are up to us as leaders. Leaders of children and young people are acting 'in the place of parents'. This is a fundamental responsibility. Parents who entrust their children to camp leaders rightly expect them to act in a way which is consistent with how they as conscientious parents would act.

This parental right applies particularly to camping. Not only does camping involve obvious hazards; camping is supremely a socializing activity. In the temporary community relationships are *accelerated* — indeed this is the main rationale for many school camps.

But what people mean precisely by 'socializing' is not always clear. Furthermore, there are few objective criteria by which the development of relationships, or the growth of social skills, can be measured. And the role of teachers in promoting personal values is itself ill-defined and controversial.

The controversial nature of teachers as 'socializing' agents is illustrated by the popular technique of 'values clarification'. Questions as to how this method of values education is used have been vigorously canvassed at times, especially by parent groups. A paper by an Australian educator, G. Partington, clearly articulates the concern for the rights of parents in education of this kind:

> Schools have always sought some knowledge about students, but the information traditionally sought has been very narrow. Sociologists, economists, psychologists or social workers who had occasion to investigate family backgrounds exercised discretion and confidentiality.

The writer then goes on to list the kind of personal information which may be elicited in values clarification strategies, and the personal nature of these processes:

> Without express and explicit parental agreement, such strategies would violate privacy rights on a scale unparalleled by other social agencies. Indeed, parents are usually unaware of the extent to which that privacy may be violated, since they generally assume that a broadly traditional impersonal curriculum is still operative.[9]

The same point is made by Professor Brian Crittenden:

For many of the techniques in values clarification there is a real risk of violating the right to privacy . . . As A.L. Lockwood points out, 'In public schools especially, we need to be conscious of persons' rights to privacy because schooling is compulsory, classroom discourse occurs in the presence of many others, and teachers have the authority to set and evaluate student performance'.[10]

Professor Brian Hill similarly supports Lockwood's stand.[11] These comments on values clarification are apposite to school camping, because camping often justifies itself in terms of its 'socializing potential', accelerating relationships between student and student, student and teacher. The way in which this is to be achieved needs to be justified.

Consider the following statement:

School camps provide an ideal opportunity to examine the whole question of lifestyles and their impact on the environment. Firstly, the students are <u>away from home in an environment more or less totally in the control of the teacher</u> . . . the teacher can discuss and demonstrate the environmental consequences of various aspects of lifestyle <u>without interfering directly in the home and without upsetting the parents</u>.[12]

The underlining is mine, and emphasizes the points of similarity with values clarification that concern parental rights. In their context these words are not necessarily sinister. But they are strikingly specific about the advantage of removing children from the home environment — as they stand, frighteningly so.

School camping is no more invalid than values clarification simply on the grounds that it raises serious questions about parental rights. But the way in which that socialization is to be achieved requires justification to conscientious parents. This places no burden on those schools which apply the same standards to the camping situation as obtain in the school itself. School camping does indeed provide a rich context in which teachers' understanding of pupils grows rapidly. It may justly be claimed that for teachers, 'the camp program is our richest source of child study'.[13] But the privilege of living with the children involves relationships and circumstances which are rather different from school.

In youth camping, the first issue is probably the basic safety question: whether the camper will return home safely or not. After that, the question of whether co-ed sleeping arrangements will be permitted is probably the most pertinent. There is little doubt that such practices contravene the legal requirements of acting in the place of parents, yet such arrangements still exist. The right of parents to know what to expect is surely undeniable in this case.

(f) The family

The stress on the family unit today was offered in Chapter 1 as a reason for rethinking camping strategy. Organized camping has, on the whole, been for young people, with family experiences left to families. Indeed, the removal of children from their families has often been argued as a very positive value of camping. The emotional emancipation of the child or adolescent from parents is said to be facilitated.[14] Personality development is considered as partly achieved through freedom from parent control.[15]

Camping is seen as a place for weaning children emotionally and morally. By contrast the home is seen as the most difficult place in which to learn 'the sense of being an effectively self-directing person, accepted by others as a worthy member of the group'.[16]

I have no doubt that traditional children's and youth camps continue to have a valuable place in the development of independence, confidence, skills and maturity for a large number of young people. But the views expressed above surely raise as many questions as solutions. For example, what hundreds of children need is not emotional emancipation from parents, but the exact opposite: some emotional bonding. Similarly, it is fatuous to talk about the advantages of freedom from parent control, where thousands of others are concerned. They don't know what it is to be under parental control. We cannot assume the kind of stable family environments presupposed by these statements. In any case, there is another perspective to be considered: the positive values of taking children and families away together. Father-and-son, mother-and-daughter and family camps provide a context for teaching different generations to appreciate one another and grow together.

Here is another significant values choice for organizations and it certainly alters the whole complexion of the *in loco parentis* question!

(g) Tolerance

Tolerance of other people and their views is so often advanced by camping and outdoor education theorists that it deserves special comment. In an age of relativism, tolerance is a prized virtue, since it is regarded as unacceptable to hold a particular set of values as being the only valid ones — or at least to insist on other people conforming to those values.

However a thorough-going ethical relativist cannot argue conclusively that tolerance is a better value than intolerance. This logical impossibility has been well demonstrated by Professor Brandt in Ethical Theory.[17] I would want to argue for the value of tolerance on other grounds, but it is vital to recognize precisely what we mean by the term:

> We may speak of tolerating a person and his opinions in the sense of empathizing with him and showing respect for his opinions. But one can respect a person and his convictions and yet believe his views to be mistaken. Further one can respect a person and yet be motivated to try and change his views, even placing legal restrictions on his ability to put his opinions into practice.[18]

Failure to recognize the distinction between respect for a person and condoning unacceptable behaviour is common. The point is that insisting on certain rules is not incompatible with tolerance. Indeed, if we are to teach tolerance to campers, it would be strange if one were to tolerate behaviour which was patently intolerant.

Those who are most deeply committed to particular values (whether traditional or modern, absolutist or relativist), have the greatest need to ensure that respect for the camper is shown in every way and that the camper who is different is not subtly isolated or rejected by leaders or the group.

Teaching values in camp

1. Values are not taught if they are merely inflicted on campers. Values education is about teaching people to make choices. The mere imposition of values may even be counter-productive by causing campers to react to values on the basis of emotion (like resentment), rather than to assess values dispassionately on their merits.

Discussion groups based on stories or case studies — or as a follow-up to a field study, role play or audio-visual — can help campers to participate in the evaluation process, but shorter camps do not always provide adequate time for this sort of activity.

2. Values can be taught through camp activities. There are skills which can be taught merely as recreational skills, but which can equally be made to include elements of challenge and group living. These will highlight the importance of co-operation, mutual support or skills of group decision-making.

3. Time for reflection on camp experiences needs to be built in to the program. Many camps have no provision at all for times of discussion during which groups reflect on experiences — analysing and evaluating their performance, and identifying values that have emerged. Even half-an-hour at the end of the day with the group can pay real dividends here.

4. Solo experiences, from a few hours to a few days, are beginning to be taken over from stress camping (such as 'Outward Bound') into more adventure/recreation type programs. This is a catalyst for personal reflection and for becoming aware of our relationship to the world around us.

5. Because of its frequent use in camp and other settings, some further comments are warranted concerning the technique of values clarification:

(a) Values clarification is a tool for identifying one's own values, seeing them in relation to the values of others. This is useful. Often people don't recognize what values they hold, the choices available or the degree to which these values are only ideals, unintegrated with their personal lifestyle.

But values clarification is but one way of beginning the process of values education. Failure to recognize this inbuilt limitation could mean that we may imagine we are teaching values, when in reality we do nothing to alter the existing values of the learners in the desired direction.

(b) The process of values clarification offers no objective criteria for assessing held values against other values. It is effective only as a sorting out process. Yet the values introduced as options may subtly influence choice by appearing to be the values of the peer group — hardly an adequate criterion for selection. Furthermore, this process, if it is 'effective', may simply confirm values which by other objective standards could be considered as immoral. Thus, if a camper concludes that he doesn't mind stealing another camper's belongings, choosing to act consistently with this position, then this choice must be accepted as appropriate.

6. Values are taught more effectively by example, rather than by pedagogical techniques. I take this to be so self-evident that it

requires no argumentation. I include it because, at the point of leadership recruitment and the development of program strategies, the importance of personal example is still sometimes overlooked.

1 *St Paul's Discovery Centre Leaders' Manual* (a duplicated document for private circulation only)
2 Neil Weatherill, *Victorian Camping Conference: Proceedings*, Department of Youth, Sport and Recreation, Melbourne 1983, p.98
3 Punton, op. cit., p.6
4 For example Penelope Fogarty, VCC Proceedings, op. cit., p.39
5 Babbage, op. cit., p.28
6 Jim Punton, op. cit., p.7
7 Alison Short, 'Values Education at Camp', in *Journal of Christian Camping*, July-August 1982, p.10
8 Punton, op. cit., pp.6-7
9 G. Partington, 'Clarifying Students' Values' in *Unicorn*, bulletin of The Australian College of Education, Vol.9, No.1, pp.34-35
10 Brian Crittenden, 'Moral Education: some aspects of its relationship to general values education and the study of religion', in Graham Rossiter, *Religious Education in Australian Schools*, Curriculum Development Centre, Canberra 1981, p.198
11 B.V. Hill, 'Teacher Commitment and the Ethics of Teaching for Commitment', Rossiter, op. cit., p.183
12 Mike Wood in *Newsletter of Victorian Outdoor Education Association*, November 1982, p.8
13 Marion J. Sack in Hammerman, op. cit., p.190
14 Dimock, op. cit., p.35
15 American Camping Association statement in Todd, op. cit., p.47
16 W.H. Kilpatrick in Hammerman, op. cit., p.20
17 Richard B. Brandt, *Ethical Theory*, Prentice-Hall, 1959, pp.288-292
18 Ibid., p.291

11

Camping and Education:
How serious are we?

WE PROBABLY ALL KNOW PLACES where we once enjoyed the enchantment of unspoiled natural beauty, but where there is now little to be seen but the evidence of wilful or thoughtless destruction. Despite the growth of community consciousness about environmental protection, many feel that the battle for the preservation of the natural world is already lost.

For eight years we lived in an area of great beauty described by the tourist promoters as 'the last unspoiled frontier'. Yet one could not escape the impression that tourism was being promoted without a care for the possibility that it would, in terms of that very slogan, be self-defeating. Tourism tends to spoil unspoiled frontiers. There is a 'credibility gap' between our pronouncements and our performance when it comes to the outdoor environment.

One might imagine that camping people would be ecologists almost by definition. One might assume that outdoor educators were environmentalists as well. The history of camping and the growth of outdoor education (whether school camping or environmental studies) might suggest that there is little left to say about organized camping and the environment. Yet in Chapter 2 we saw that the outdoor emphasis of popular camping philosophy was not always reflected in actual practice.

Internal inconsistencies
Twenty years ago William Howenstine recorded his conviction, based partly on a detailed study of the programs of eight Michigan and Ohio schools, that there was a substantial contradiction between the stated objectives of teachers about environmental education and the way they conducted school camps.[1] It seems

probable that this is still the same today in this country. The credibility gap is still with us.

Historically, outdoor education (and with it school camping) has had two different roots. One is the physical education area, the other is natural science. The growing emphasis now is very much on an 'inter-disciplinary' approach, where the various disciplines from maths to languages to biology or physical education enhance· one another or are taught more effectively.

> Most outdoor educators claim no body of subject matter as their own. They are methodologists and lay claim only to places for learning and methods appropriate to those places.[2]

> Outdoor education is not a discipline — it claims no subject matter. Outdoor education is a place, an attitude, a method; it is not a subject.[3]

It is not our intention to define outdoor education here. But it may be pointed out that, while some educators in this country define it specifically in terms of environmental education,[4] others see the two as quite distinct (though complementary) entities.[5] The latter appears to be the predominant view amongst those involved in school camping. If that is so, it would help to explain why school camping so often takes little advantage of the outdoor setting to teach young people to understand, value, conserve and live in the outdoor environment.

This reflects a 'Model A' perception of camping, described and rejected in Chapter 3. That is, it is a perception which focusses on one or other of the three major attributes of camping — in this case 'education' (narrowly-understood) or 'recreation in the outdoors'. It does not take adequate account of the way in which the attributes of community, education and the outdoors can and should interact in camping.

Putting theory into practice

A narrowly conceived view of camping has certain dangers. Camping activities may contribute to the destruction of the environment or raise questions in the community concerning the value of school camping. In this context a number of specific issues deserve consideration.

1. The need to take environmental education seriously

Environmental education has two facets. The first is the scientific basis, the attempt to gain an understanding of how human life depends on and affects the natural world. Much of this can be achieved in classrooms and laboratories, but much can be achieved in the natural environment itself. Outdoor educators should be providing the inspiration and the structures to make this happen more.

Howenstine's study showed that, despite a general recognition that the outdoors provided unique teaching opportunities not available in the school for direct experience in experimental projects, the camps studied did not, on the whole, offer such experiences or use such opportunities. He attributes this to lack of adequate teacher training.

The scientific core of environmental education is the province of those who are teachers of science. Nevertheless, many adult camp leaders know enough to impart some significant knowledge to campers in the camp situation. If we are going to survive as a race, then we ought to take the opportunities given us in the camping environment to teach — whether we are running a marine biology camp for senior high school students or a holiday camp for eleven-year-olds.

The second facet of environmental education is the development of a conservation ethic. This involves acquiring a 'feel' for the natural world; a sense of belonging in it, depending on it and wanting to conserve it, not simply for ourselves but for future generations.

This does not require sophisticated scientific understanding, helpful though that may be. I've learnt to value unspoiled beauty because wherever we went as kids, my parents would call our attention to various details, expressing their appreciation for them. These early attitudes were reinforced by other experiences, ranging from cooking sausages on a fire in the backyard to fully-fledged camping expeditions.

2. The need to appreciate the environment for what it can provide
I remember seeing, in the soft light of evening, an owl sitting on top of a post. At the foot of the post was a kangaroo, grazing peacefully. I drew the attention of a passing camper to this magic scene. His response was to pause just a moment, perhaps for the length of time he felt politeness required, and then move off with his back turned.

One of the reasons we don't try to communicate more of our sense of wonder is that it is painful to find that our excitement is sometimes not reciprocated. In fact if we're not told it's boring, we may be given that impression unmistakably. In an era where instant satisfactions are vicariously available via the giant zoom lens of the TV camera, people have to learn to look and listen patiently for themselves.

One of the rewards that camping can provide is quietness. But if we are serious about giving campers even this experience, we must not only plan for it, but patiently educate the campers to it.

As I write in the leafy surrounds of a Melbourne suburb, I am engulfed by noise. The earsplitting sound of a motorbike without a muffler roars from behind the back fence. More penetrating still is the rumble of the washing machine, mistaken first for a large truck and then for a low-flying jet! I find myself almost incapable of logical thought with all this going on. It's not always like this, of course, but for most of us times of real quiet are precious because so rare. Perhaps we cannot expect much else in the city, but it angers me that an otherwise noiseless night in the open country can be so savagely invaded by a hand-held radio from a hundred yards away.

In the camping situation there is usually greater control over the intrusion of unwarranted noises. Wasn't it great when the old camp generator used to be turned off at night? Silence. Peace. The growing awareness of quietness and perhaps the far-off howl of a wild dog. In camp there are still difficulties in tuning in to quietness, but the possibilities are there.

Here at home my options are more limited. Short of pulling the washing machine cord out and strangling the neighbour's dog with it, I can't do much. I may dream about encasing that motorbike in concrete and dropping it in the middle of the Pacific, but that's not practical.

At camp, we can do more to structure our environment. If we're mobile, the chances are we can find a camping spot remote from other groups. Yet how many camps make a quiet moonlight walk, a 'solo' or a quiet time during the day a matter of priority?

Run your disco back at school by all means! Have a youth group night where you lift the roof with records for a few hours. But why do it at camp? What's wrong with watching stars, even satellites? What's dull about listening to the hooting of an owl in the distance or the lapping of water on rocks? What's corny about a quiet chat around a campfire with friends?

We have to educate ourselves and then our campers away from

the television and the hi-fi set for them to gain a sensitivity to the natural world. Many city people hardly know what it is to be working out in the weather. We wouldn't know what it is like for the farmer to deliver a calf in the pouring rain and biting wind. How many city dwellers see the sunrise? Even those who are up early enough can't see it for buildings.

A serious commitment to use of the outdoors cannot be sustained on the basis of mere nostalgia, especially since fewer and fewer urbanized people have the memories in the first place. On the other hand, there is a common justification for outdoor living which doesn't altogether ring true either. This is the idea that it is 'out there' in the bush where we human beings 'really belong' — the idea that the world of nature is real, the world of the city is not.

It is possible to concede that urbanized living isolates us from the 'realities' of our dependence on nature without attributing to city living an almost evil connotation. City people are isolated from many of the realities of nature and their overall dependence on it. Just watch the suburbanite hosing down his concrete pathways at the height of the summer while the farmer cries out for precious water. But to claim that the world of the city dweller is unreal smacks of unreality itself.

The dropouts, the hermits and the back-to-nature freaks are not understood by the average urban dweller, because everything is so black-and-white. The ordinary person can't relate to a philosophy which denies the reality of city living. An interesting reflection on wilderness adventure from a Christian viewpoint is given by two of the founders of *Australian Wild* magazine:

> Some Christians explain these experiences (at times almost mystical in their intensity) by saying that God is 'closer' out in wild places. But this cannot be the case: God is with us wherever we go... Some see it as escaping the evil influences which exist where man has shaped his environment. But we cannot escape evil by moving to another place; it has affected every part of creation, and it is even within ourselves![6]

The authors reject the idea that cities are, *per se*, inimical to the idea of God's creation. But they do argue that the sophistication of city life alienates us from our earthy origins and that, in experiencing the earth, we become more whole as people. There is a sense of balance in this more modest claim for the value of the wilderness, but it is no less authentic and important for all that.

In summary, the outdoor environment has rightly been seen to offer experiences which minister to the human spirit. But we have also acknowledged that those experiences are both elusive and capable of widely varying interpretations, from pantheism to Christian revelation.

But there are values even in the mere change of surroundings. One of these is the greater appreciation of the benefits of civilization. To quote Walters and Collie again:

> An acute appreciation of the gadgets and conveniences [of our civilized lifestyle] is gained when you don't have them. Living with few resources beyond one's own native strength prompts one to wonder whether plumbing, hot water, electricity, a familiar mattress, TV and take-away food are necessary to our enjoyment of life at all. Curiously, the very perils and privations become one's fondest memories.[6]

Another aspect of this change of surroundings is the change of perspective it can give to life back home. For some it will be a renewed appreciation of one's family and one's circumstances. To another it will be a realization of the gaps in his view of life, or the inadequacies of his relationships with others at home. The end result may be that campers who have been able to enjoy a thoroughly different lifestyle and environment will return home resolved to live differently.

This view of the natural environment sees it not as an object of education, but as a context for reflection on one's on-going way of life. The impact of such an experience, for the great majority of campers in an urban society, must be to help them live better where they are, not make them restless and negative. Some may have the vision to dramatically alter their lifestyle, and the financial resources and necessary business and social skills to do so, but most won't.

3. The need to minimize impact on the environment

Again, this is an issue which has been well canvassed, but which still cannot be taken for granted. Again, the observations of Howenstine regarding school camping programs still ring true. He speaks of the tolerance of negative 'conservation activities' (like each camper being asked to pick a certain plant) and the 'inconsistency between what staff members tell the campers and what the staff members do'.[7]

He goes on to make a fundamental point: that a sense of

stewardship of our natural resources begins with little things. We don't have to be professional environmentalists to recognize many potentially damaging habits and activities. Kids like breaking branches off trees, taking short cuts through young tree plantations and dropping plastic wrappers or other litter. Three suggestions can be offered to help camping people minimize their impact on the environment:

(a) Develop a mental attitude that 'the little things matter'. In principle I see no difference between dropping a lunch wrapping in the bush and dropping a truck-load of rubbish there. The acceptability of the first becomes the reason for the second.

(b) Don't just lay heavy rules on people, but explain reasons, demonstrate consequences and give experiences which make sense of the rules.

(c) Anticipate potential impact areas, especially in fixed site camping, and take preventive measures where possible. For example, prickly grevillea bushes or attractive but unobtrusive forms of fencing and landscaping can be located strategically to prevent foot traffic where it isn't wanted. Rubbish bins can be located in the places where litter is likely to occur, screened if possible or painted to blend in with their background.

In setting up a campsite or camping area, attention should be given in advance to where the foot (and other) traffic is likely to be most heavy. It is sometimes best not to lay out pathways until some camps have been run and you can discover the route naturally taken from one area to another.

The basic ethos of bushwalking and lightweight camping is well-known, accessible in books and other outdoor publications. The replacement of a 'pioneering ethic' with a 'wilderness ethic', with the concomitant notion of 'no trace' camping, is well-established. Outdoor educators are being urged not just to minimize the impact of their activities, but to try to eliminate any effect on the natural environment.

4. The need to justify camping educationally

A basic weakness in camping philosophy and practice is the tendency to ignore other dimensions of camping. It is not sufficient to justify camping purely in terms of say, environmental education. That begs the question of why it needs to be residential.

Similarly if camping is justified simply in terms of its socializing or personal development possibilities, it begs the question of how that is to be understood and why that should be undertaken in schools.

If outdoor educators want to justify camping even as a tool for education, then it is clearly reasonable that they can be expected to show how it works. That is, how do particular residential outdoor study programs enhance students' understanding and appreciation of the environment?

In the literature of outdoor education there appears to be a paucity of hard data to demonstrate the educational values of outdoor education in general, let alone of camping in particular. Clifford Knapp has issued a number of challenges to outdoor educators:

> More empirical research is needed to substantiate the place of outdoor education in the school curriculum. Justification of the values of outdoor education should be based on valid statements. Exaggerated, intuitive and authoritarian claims must be evaluated for accuracy.[8]

Other issues have been raised in this book concerning the ethical as well as pedagogical values undergirding school camping. In terms of the need to build, re-establish or enrich the most fundamental relationships in which children grow up, school camping should be justified in relation to other camping opportunities.

There are school camping programs, for example, where the following characteristics would apply:
(a) the proposed activities are readily available to families
(b) the proposed program is not related directly to the curriculum of the students
(c) the proposed camp places a considerable financial burden on parents.

Any school should accept the responsibility of justifying to itself and to the parents the inclusion of camping in the normal course of the school year.

This is not to suggest that school camping necessarily lacks validity. But there are still many cases where a valid case for the school camping program is not put forward. It surely is significant that there is generally provision for parents to opt children out of school camps, with various arrangements for those who don't attend back at school.

On the face of it, it seems curious that students are given the option of not attending what is in effect a normal class program.

Is this tacit admission that educators are not entirely convinced that the school camp is fully justified on educational grounds? On the other hand, if the cost burden on parents is the chief reason for the opt-out provision, why isn't the cost of the school's camping program borne by the school (or the State) in the same way as normal tuition?

Until these questions are answered, the opt-out possibility should not be merely retained, but clearly indicated to parents. The question is not so much whether camping in education can be justified, but whether educators do so to parents and the community. Only then will school camping deserve the status of belonging in the educational experience of the child — and justify the cost for parents and taxpayers.

1 In Hammerman, op. cit., pp.400-409
2 George W. Donaldson and Oswald Goering, *Perspectives on Outdoor Education*, Wm C. Brown Publishers, 1972, p.96
3 Ibid., pp.149-150
4 See for example Bob Easther, 'The Nature and Scope of Outdoor Education', in *VOEA Newsletter*, Vol.2, No.1
5 e.g. Mike Wood, 'Outdoor Education and Environmental Education: Partners', *VOEA Newsletter*, November 1982
6 Brian Walters and Michael Collie, 'Wilderness Adventure' in *On Being*, Vol.9, No.9, October 1982, pp.15-16
7 Hammerman, op. cit., p.404
8 In *Perspectives on Outdoor Education*, op. cit., p.120

12
Family Camping:
What does it offer?

THE GROWTH OF ORGANIZED FAMILY CAMPING has been a very obvious feature of the Australian camping scene in recent years. This has also been the case in other Western countries. Why has this been so?

The idea of families going away on individual camping holidays is not so new, of course. There are various indicators to show this growth, including the boom in sales of caravans (prior to the fuel crisis) and recreational vehicles, usage of national parks and growth in the number of caravan parks.

One of the obvious but key reasons for the increase in individual family camping, apart from increased leisure-time available through increased holidays and 'flexi-time' employment, is the camping technology now available. Dad doesn't have to be a former Scout to feel confident about managing a camping trip. Caravans and campervans provide mobility with all the comforts of home. But tent gear is now also sophisticated. Colourful continental-type tents have almost replaced the green roof and white walls of the old 'auto-tents'. There are room dividers, easy-to-assemble frames, built-in zip-up mosquito netting and sewn-in floors to eliminate creepy-crawlies of all kinds.

Indeed, there is something faintly ridiculous about the camping scene at times. We can sit around in comfortable aluminium-framed chairs, eating food taken from the portable camp refrigerator and cooked on a portable gas stove by the light of a portable gas lamp. A friend of mine stumbled on a man in a quite remote piece of bushland, sitting in a clearing by a little stream, watching a colour TV set powered by a portable generator. Even the lightweight camper is apt to forget that his own ability to be 'lightweight' is a result of amazing technological advances — from the space-age sleeping bag to freeze-dried food.

We are concerned here, however, only with *organized* family camping. The term 'organized' as before denotes camping programs conducted by groups or organizations, not simply on an *ad hoc* basis by small groups of friends or individuals. Nevertheless the growing trend for individual families to 'go camping' is an interesting one. If camping experiences are increasingly available to individual families, why is organized family camping on the increase?

The growth of organized family camping

Now here's a research project for some budding recreation consultant! I suspect that we won't need to wait for statistical evidence before we can claim that the growth in organized camping is a response to a felt need. Organizations have been running family camps not just because they have decided that they are, in principle, a good idea, but because there has been a demand for it. Why?

First, there is a large number of families who still don't have the necessary wealth, mobility or confidence to organize and fit out a camping expedition for their own family. A significant proportion of 'family camp' families are in this category. This does not necessarily mean they are what we would call 'disadvantaged families' either — although, once again, a number are.

Second, families are under pressure — ordinary families as well as those finishing up on the files of a social welfare agency. Families are recognizing the need to holiday together as families and with others, where organized activities make it possible for parents to share the load and responsibility and get a little rest themselves. Organized camping programs provide 'things to do' — and a generation of bored kids needs that. Parents see an organized camp as an attractive focus for a family holiday and a way of finding help with the supervision of children.

The needs of families in society

In November 1977, the Australian Government's Commission on Human Relationships made its report public. It contained 511 recommendations, of which 131 dealt directly with the family — covering general policies, support services, child care, divorce and property, lone parents, adoption and fostering, refuge housing, education about conflict and violence in the family setting, child abuse, crisis counselling and the profound effect of alcohol on human relationships. In addition, scores of other recommendations had direct bearing on the quality of family life.

In the book *Australians at Risk*, Anne Deveson, one of the commissioners, said:

> Of all our institutions, the family is the most influential in terms of human relationships. It is universal, being found in both sophisticated and primitive societies as far back as our knowledge takes us . . . Yet the family, which can give a child so much, can also bring it harm.[1]

Margaret Mead has said:

> We have never discovered any other way to produce responsible human beings except through the family.[2]

It is obvious that there is considerable disparity between our ideals about the family and the realities of family-life in society. Furthermore, many problems arise because the nuclear family is such an isolated unit in society that it doesn't have the resources to cope with the problems it confronts. There is an obvious need for a variety of social settings which can help families resolve some of the challenges they face. Family camping is one such setting.

We must not suppose that it is only the odd, 'abnormal' family that we have in mind. In any case, there is now such a large percentage of single parent families that it is difficult to use the word 'normal' for the traditional two-parent family without sounding a little out-of-touch. The pressures on almost all families are well-known, as are the social changes affecting families (e.g. contraception, women in the workforce, mass media influence, narrowing family structure, immigration and urbanization.)[3] What can family camping offer in such an environment?

Family camping distinctives
Organized family camping should be more than just a profitable way of cashing in on a community need for providing access to attractive family holiday activities. At an organizational level, sufficient thought needs to be given to creative ways of programming for a family camp. Obviously, if we take the educational and social aspects of the temporary community seriously, a good family camp needs more than a distinctive clientele.

We must ask what are the particular needs of that group of campers and how can we meet them? There will obviously be variations between particular families. The following suggestions provide a starting point for planning a camp to meet the distinctive needs of families.

(a) Activities should involve family units
Some camp activities should involve families as family units. These family units may at times be wider than immediate nuclear families — through the inclusion of other (perhaps single) members of the total camp community. The leadership of a family camp can include some people free from family responsibilities of their own and therefore able to help a single parent or be involved with organizing and leading activities.

There are many activities in which families can work as a unit. For example, this morning the Johnsons could be making pottery, the Smiths take a rowing boat out and the Lings do some kitemaking. This could be a regular daily feature each day, families rotating through a variety of activities. Special features could also be included, such as asking families to each present an item at the camp concert.

Not only will surprising talents be unearthed in this way; memorable experiences will be shared intimately as families. This is something which may not occur by merely accepting family enrolments for a camp. Social factors militating against family enrichment will be at work in camp, just as they are in the community at large. The little kids will play together, the teenagers will go off and do their own thing and the adults will be left around to talk, read or look after someone else's kids.

Family camping requires planning to structure activities in which there is a common expectation that families will participate together as families. These activities will not fall into place accidentally. Programming them may be the only way to make them happen — and therefore the only way in the camp situation to advance family understanding, interaction and co-operation beyond what normally exists in the home situation.

Creating situations where families work together may help camp leaders achieve the greatest gains. The discoveries that family-members make about each other ('Gee Dad, I didn't know you could make one of those!'), the memories of shared experiences ('Wasn't it funny the day Mum fell in the creek and we all had to pull her out!'), and the tangible proof of joint activities (That jam dish is the one we made at camp that year') all become fixed points or significant markers in the life of any family.

I have been amazed more than once by letters received from families who already seemed to have outstanding relationships when they came to camp. They have talked about the benefits to them as families of going to a family camp together. Interestingly, such families are often nowhere near the 'top of the heap' socially. The families which appear most in need of valuable shared experiences are often the wealthy and socially successful, where human relationships have run a poor second to material acquisition or frenetic lifestyle.

Even during camp there should be provision for families to reflect on their experience together. This can be facilitated by a question or an activity: making a family 'coat of arms', drawing a picture or simply asking families to discuss a given question. What matters is that family-members think about their relationships and perhaps make resolutions together about the way they might relate to each other in the future. In this way, positive growth experiences can be integrated during camp rather than delayed until the campers return home. We repeat that structured family experiences are beneficial to other than 'needy' families. Many people are looking for experiences which will enrich their family life:

> We don't want to just go to camp and goof around and have recreation; we've done that. We would like to have some growing experience with our children.[4]

Another aspect of the growth potential of family camping is the way camping 'offers parents an opportunity to become vulnerable, to join the children in an uncertain world'.[5]

The author of this comment is a grandfather, veteran of hundreds of camping trips. Family camping can provide experiences where parents and children are on an equal footing, where children and parents grow as friends, where parents are not required all the time to be teachers and supervisors. A change from normal roles gives new perspectives on relationships.

(b) Activities can 'free' parents and children
We have often winced at the cost of a family camp, yet organized family camps generally provide unparalleled value-for-money as a family holiday. Some of the shock of camp fees amounts simply to a recognition of how much it costs to feed and provide adequate shelter for a family for a week. Many camps provide food fit for

kings and a range of highly exciting activities for the whole family for a week — at the cost of just a few nights' sleep in a motel.

But there is more than freedom from the normal limitations of finance. As well as activities which families can enjoy together, family camps provide activities in which parents can be freed from their children and vice versa.

I remember a single mother with four small children who was having her first real holiday at a family camp. She 'had a ball': went horse-riding, swimming, canoeing and a dozen other things while other people looked after her children. Much of the benefit of the camp for her derived from the readiness of others to give her this well-earned break — by doing more than their fair share of wiping dirty faces, taking her kids to the toilet and occupying them in satisfying activities. In this case, 'freedom' for one parent was provided by others.

Meals are an important feature. Some meals can be eaten casually in the outdoors, where people will congregate with whatever friends they choose. At other meals, place-cards can be used to ensure that people sit with other family members. Again, families may be asked to sit as families at some mealtimes. (Some camps make it known that this applies for one meal each day — usually the same meal.) Many parents have echoed the words of this mother:

> I just enjoyed meeting other people and doing nothing in particular — and to have meals served up so beautifully was perhaps the best part as far as I was concerned!

There is also value in 'freeing' the children from the parents. The same mother said:

> The children really had a lovely week doing things they never do at home; it's still talked about a great deal. I know that our children have often had fun and done things on camps which were made possible because someone else was willing to supervise them. Where they would have had to drag me out of a chair or a book, to keep an eye on them out of a sense of duty (and there's no fun in that for them), they've been able to enjoy these things with greater freedom.

(c) Family camps can provide the opportunity for adult reflection and interaction

As with most features of camping of any sort, adult interaction will occur whether we plan it or not. In the normal course of events, parents will share ideas and frustrations, plans and uncertainties with other adults while they knit, walk or just sit around a campfire when the children have gone to bed.

But organized family camping can provide specific opportunities for fresh insight. For example, evenings often provide opportunities where particular issues can be aired. A short talk by a psychologist, teacher, doctor or anyone else on 'bringing up kids', 'coping with conflict' or any one of scores of problem areas may give parents not just access to ideas, but access to people with whom they can share mutual concerns.

(d) Family camps can provide the opportunity for inter-family, inter-generational activities

There is value in having children interacting with other parents. They will develop confidence in other people, they will enrich other people and they will observe other models of parenting. Sometimes kids will discover that their own parents are not so bad after all! On the other hand, children who, for example, lack one parent may gain from warm contact with another father or mother. If the families involved have on-going contact with each other (such as in a local church situation), these bridge-building contacts can have considerable long-term significance.

There are families who have supported one another in very practical ways as a result of family camping experiences. I think of a family who gave a lounge suite to another family experiencing financial struggles. I think of a couple who supported a mother through the trauma of her divorce proceedings, talking patiently on the phone and visiting the family from time to time. And many families have formed permanent friendships which have enriched their lives.

(e) Family camps can provide education for family living

The family camp is a way of shifting gear out of the workaday television-watching, meaningless humdrum into which we can find ourselves slipping. It is an opportunity to try out a more dynamic family life.[6]

Television watching has become something of a way of life for most of us. With it comes passivity, boredom, detachment from issues and a loss of the ability to imagine and entertain oneself. Many's the kid whose first question at camp has been 'Have you got TV here?' The howl of dismay indicates the extent of the addiction. Yet the same camper just won't miss the TV if the camp program is good.

The television has three obvious privatizing effects in relation to families. First, it isolates families from other families. Visiting one another's houses is replaced by watching the box in the lounge-room. And don't dare phone up in prime viewing time!

Second, it isolates family-members from one another. Sitting in front of the TV for meals, conversation hardly exists.

Third, it projects an image of life and a set of values which have little in common with those of the family. It conveys images which constantly exploit sexuality, promote the acquisition of innumerable luxuries as the way to happiness, worship eternal youthfulness, and locate a sense of self-worth in the absence of acne, grey hair or any form of physical imperfection.

The headphones are even more a symbol of isolation of people from one another. One can now be anywhere at all, it seems, and be in a world of one's own, blissfully insulated from other people by virtue of micro-technology.

The family camp program is an agent of change in that it can provide structures in which families begin to relate to each other in new ways. Families may also be introduced to activities which are repeatable events in their ordinary life back home. I can think of a father who got a taste of sailing at a camp, subsequently buying a small yacht which has provided a focus of family recreation ever since. Other families have become addicted to family camping itself as something to look forward to each year — a significant event for the whole family.

Some possible family camp models

Much of what has been said in this chapter presupposes a fairly structured and intentional approach, with a base-camp model in mind. This need not be the case for all family camping programs. While our concern here is more with broad principles, we will illustrate something of the range of possibilities with a very brief sketch of five successful programs which have been run. The first four were of seven days' duration; the fifth was a weekend church camp.

1. Mobile 'safari'

Families for this camp were required to have their own vehicle and camping gear. The group toured to various places, camping grounds having been booked in advance by the organizing team.

The tour was a camp by virtue of an unwritten 'contract' between the families that they would travel together, joining in communal meals and activities each day.

2. National park base-camp

This camp was similar to the first in that the 'contract' between families was fairly limited and the program very *ad hoc* and low-key. Sites were booked for eight families in a small national park camping area, again families supplying their own food and equipment. There was virtually no pre-arranged program, families being free to join in any activities as they wished or to choose alternative activities.

In both these cases, the specific objectives of the camps only involved family units — see distinctive (a) above.

3. Base camp for families with teenage children

This was a camp where a good deal more communal activity was planned. The campsite had a communal kitchen, dining-room and meeting-room with an open log fire. The sleeping accommodation was in eight-bed cabins. In general there was to be a family in each cabin, but the kids who chose to were able to sleep in separate cabins. After the first night, all of them chose this option.

Because of the communal setting, there was a great deal of shared activity every day, with the teenagers and parents doing some activities as separate groups and sometimes as family groups.

A number of families who came didn't have the confidence, mobility, equipment or experience for the first two types of camp. Decision-making about activities here was a daily, corporate process. Some good discussions were held around the fire at night about issues of concern to the campers.

4. Base-camp for families with younger children

The base-camp format again attracted a number of families with a single parent or who, for other reasons, would not have managed other camping styles. Two families did not have cars at all and the site was suitable for smaller children.

The program was highly planned, although parents had an element of choice in what program options to take. Some activities were specifically designed to be taken in family units. Others were 'whole group' activities, like a walk along a beach in the afternoon.

Older children enjoyed looking after the very young ones and there was a mixture of fairly organized activities, free time and low-key optional activities. A bedtime story for the children, brief adult discussions and some family entertainment made up the evening programs.

5. Weekend church camp

Here the families were known to each other, the group including older and single people not attached to families. The weekend was highly organized, but elective sessions and a generally informal approach left people free to sit and talk if they preferred.

Friday evening saw a welcome and warm-up activities, including a bedtime story for the very small children, square-dancing for all and a devotional session after supper.

Saturday included an early morning walk for the early risers, an all-age worship time, free time for trampolines, cricket and other outdoor sports, and a walk to the lunch-spot away from the camp.

The afternoon consisted of the walk back to camp, followed by a number of electives from crafts to music making. The evening included some games and quizzes, an earlier bedtime for children and a later discussion for adults.

Sunday began with 'sunrise on the mountain' — a short drive from the campsite. An inter-generational worship service and some more free time (including a children versus adults cricket match) completed the morning. An informal gathering for everyone after lunch rounded off the weekend.

Some practical hints

Before concluding this brief consideration of organized family camping, a few practical hints may be useful to those who may be planning a family camping program for the first time:

(a) You should have a core of leaders, including if practicable at least one family. Most people appreciate guidance, even when major decisions are made by the participating families. Family camping needs planning as much as any other kind of camping. If certain people are recognized as the leadership team, they will provide a recognizable channel for feedback and suggestions. There is little reason to fear the development of an 'us and them' mentality if the leaders are well chosen.

(b) The value of leaders meeting the families (either as a group or through individual visitation) before the camp has been proved. It helps leaders form an impression of the needs of the group and helps ensure that camper families will ask questions, feel more relaxed from the outset, and come equipped with the necessary clothes, bedding and equipment.

(c) It may be desirable to suggest an age-range into which children of families should fall. Some sites, for example, may be quite unsuitable for very small children, because of the dangers of the environment, lack of bathing facilities or other factors. Again, it may be awkward if there is a large age-range of children, but few children in certain age-groups. Younger children won't mind so much, but the teenager doesn't want to feel conspicuous or lonely.

(d) It is better to over-organize than to under-organize, providing that you don't insist on doing things just because you have organized them. It is better to have several options available than one or none. Even where choices are available, most people get frustrated with too much lengthy discussion and decision-making. They prefer someone who has appraised the various options well to say, 'I think X would be better than Y this morning. Why don't we do X?'

1 Anne Deveson, *Australians at Risk*, Cassell Australia, 1978, pp.67-68
2 Quoted in Anne Deveson, ibid., p.68
3 See Deveson, op. cit., pp.68-69
4 Graendorf and Mattson (ed.), *An Introduction to Christian Camping*, Moody Press, 1979, p.112
5 Lloyd D. Mattson, *Family Camping*, Moody Press, 1973, p.20
6 Ibid.
7 Graendorf and Mattson, op. cit., p.111

Part Three:
'Coolamatong'
— a Philosophy in Practice

coolamatong

13

Camp Coolamatong:
How is it distinctive?

SINCE IT FIRST OCCURRED to me to use 'Coolamatong' to illustrate the philosophy of this book, I have been beset by doubts. Would readers assume, regardless of what I actually said, that I was holding up Coolamatong as a perfect example of a camping concept? Would the use of one example only (i.e. a site-based program) be restrictive, either limiting the thinking of readers or seeming irrelevant to people involved in quite different camping styles? Could I describe it in a way which really dealt with the issues, without embarrassing the people involved?

As I discussed the problem with numerous people I was consistently urged to take the risk. I do so now with considerable hesitation.

First, some readers may feel that the example is being held up as definitive or as singularly important. Let me say as emphatically as possible that this is not so. Of course I am a believer in the 'Coolamatong' concept as an expression of the particular philosophy to which I am committed, but that is not why the example is used. The point is that Coolamatong provides one concrete example, which is familiar to me and which illustrates some of the most fundamental ideas advanced in this book.

Second, there is the fundamental inadequacy of words to convey the spirit or feeling of this experiment. It is possible for someone to read a statement about a subject and, from then on, to have a completely fixed idea about the matter which is quite wrong. The fault may be with the writer, who has expressed himself ambiguously. It may be with the reader, who imposed his own interpretation on the words read. In any case the Coolamatong concept is not fixed for all time. It will be adapted to changing situations and reflect the convictions of future personnel.

On the other hand, 'one in the eye is worth two in the ear'. Speaking of the mind's eye, a word picture can often illustrate something more effectively than books full of abstract ideas. There are ample precedents for making a point with a story and there is a story here, too. So we begin.

A dream unfolds

The Coolamatong story could be said to begin with the arrival of the Barton family last century in Gippsland, Victoria, Australia. The Bartons took up land around Lake Victoria, one of a system of lakes covering nearly four hundred square kilometres and separated from the ocean by a thin barrier of sand dunes constituting the Ninety-Mile Beach.

Fred Barton, grandson of the original settler, lived with his wife Joan on an otherwise uninhabited peninsula of land known as Sperm Whale Head, surrounded on three sides by the water of Lake Reeve and Lake Victoria. Here they brought up two sons. On this poor and remote coastal country covered in banksia trees and coastal scrub, they raised stud Angora goats, the progeny of which have formed the basis of Angora flocks all over Australia. The story deserves telling elsewhere of the way of life of this remarkable family. From 1927, at Fred Barton's initiative, part of Sperm Whale Head came under the control of the National Parks Service and from that time until 1957 Fred became honorary and later part-time ranger for the park. His records have become the accepted authority on the species of plants and birdlife on Sperm Whale Head, the whole of which is now a National Park.

But we must not digress here. Just one other feature of the Bartons' influence on our story must be noted. Fred proved to be not just a remarkable naturalist and a conservationist ahead of his time, but also a philanthropist as well. He had acquired a farm property on the mainland, on the other side of Lake Victoria, including another sandy strip of land known as Banksia Peninsula. This peninsula projected out from the mainland and then ran parallel to it for two-and-a-half kilometres, forming the sheltered waters of Duck Arm in between.

In 1951 the Bartons conceived the idea of dividing the peninsula into four-hectare campsites and giving these blocks of land to interested organizations as a way of marking Australia's Jubilee year. Some idea of the generosity and far-sightedness of this scheme can be gauged by the fact that the Bartons received a firm offer of ten thousand pounds for the land from a real estate developer — at that time a very attractive sum of money.

Several organizations were offered land but declined, for reasons which are hard to determine. No doubt some thought there must be a catch if someone was trying to give away land. In 1952 the Scripture Union was offered a site and chose the first one on the peninsula, with access to Mason Bay on the south side and Duck Arm to the north. The organization already had a camping program and owned a well-developed site near Toolangi, in the mountains to the north-east of Melbourne. But the new campsite (named 'Coolamatong', an Aboriginal word for 'hill beside water') soon became the focus of adventure camping, with watersports as the feature attraction. (Further information about Scripture Union and the management structure of Coolamatong appears in Appendix B.)

By 1972 Scripture Union had developed a third campsite at Lake Eppalock, and all were attracting large numbers of holiday campers. But finance for capital development was stretched and the camps were largely idle during the school year.

At this time, someone heard that the Bartons' farm was for sale. The Bartons had been living on the mainland since 1957 and the farm (through which the track to Banksia Peninsula passed) was still the home of the 'Banksia' Angora stud, running goats and some Corriedale sheep. The possibility was mooted of selling the camp at Lake Eppalock and putting the proceeds towards the purchase of the farm. Such a move would mean the consolidation and rationalization of staff and facilities, while still offering two distinct types of camping (water-based and farm-based). Furthermore, the new site would be built for year-round use and the economic viability of the development could be assisted by a year-round camping program for schools.

It was agreed to enquire of the Bartons as to the asking price for the farm. As it happened, the farm was not on the market at all, but the development proposed excited the Bartons and, in June 1973, Scripture Union took possession of the farm on typically generous terms, having found a buyer for the Lake Eppalock campsite. In November of that year, the Slater family — Tom, June, Peter (almost four) and Jocelyn (twenty months) took up residence at the farm, to begin the work of making the new Coolamatong dream come true.

Coolamatong now

It is tempting to tell some of the story of the next ten years, of the fascinating characters, minor disasters and major excitements which constitute the transformation of a goat farm named 'Bonnie Banks' into the Coolamatong of today. There have been droughts, floods and bushfires, snakes in the house and foxes in the chookhouse — all the ingredients of a good bush yarn. I'm going to write them up one day, but this is not the place.

(a) The property

But what is Coolamatong now? We must begin with geography, though that is not the most important thing. Coolamatong could be somewhere else and be fundamentally the same. It is really the philosophy of Coolamatong that we are concerned with.

But Coolamatong is a property, too — a 'piece of dirt' as farmers sometimes say. It consists of seventy-five hectares of land, including the original campsite of four hectares on Banksia Peninsula. The farm consists of some improved pasture and some largely untouched bushland, including a swamp. The property is a farm in practice, with Merino sheep being raised for wool production. The bush areas abound with kangaroos and the whole area is rich with a stunning variety of birdlife. Milking cows and poultry supply the families who live there, while ducks, geese and turkeys provide new sights and sounds for city campers.

The property includes two campsites. The original site on the Peninsula is now known as the Coolamatong 'Lake Camp'. Here campers sleep in tents, sail, kayak and explore the lakes by small motor boat, as well as do some waterskiing and other activities. Expeditions off the site include trips to the nearby mountains for short bushwalks, trips to nearby rivers for kayaking, and camping expeditions by boat to other lake shores and the Ninety-Mile Beach.

The other campsite is the 'Farm Camp'. This is quite distinct from the Lake Camp; you can be at one campsite and be almost oblivious to the existence of the other. The two environments are remarkably dissimilar — almost two different worlds. The Lake Camp is dominated by the water and covered with banksia and wattle trees. The sights and sounds of the lake are visible and audible wherever you are. The Farm Camp, on the other hand, is dominated by open pasture, bounded by forested areas and dotted with great gum trees. A short walk in any direction means an encounter with the sights, sounds and smells of a farm. The lake,

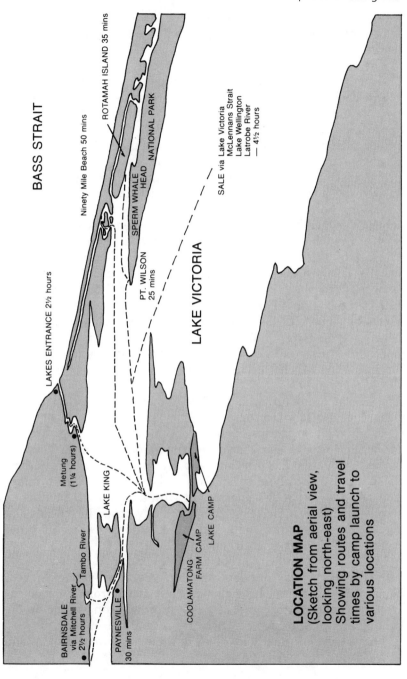

BASS STRAIT

ROTAMAH ISLAND 35 mins

Ninety Mile Beach 50 mins

SPERM WHALE HEAD

NATIONAL PARK

PT. WILSON 25 mins

SALE via Lake Victoria
McLennans Strait
Lake Wellington
Latrobe River
— 4½ hours

LAKES ENTRANCE 2½ hours

LAKE VICTORIA

Metung
(1¼ hours)

LAKE KING

Tambo River

BAIRNSDALE
via Mitchell River
2½ hours

COOLAMATONG
FARM CAMP

LAKE CAMP

PAYNESVILLE
30 mins

LOCATION MAP
(Sketch from aerial view,
looking north-east)
Showing routes and travel
times by camp launch to
various locations

though visible, is a more distant view, down below the steep hill which intervenes between the camp and the low-lying land of the peninsula.

The farm campsite itself consists of only three buildings: the main building, the sleeping accommodation and the recreation room. Each is designed with quite specific aims in mind. The first two buildings are of brick construction to withstand the impact of year-round use. The Farm Camp offers a distinctively different program from the Lake Camp. Horse riding, a large and complex obstacle course, cross-country cycling, farm demonstrations, orienteering and bushcraft activities are the attractions of this site, as well as kayaking, swimming and boat trips.

Serving both campsites is a large fifty-passenger motor vessel, which is owned by Coolamatong. This is an enormously valuable part of the whole program. Moored at the Coolamatong jetty in Duck Arm, this boat is capable of taking a whole camp group out on the lakes safely in all weathers. This in effect means that hundreds of square kilometres of lakes, as well as rivers, ocean beach, the National Park and the busy port of Lakes Entrance are accessible. The *C.C. Neill*, as it is named, goes to all these places. Most campers return to the railhead at Bairnsdale on a two-and-a-half hour cruise via Lake Victoria, the village of Paynesville, Lake King and the Mitchell River.

(b) The program

The Coolamatong program falls into two broad categories: holiday programs and school programs.

The holiday programs operate at both campsites. They are run in the same way as other Scripture Union holiday camps. They are staffed by voluntary directors and teams of voluntary leaders. They usually last about seven days and cater mainly for primary and secondary school students, but with a significant number of family camps as well. These camps are advertised in schools and by direct mail, along with Scripture Union's camps in other locations. They are open to anyone.

Much of the philosophy of this book could be illustrated by reference to the way holiday camping programs operate. Indeed, numerous illustrations have already been drawn from involvement in these camps. But the rest of this section will concentrate on the schools camping program. There are several reasons for this:

* I have been personally involved in these programs, week in and week out, for over five years.

* Because they are run professionally by a group of paid staff, they reflect a consistently applied and evaluated approach used over a large number of camps.
* The actual physical design of the Farm Camp (where the schools program happens) has been deliberately built around the philosophy of the schools program.
* School camping is a form of camping where the educational and recreational attributes of camping can be shown to be attainable, even where the community dimensions are given prime importance.

Camping with a difference

The first advertising brochure and teachers' handbook produced to explain the school camping program made the claim that Coolamatong offered 'school camping with a difference'. There were three features of the Coolamatong program we considered significant.

1. The diversity of options

In terms of environmental studies, there is easy access to a wide range of eco-systems: improved and unimproved grazing country, bushland, swamp, coastal dunes and various marine environments. The area is rich in wildlife. There is a variety of animals on the farm. Farm experiences include milking cows, handling sheep and poultry, watching demonstrations in sheepdog work, shearing and the whole range of sheep husbandry. Almost all of this is available without leaving the property.

Local studies can include timber milling, irrigation farming, forestry, the fishing industry and lifestyle in a country town — though these have been rarely explored because of choice and time constraint.

Then there is the range of recreational choices already mentioned, as well as the usual variations of having a campfire, cooking damper, organizing a woolshed dance or a night walk. On a tour of campsites in North America a few years ago I came to the conclusion that there must be few places in the world where a more diverse environment exists within range of a single campsite.

There is, of course, no cause for boasting on that account. For one thing, we have by no means explored all the possibilities of the environment. But, more importantly, we can hardly claim credit for them being there anyway! Certainly we have deliberately developed the potential of the farm for teaching purposes. Certainly the purchase of the *C.C. Neill* has opened up the whole area, but we can't claim credit for the donations which went towards its purchase. And we certainly didn't put a farm next to a lake, within sight of a National Park and within sound of the ocean.

Any human credit for our good fortune in being there should go to Fred Barton, without whom there might well have been a conventional subdivision for holiday housing where the Lake Camp and the National Park are now. In any case the 'school camping with a difference' idea didn't refer primarily to the study and recreational possibilities of the site at all.

2. Program role of resident staff

Another important feature of Coolamatong is the role of resident staff. Besides the director, there are three other permanent staff and usually a short-term assistant as well. Although the three other long-term staff have specialist contributions (cooking, maintenance and farm management), they are fully involved in the camp program whenever a school is in.

The presence of competent resident staff has meant three things: (a) We have tried to tailor programs to the individual schools, and the objectives that their teachers have for the camp. This means taking the time to understand what teachers want, not simply to run a routine program regardless of which group is in.
(b) We have been able to offer activities which are sometimes beyond the scope and abilities of the teachers concerned. Butchering a sheep is a good example. Another is various boat trips, which require licensed drivers.
(c) We are able to relieve the teachers of a significant amount of organizational work by offering leadership in the main camp activities. This relieves teachers of some of the pressure of organization and enhances the potential for relationship-building between teachers and students.

But even the program role of resident staff is not the key distinctive to which the 'camping with a difference' idea refers. That key distinctive is the relationship which obtains between campers (students and teachers) and the members of the resident staff community. This has to do with the way staff on the one hand and visiting teachers and students on the other, perceive their relationship with one another.

3. A 'guest' relationship

Right at the beginning of a camp, the Coolamatong director explains that the staff see the campers as guests. They do not see the school as merely hiring a campsite or the staff as simply offering a service. They see themselves primarily as hosts and the campers primarily as guests, who will share in a small way in the life of the resident community.

Perhaps this sounds like a superior attitude, but it is quite the contrary, both in its intention and in the response of the campers. The Coolamatong staff clearly signal that they want to develop a friendly and respectful relationship with their guests. This will involve them in a degree of interaction with the campers which goes beyond the requirements of a merely commercial 'client' relationship.

With this brief description behind us we may now proceed to an examination of the way in which this underlying philosophy is translated into the buildings and program which are 'Coolamatong'.

14

The Farm Camp Development:
How did the design reflect the philosophy?

NO ONE WILL EVER BUILD the perfect campsite. We have often told ourselves that if we were building again, we would do this or that differently. But then we would overlook something else instead. The important thing is that the design of buildings (including their location and relationship to each other) and the design of programs, staffing policy and organization structures should reflect the basic philosophy and objectives which they are supposed to implement.

In building the Farm Camp we had an exciting opportunity to 'start from scratch' on the basis of a well-defined philosophy and a good deal of experience in running camps at our own sites and elsewhere. A master plan committee was formed, which included a good number of voluntary workers as well as one or two paid staff. All of them, however, had a strong involvement with the organization and an understanding of its philosophy. There were people with mainly camping expertise, while others contributed ideas and experience of a specialist kind: an architect, a builder, two farmers and three teachers.

The committee also called on the advice of an environmental scientist, an agricultural scientist and a horticulturalist. Eventually, the master plan was produced — some forty pages of findings, from a statement of basic aims to lists of suitable trees for planting at different sites around the property. When this basic policy document was approved by the state council of Scripture Union, the committee then set to work to design the farm campsite buildings. The philosophy clearly dictated the design they came up with.

1. Location of campsite

Three alternative sites were proposed — a remote site in the 'bush paddock', a sandy rise in the centre of an open paddock and a site right in the middle of the farm, close to the shearing shed and a small orchard. Naturally, practical considerations like drainage, access, power and water supply were important, though not altogether decisive.

The choice of the central site both reflected and affected our philosophy. I was off the mark in my own initial preference for the bush site — as subsequent developments quickly showed. But the central location had two clear advantages. First, everything about it said 'farm'. The chosen site for the new buildings was only a stone's throw from the old shearing shed and sheepyards, with paddocks on all sides. Second, the site was close enough to and in full view of the existing staff houses, but just far enough away from them to maintain a necessary degree of privacy for staff and their families. Indeed, the access road to the peninsula provided a ready-made psychological barrier, so that going into the staff residences area was a fairly conscious act.

The reader can see how important this has been in terms of the 'guest' idea. When the director said, 'Welcome to our place; this is where we live and we're glad you're here', the whole feeling of the camp soon reinforced this idea.

2. Location of farm buildings

The cowbail and poultry sheds were originally in what became the staff residence area. When they were rebuilt, they were located in the farm area in the general vicinity of the campsite. This involved some relative inconvenience for the staff who milked cows, fed poultry and collected eggs. But it was a deliberate choice, chiefly to create a situation where staff in the course of their daily tasks had to move naturally in and out of the camp area.

This meant that the 'being-on-a-farm' and the 'being-at-our-place' feelings were both reinforced automatically during the course of the daily schedule.

3. Size of the campsite

A very significant decision was that of size. The first consideration was the total numbers which should be catered for. In other words, how many beds would we provide? This was the key point at which purely commercial considerations were rejected and a fundamental principle given top priority. Respected advice was that, to make money, accommodation for about ninety campers was necessary. This was reinforced by advice that many schools liked to take a whole form-level away on camp, rather than one class. Therefore, ninety to one hundred was a sensible number to accommodate.

This number of campers ran completely counter to a growing preference in the organization over many years for smaller total numbers of campers. It was felt that when the number of campers got over thirty-five to forty, it became significantly more difficult to develop a real personal dimension in the group, or even to learn everyone's names. Significant relationships between leaders and campers are sometimes hard to achieve in seven or eight days, let alone four or five.

The committee settled on forty-two beds for campers, with an extra seven beds in three separate bedrooms used mainly by staff. The number fifty then became the key to size of dining-room, kitchen and other facilities. This was a number which would also accommodate the typical holiday camp, with around thirty to forty campers and twelve to fifteen leaders, including cooks.

A second aspect of the size consideration was the number of beds in each sleeping unit. The holiday camps had long worked on the basis of a leader sleeping with each group of five to seven campers. This configuration seemed appropriate for school camps, too. There are six cabins with seven mattresses in each, arranged in double bunks. One bottom bunk is normally wardrobe space, but can become a bed simply by placing a mattress in the space. This was a plan to give more flexibility, in case of uneven numbers of boys and girls, and has been used quite often.

The third aspect of 'size' was a commitment to the concept of simplicity. The aim was to provide basic facilities that were attractive and of good quality, but were relatively unsophisticated. There were two factors involved here. One was the need to keep the total cost down; the other was to actually 'say' something, in the design, about lifestyle and priorities.

On reflection, we probably went a little too far in this direction. For example, more pantry and cold-storage space, more room in the shower areas and a slightly bigger dining-room/lounge area would have improved the functional quality of those areas. But these are relatively small considerations in the overall picture.

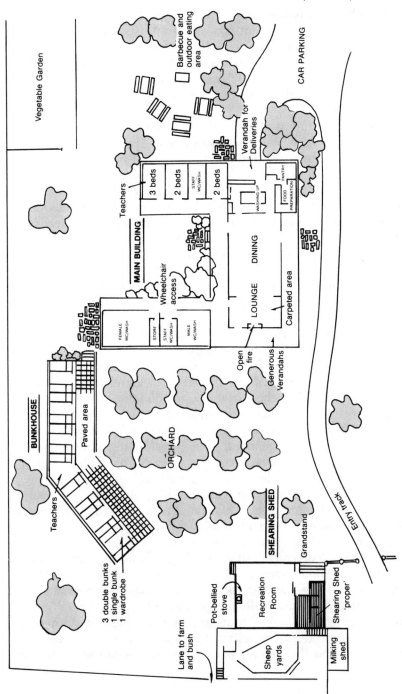

4. Number and relationship of buildings

By far the most important consideration was the desire to make people feel at home in the place. It was agreed that maintaining the 'human dimension' was of prime importance. Many campsites have a large institutional feel; it was agreed that the main building should reproduce the feeling of a 'homestead' in keeping with the farm location.

After an enormous amount of work by our architect on various possible layouts, a courtyard design was agreed on. This would cater for the basic communal functions, leaving only sleeping accommodation and indoor recreation to be catered for in other buildings. It is a matter of speculation and subjective evaluation as to what effect the layout actually has on the camp or individuals. It seems safe to say that, at the very least, there is a feeling of security and intimacy about the place - especially for younger children. There is a 'family' feel, too.

Other considerations included the reduction of the impact on the environment to a smaller area and the need for convenience in movement between areas, especially for families and at night or in wet weather.

However, there was some conflict here with a tradition of having sleeping groups dispersed throughout the site in quite separate cabins or tents. This was just one of the many areas where compromise was needed. In the end it was felt that the above considerations plus the economy in building outweighed the importance of a sense of independence in each sleeping group.

The 'boomerang' shape of the sleeping accommodation is another attempt to engender a sense of belonging and community. The building moves away from the main courtyard building, but bends around to enclose the original orchard (still bearing a variety of fruit) to meet up with the third building, the shearing shed and recreation room. This layout also enabled us to preserve a beautiful gum tree, which shaded a breezeway between the two halves of the sleeping accommodation.

There was a divergence of views about the actual location of the sleeping accommodation. One view was advanced that the placement of this building to the north, forming a fourth side of the courtyard, would really create that sense of community — of all belonging together — in a quite inescapable way. Others felt uneasy about this. The clinching argument was the desire to preserve a view through the big dining-room windows to the farm and the bush areas beyond. Thus the courtyard remained open.

An unforeseen consequence of this decision was that the sleeping cabins were removed from the immediate area of the teachers' bedrooms. This meant that it was possible for campers to create a disturbance at night while teachers slept unaware. This now seems so obvious that we wonder how we could have missed it, but we had begun with the mentality of the traditional holiday camping program, in which there is always an adult in each sleeping group. Thus the 'breezeway' in the middle of the sleeping block is now a staff room as well!

5. Appearance
The master plan stated that buildings should be 'ground-hugging, rather than ground-alienating' — an important consideration for a flat environment. One especially exciting sketch plan was rejected because it did not meet this requirement. It was felt that the buildings should really belong in the environment as far as possible. Not only should they be ground-hugging; they should also look like farm buildings.

Each building has fulfilled this requirement perfectly. As the main building rose from the ground, numerous passers-by would ask, 'Who is going to live in the house over there?'. Plan successful! When a family arrived for an early family camp, a child asked, 'Mum, do we have to sleep in those sheds over there?', pointing to the sleeping cabins. Aim achieved again! And of course the shearing shed looked like what it was — a typical shearing shed.

It may seem strange to any camping person that we should actually be pleased that the campsite looked like a house. If camping is about escaping from an urban environment, surely the aim should be to studiously avoid the replication of urban images in a campsite? This is a reasonable question, particularly as we have argued that camping should give urbanized people a taste of living close to nature.

At this point personal preferences about camping styles and personal images of what constitutes a suitable camping environment come into play. To some extent when we set up a base campsite, we quite consciously create a certain environment. In North America, the Western 'cowboy-and-Indian' image influences the camping movement. Camping was a search for adventure, a pioneering challenge, with Daniel Boone and Davey Crockett heroes to be emulated.

This concept has been faithfully reproduced in Australia. Though it is not my personal preference, it is superficial to criticise it as merely corny or irrelevant. When a camper enters such a place, there is a 'willing suspension of disbelief'. The campsite becomes a place of imagination — perhaps a form of escape, but one recognized as such. There is a sense in which it is authentic as a consistent expression of a camping philosophy, even if it seems alien to our culture.

Thus, in regard to our Farm Camp, whether a house-like building is appropriate or not is not to be judged by whether it fits the general public's preconceived notions about that a campsite should look like. The question is whether it satisfies clear criteria which reflect the broad philosophy of camping and the particular objectives which lie behind it.

In this case it was felt that a 'farmhouse' concept was an authentic expression of the desire to be true to the environment and true to the basic principle of developing a homely atmosphere. It is not essentially different from a traditional tent or rough cabin format in providing the necessary shelter from the elements, and it is functional and robust enough for year-round use.

Features of the design and layout of the campsite which fulfil these criteria include:

* Wide verandahs around the main building, with a typical Australian profile. These provide shade in the summer, shelter from the rain and pleasant places out of the wind to sit and talk.
* Gardens of native shrubs in the courtyard and around the buildings, creating a pleasant, lived-in feel to the place.

6. The lounge-room at the camp director's home

The lounge area at the campsite is quite small. It is carpeted, with an open fireplace, but it is just an annexe to the dining-room, designed as a quiet spot to read or place to gather quietly before a meal. When the camp director's house (the former farmhouse) was renovated and enlarged a large lounge-room was added, specifically as a place where a whole camp could be invited to spend an evening.

This was part of the concept of building personal relationships with the camper 'guests'. The lounge includes a large open fireplace, where big logs crackle on cold evenings, with a massive piece of old bridge timber for a mantelpiece. It is carpeted with fairly cheap carpet, but with a thick 'sandwich' underlay, so that campers can sit on the floor quite comfortably for a couple of hours.

7. The shearing shed/recreation room

The original shearing shed has been incorporated into the 'new building', though with some modifications. Our architect waxed lyrical about the qualities of this old shed and the surrounding sheepyards. In particular, he felt they demonstrated the Australian farmer's capacity for ingenuity, and ability to adapt to suit his purposes. A classic example was the way the exhaust pipe from the old petrol-driven shearing plant was suspended with a piece of fencing-wire from the spouting!

However, compromise was again required. While the development of the shed retained the plain corrugated iron construction, the main roof truss was suspended from two great poles, cut from the forest in the nearby mountains. There were some windows on one side, but along the other side, overlooking the sheepyards, large hinged shutters opened up to let the breeze in or provide a grandstand view of the sheepyards.

The yards and shed are designed around people as well as livestock. The shearing shed proper is separated from the recreation room by a large sliding door. It is out of bounds, except when an organized activity takes place there. Features of the shearing shed are the tiered seating at one end, to provide a view of shearing for all campers, and removable sides to the 'catching pen' for an unimpeded view of the butchering.

The recreation room is 'rough' insofar as it is largely unlined. For one week of the year it is the woolroom while shearing is in progress; otherwise it serves as an indoor area where campers go freely at any time for table tennis or other activities. It is efficiently heated by a pot-bellied stove which is fuelled from the abundant supply of dead timber in the bush areas of the property.

The decision to add a separate indoor activities hall was not made because the weather is unfavourable (it is in fact relatively warm in winter and cool in summer), but because we wanted to keep the dining-room set up as a clean, well-organized, homely place, rather than having to double as an activities centre as well.

8. Around the property

Naturally, these basic objectives had their implications for the whole property, not just for the immediate area of the campsite.

Important choices were made about delineating the areas where campers had free access at any time, from those which were restricted in some way. The bush paddock was reserved for ecological studies, the pasture areas for grazing (though campers were free to enter them), and other areas for activities like orienteering, obstacle course, wide games and horse-riding trails. The lane which runs up the middle of the farm is not only an asset for moving stock, but gives easy access with a minimum of interruption by fences. There were few directional signs anywhere, inside or out, which might create an institutional feel about the place. The sleeping cabins were named after local birds and animals. These and other signs were generally in routed timber, all painted in an earthy yellow lettering on a sage green background.

Tree planting has been a high priority, plantations of native trees and shrubs continually being established. These are not only suitable for screening less attractive areas and providing windbreaks, but also for beautifying the total environment.

All this, of course, is 'nuts and bolts' stuff. Of greater significance is the way in which the program promotes the development of a personal relationship with camper guests. It is in the relationships between staff, and in their basic motivation, that the underlying Christian ethos of Coolamatong is most clearly seen. The through-the-year camping program is not religious in the ordinary sense of the word, but it does reflect a Christian attitude to people. We now look at how this concept works out in practice.

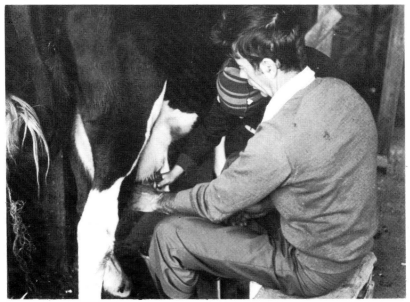

A camper takes over milking from Brian Gray

Enjoying visiting the poultry

Young riders get ready for a trail ride

Horse-riding — more than a means of transport!

Inner-suburban girls at bushcraft activity

Kayaking in Duck Arm

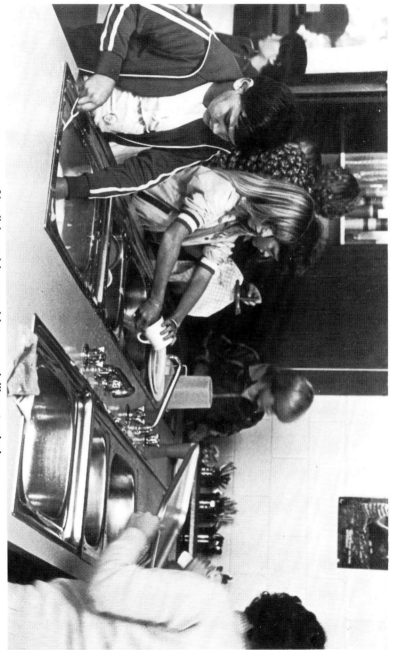

No dishwashing machine — a deliberate choice

The lounge carpet — an important place for quiet recreation

Off on a trip in the C.C. Nell

Campers enjoy the wide open spaces of Ninety Mile Beach

Fun on *Wednesday* night in the director's house

Aerial view of Camp Coolamatong: the Farm Camp upper left, staff housing centre and Duck Arm top right

The original Barton homestead overlooking Banksia Peninsula

The Barton homestead after renovations for the Slaters

The director's home as it is today, landscaping complete

The view from the Farm Camp towards Lake Victoria

The Farm Camp showing main building and bunkhouse

Camp-site buildings blend with farm surroundings

Fun on the obstacle course

Crawling along a suspended pole is harder than it looks

Farm studies at Camp Coolamatong: Ken Hutton

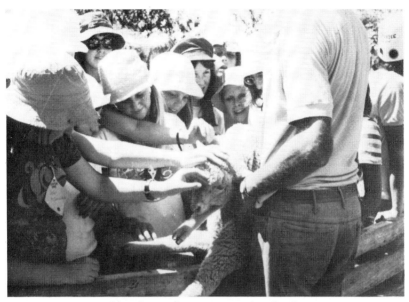

Hands reach out to touch a lamb

Ken Hutton shearing — a highlight

Author and Ken Hutton skinning a sheep

The shearing shed: retaining its original rough character for indoor games

15

Relationships in the Community:

How do they develop?

COOLAMATONG IS A 'COMMUNITY' in two senses. There is the sense of it being a temporary community whenever a camp is in progress, and there is the on-going community of residential staff. For any school group coming to Coolamatong, there is a mutually enriching interaction between the temporary and the permanent community. In this chapter we will outline the way in which the philosophy of Coolamatong, and in particular the idea of the 'host-guest relationship', has been put into practice. But first, an introduction to the resident staff community.

Coolamatong staff

The first staff member at Coolamatong was the director — that was where I and my family came into the picture on a full-time basis. My own background was teaching. Ken Hutton began work soon after as a part-time farm manager, working initially for a day a week. When the farm camp building project began, Ken agreed to work three days a week on the project, putting his practical farmer's skills to work as a builder's labourer.

When the building was completed, two further staff were appointed full-time. Dianne Husted took leave from working with a bank in Bairnsdale to try her hand at cooking for large numbers, after which she resigned from the bank to work on a permanent basis at Coolamatong. Brian Gray, with his wife Barbara and three barefoot sons, fresh from Papua New Guinea, completed the staff team. Brian's particular skills were in the building and maintenance area, and they were the skills which had originally taken him to PNG with Australian Volunteers Abroad.

Of these four staff members, I was the only one who was a camping 'professional', having been full-time camping co-ordinator for Scripture Union of Victoria for five years. What some might see as a limitation was in fact a strength. It gave the community an entirely authentic feel — a feature often noted by visiting teachers and others.

Ken lives about thirty kilometres from Coolamatong and now comes to work four days a week.[1] The rest of his time he runs two family properties with other members of the Hutton family. He is a tall, strong man — every inch a farmer — and, besides managing the farm, he utilises a lifetime of experience with horses to supervise the horse-riding program as well. Dianne lives in the old 'Cottage', an attractive little home built years ago from locally made bricks and close to the director's residence. The Grays live in a house which Brian built a little further around from the 'Cottage'.

When the Grays arrived they knew very little about Coolamatong. A letter of invitation to them had spelt out three basic facets of the job:

(a) Membership of the staff community
This meant a commitment to the life and welfare of the other staff and to living in harmony with them. This was the most important requirement.

(b) Involvement with campers in the camping program
This meant not just being prepared to work with people around them. It meant being involved fully in the programs whenever a school was in (i.e. for about twenty-six weeks a year) and in school holidays as well.

(c) Building and maintenance
Although this was Brian's particular area of expertise, this was the third priority.

I have mentioned these requirements because they are the basis on which every staff-member is appointed. Staff-members are first and foremost members of a staff community, one which is involved in a service role — to assist visiting camp groups. In Dianne Husted's case, her role at Coolamatong is quite different from the career she was formerly pursuing. However her earlier involvement in local youth work and welfare work clearly showed a person who could relate to young people as well as adults. She was regarded as a friend and confidante by many kids, who held her in the highest regard.

Brian Gray was an accomplished skier and bushwalker and had run a YMCA centre in New Zealand.

At the beginning of 1982, Jim and Julie Rees and their children replaced us in the director's house. (We had reluctantly agreed to return to Melbourne, where I took up a wider supervisory appointment with Scripture Union.) Jim was a primary school principal with the Victorian Education Department and Julie was also a teacher. Both had extensive experience of camping and youth work.

This completes the current picture. We have introduced the staff by name because it is the only sensible way to describe how they relate to the campers during the week. And Jim and Julie will, I know, forgive me if I speak sometimes from my own experience in the past, rather than of the present situation.

The staffing picture would not be complete without a mention of the invaluable role played by short-term staff. Len Creek, with his wife Bev and their children, lived for six months at Coolamatong. Len used his amazing range of building, mechanical and farm skills to set up the major sheds and put our machinery in good working order. Ian Fuhrmeister, a maths teacher and now an outreach youth worker, was with us for twelve months.

Since the middle of 1979, there have been short-term staff continuously. They have spent from three to eighteen months, providing back-up in the kitchen and in activity leadership as well. Some have been teachers on leave, such as Ted Endacott, who fitted in three months following a camping trip in South America, North America and Europe, and later became camping co-ordinator for Scripture Union in Victoria. Others have been locals like Susan Cox, who gave invaluable help in horse-riding and cooking for eighteen months.

The staff community

The goal of creating a community rather than simply a staff is a product of three key ideas:

(a) Community is seen as being, in essence, the expression of the corporate nature of the Christian faith. It is not just an outcome of a shared faith, but an obligation to care for one another. We see it as something of a contradiction for Christians to work closely together without sharing their lives more deeply than is common in our society.

(b) The demands of living as well as working closely with other people make it necessary to develop a considerable degree of tolerance and understanding. To put the matter simply, real love for one another is required — something which can be learned and worked at with God's help.

(c) The ability to love one another and cope with the demands of living is rightly regarded as an authenticating feature of Christian community. As we see it, the Christian faith has often been rejected not because people didn't know the facts, but because they haven't seen it working — not because it is not intellectually true, but because it sometimes lacks credible witnesses. If Coolamatong was to be known as a Christian enterprise, it had better look like one!

The way in which this community ideal is pursued is essentially practical and humdrum. It is not a religious community in a monastic sense. It makes no claims whatsoever to be innovative, or even especially successful. It has no practical expression in the school camping program in terms of worship or religious observance. It is simply a group of staff members who are committed to caring for one another and their guests, not merely to working together.

Nevertheless, to satisfy the curious and to do justice to the idea, the following brief comments may help fill out the picture. The community is wider than the staff. It includes their families and other people closely involved with them. One couple, Joe and Ann Scull, came to live on Banksia Peninsula in the early years of the Farm Camp development to contribute their skills directly to the project in a voluntary capacity. The fact that the group multiplied biologically made for increasing difficulties in meeting together. Not many homes can sleep up to fourteen children while eleven adults are meeting in the lounge-room!

The total group generally meets weekly to share burdens and news, study the Bible and pray and worship. Sometimes the gathering will begin with a meal; at other times it will be at a weekend and include 'all-in' games and other activities which involve adults and children alike. Sometimes the meetings have been routine; at other times matters of considerable personal significance have been shared in the group. Most of us have struggled with being honest and open about our feelings, but the commitment of working at that has always been of fundamental importance to the health of the group.

The staff also meet regularly during the week to adapt plans, share news and evaluate progress, as well as to pray about the day's affairs. The routine planning and management decisions, budgetting and communication processes are handled at these meetings.

The practical dimensions of community were, for us, a matter of constant satisfaction. Affirmation from others often took the form of a birthday celebration, a letter while on holidays or flowers in a vase when you returned after an absence. But most of the time the expression of love was essentially practical. You rarely had to ask another person to milk the cow or feed out the hay when you were away for the day or had another commitment. Help was offered before you could ask — or more often the job was done before you thought about it. It is a rare privilege to work and live in such a situation.

The 'wider community' is not only functionally important to the program, but enriches the experience of camp for a visiting group. For example Dianne's parents, well past retiring age, are usually around on the first afternoon — Mrs Husted baking as only she can in the kitchen and Mr Husted, a retired orchardist, working in the camp's vegetable garden. The affirmation and involvement of elderly people is a significant educational act in a society which, on the whole, tries to pretend that the elderly don't exist.

Again, Julie Rees and Barbara Gray are involved not only in the corporate life of the community wherever practicable, but in the camping area as well — whether managing the poultry, helping in the kitchen, selling T-shirts and postcards to campers or just cleaning windows. And the little girls who comment on Ken's big brown eyes are always interested to meet his wife Faye and the children if they drop in!

Making it happen in relationships

We now have a sufficient understanding of what is meant by the resident staff community to explain how that group interacts with temporary communities, the school camps. How are relationships established and built up between Coolamatong staff and their guests? Here are the key elements of a typical program in the order in which they most often occur:

1. Pre-camp contact

Where possible, one or two Coolamatong staff visit the school and talk with teachers about the program options. The aim is to tailor the program to the needs of the particular school. Often this contact is only with the teacher in charge of the camp, though occasionally it includes others. In all cases, a substantial teachers' handbook goes to the school when the booking is confirmed. This contains biographical information about the staff, as well as background information and a prospectus of the program options.

Occasionally the staff visit a meeting for parents, showing slides and explaining what usually happens at a Coolamatong camp. The staff are really 'exhibits', especially in places where parents are unwilling to let their children go to camp.

2. On arrival

The staff are on hand to greet the 'campers' (including teachers) when they arrive by bus from the railway station. It is fascinating to observe the different groups when they arrive. Where staff have already been to the school, there is often a heightened sense of excitement as the kids pour off the bus. Where teachers are returning from the previous year with a different group of students, they have obviously communicated their own sense of expectation to the kids.

At times everyone is quite new and the challenge is to make them feel comfortable and relaxed straightaway. Jim, Brian and Ken help unload luggage and put it on the verandah. They are already flat out introducing themselves and answering questions from excited kids. Before the group disperses to find bedrooms and unpack, they sit down to hot scones and drinks in the dining room.

3. Introductions

After the staff have served drinks and scones at the tables, the teacher-in-charge introduces the camp director, Jim Rees. He welcomes the group and then introduces the other staff. A short explanation of the 'Welcome to our place — we think of you as our guests' idea follows. Only two rules which apply immediately are mentioned. (Most rules can wait until later.) These few minutes are designed to establish two points for the campers: that there are some rules; that the staff want to be friends with them on the basis of mutual respect.

4. Orientation activity

The first afternoon consists of an orientation activity in which the group is generally subdivided into three groups. These groups rotate through three activities conducted by the Coolamatong staff: a walk around the farm property, an introduction to horse-riding safety, and a tour of the lake frontage and the staff housing area. Each of these activities takes about half-an-hour. During this time two things happen:

(a) Coolamatong staff learn names
We have found that it is possible to learn the first names of thirty children, sometimes even forty, during that hour-and-a-half in which we have the campers in three groups. It takes intense concentration, repetition and writing down, but it is a skill which can be learned.

The significance of this process is that it signals to the campers that the staff care about them. Also it enables the staff to call campers by name during the rest of the week (though inevitably one or two people have similar names or appearance to confuse us for the whole week). This has a great personalizing effect on relationships; people like to be called by name.

The risk is that you may forget just one person — and that person knows you have forgotten! It is essential to get names early; the longer it takes, the more embarrassing it is to ask again.

(b) Campers learn the rules
This is what we call learning by 'the slow drip method' (a reference to the process, not the person teaching). As the groups move around the campsite, they learn a number of important rules: don't come into the horseyard unless you've been told to; go through gates not fences; only drink water from these taps; wear a lifejacket when kayaking; keep out of the workshop; use the jetty but not the boats; put the bridle on this way.

The beauty of this method is that there is no tedious listing of rules and regulations, no sense of being lectured about restrictions. The reasons for each instruction are obvious and can be pointed to rather than merely talked about. There is also a bonus for relationships with campers; the limitations can be pointed out in a non-authoritarian way and the whole process is conversational.

By the time the orientation is over, relationships have already begun. Coolamatong staff have already identified the conspicuously helpful or troublesome campers and this knowledge becomes a basis for discussion with teachers about the needs of particular campers.

5. First night
The first evening meal is important, not just to satisfy curious or anxious campers about the quality of the food or to establish

mealtime routines, but because it is the cook's first opportunity to get to know the campers' names.

Evenings are usually organized entirely by the teachers, but at least one staff member usually goes over to the campsite at an agreed time to show slides of the area and its wildlife. This provides valuable background information for the campers, alerting them about things to look for. It also gives the staff member an opportunity to revise names again!

6. Milking the cows

It is much easier to milk a cow without the help of half-a-dozen kids. It is even easier without an audience of noisy and excited campers. So milking time is another small evidence of the commitment to involvement with campers. It has considerable educational value as well!

Usually one group of campers is allocated to milking each morning. Campers are invited not simply to watch but to 'have a go'. The risks to Jim and Brian range from having a stream of milk misdirected into their gumboots to having an agitated cow mess up the bail. But the cows seem to adapt to the extra attention and it is worth the effort.

7. Meals

Because they need to maintain some family life, when camps are in, married staff eat at home except for the midday meal. Lunch is held outside whenever the weather is suitable — which is nearly always. This is a good hour for relaxed conversation and listening.

.Meals are almost always served by the 'file past' method. This gives campers the chance to choose what they want to take or leave. Besides being a thoughtful gesture, it helps eliminate waste. It also gives Dianne another regular contact with the campers.

The kitchen is an important focal point in many a camp for not just physical warmth but emotional warmth as well. The kindly cook often becomes a substitute 'mother figure' for the lonely camper and the kitchen a place of homely activity and security. There is a common image of the camp cook as a tyrant, waving a wooden spoon threateningly and promising dire retribution for some cowering camper who didn't do the washing up. Such an image has some justification in my own memory. Needless to say the cook who can not only produce adequate quantities of delicious food, but remain friendly and firm as well, is a real asset.

8. The main activities

While teachers are involved in all the activities with their students, sometimes running their own program as well, most teachers choose some basic program options led by Coolamatong staff. Ken generally runs the horse-riding program, Jim the kayaking and Brian a major and complex obstacle course, or an intriguing bushcraft activity in which campers learn to get drinking water from gum trees, cook in the open or survive a night in the bush.

From time to time, short-term staff give leadership in activities in which they are skilled. Occasionally the permanent staff rotate activities to break the pattern of repetitive teaching.

While activities don't usually provide a good context for conversation, they do provide a passport to good relationships or, better, a vehicle for the development of relationships. Monumental patience is sometimes demanded, and many campers recognize that staff often act in ways which go far beyond 'the call of duty'. The staff are acutely aware of past failures and it is here that the fellowship of their own community is often a sustaining influence.

9. The boat trip

Most camps include a day which features a trip in the *C.C. Neill* to the Lakes National Park, Rotomah Island, Ninety Mile Beach, or other places around the Lake Victoria area. Such days provide ample opportunity to share with campers, the Coolamatong staff also showing campers around these areas in small groups. A favourite group activity is bird observing, a friendly competitive element often adding stimulus to the search. One group of sixteen-year-old boys spotted thirty-one species in an hour. Again the local knowledge of staff enhances the experience.

Mind you, there are disappointing experiences too. Staff often struggle to communicate their appreciation of the environment to campers, sometimes having to give up on encouraging them to be quiet and observant. Teachers are usually consoling at this point; it is sometimes a relief to know it isn't all our fault!

The challenge posed by the occasional unresponsive or rebellious group of kids is often the best test of whether there is some real fibre in a relationship, or whether it is based on mere sentiment and the desire for approval. If a teacher or a Coolamatong staff-member doggedly persists in attempting to direct and motivate kids in a certain direction, it may simply indicate a failure to perceive the reality of the situation, but it need not. It may be a valuable indication to the camper that the adult cares enough to move the camper on to a new experience.

Other features of these trips include games and singalongs on board, serving lunch, boiling the billy and having your hat 'stolen' over and over again by a camper who doesn't know when to stop! It's all part and parcel of sharing in the life of the temporary community in the hope of contributing in a small but significant way to the growth of persons.

10. Farm afternoon

A distinctive feature of Coolamatong school camping is 'farm afternoon'. Almost every group chooses to include this in its program. Ken is naturally the key figure in this. His diploma of agriculture and his experience both as a farmer and a soil conservation officer are fully utilized. But what really comes to the fore is his ability to patiently and clearly explain what he is doing and to answer innumerable questions.

The program usually begins with an introductory talk in the shearing shed about what a farmer's life is really all about. Everyone is aware that Ken is speaking from a lifetime of experience, from a boyhood in the remote sheep-and-cattle country of Swifts Creek onwards. The scene changes to paddocks, where the sheepdog demonstrates his uncanny ability to control a mob of sheep. These are brought down to the sheepyard for drafting, crutching or drenching.

Where practicable, campers get a chance to operate the drafting gate, catch a grown sheep, nurse a lamb or even brand a sheep (with paint) after shearing. Most of these jobs are stretched out over a much longer period than they would ever be on a normal farm to provide continuous opportunities to demonstrate various facets of animal husbandry.

Shearing is a highlight. Again a demonstration out of season is often possible. For hundreds of children this is a first experience of seeing wool come off the sheep and the fleece skirted and rolled up for the press.

Time does not permit a full account of farm afternoon. A feature worthy of more lengthy treatment is the butchering of a sheep, a regular demonstration which has fascinated hundreds of campers who didn't think they would ever be able to watch it. Sensitivity to the feelings of younger children in particular is always maintained, the actual killing sometimes being done before the children come in. No one is ever forced to watch, but few opt out.

A careful introduction prepares the campers and puts it all in perspective. The only ones who ever seem to experience any sort of shock are adults and older girls who seem more liable to respond to conventional expectations. One primary school teacher wrote, 'Again we had a marvellous camp, the highlight of which was the anatomy lesson on farm afternoon'.

11. Wednesday night

'Wednesday night' is what we have come to call the most distinctive feature of Coolamatong — an evening program in the lounge-room of the director's house. Otherwise known as 'an evening at Jim's place', this program usually happens on a Wednesday night — hence the name.

It most often takes the form of an 'Aussie night', and includes singing traditional Australian songs to guitar accompaniment, a few tall stories and bush yarns, and some tales about interesting characters in the history of the area. Some games invented around Coolamatong objects and activities are sometimes played, a 'kangaroo feather' award often being made to honour special achievements by campers.

An important segment is a slide-show, consisting of a few slides from the private collections of each of the resident staff. This lets the campers in on the lives of the staff a little more — their families, previous background, travels and interests. The guests find it fascinating.

The program also provides an opportunity to explain the ownership of Coolamatong and the nature of the organization which runs it. This is the only time during the week when the Christian basis of Coolamatong is talked about formally. While some groups are a little suspicious in advance about even this much explanation, we have consistently found that such fears are completely allayed and the universal response is that the evening has been a real highlight. The enthusiastic acknowledgements of 'thank you for having us' as the kids leave to return to the campsite has always been ample reward for sacrificing a night with the feet on the mantelpiece.

12. Follow-up visits

With a busy year-round program at a site nearly 300 kms from the city that most campers come from, it is impossible to maintain any significant contact with the majority of campers in the school camping program. From time to time, however, Coolamatong staff have visited schools and renewed acquaintance with young people, particularly those from primary schools and from less privileged areas of the city. These visits have often been most rewarding for the staff, who are generally mobbed by former campers, all of whom want to know whether the staff remember their names!

In all these ways, the philosophy of Coolamatong is implemented week by week as campers participate in a small way in the on-going life of the Coolamatong community. But this is an incomplete picture. It is written from the point of view of the resident community to illustrate the particular approach adopted. It must be remembered that the community of students and teachers is significant without the Coolamatong staff.

In one sense the resident staff are the guests of the temporary community, privileged to be included as facilitators of their program. In the long-term it is more important that the relationships between teachers and students develop. These are the relationships which are of continuing importance. The responses of guests, whether teachers or students, suggest that the particular contribution of Coolamatong has been pivotal.

---

1 At the time of publication, Ken had been granted leave for at least twelve months to concentrate on the family property

Part Four:
The Temporary Community and the Church

Part Four

The Temporary Community and the Church

16
The Theory of Christian Camping:
Is it relevant?

A CURSORY STUDY OF THE HISTORY of organized camping indicates that the Christian church has had a big stake in camping from the earliest days. Until the recent boom in school camping, 80% of all organized camping in Australia was done in the name of Christianity.[1] The church has often been a pace-maker in taking groups of people into the outdoors for residential experiences, while many of the most creative and well-developed camping programs are run by Christian organizations.

Traditional reasons for Christian camping
The commitment to camping involves more than just investment in real estate. Enormous time and energy has been expended on maintaining sites and equipment, planning and conducting programs. Why is this so? There are at least five perceptible strands in the history of Christian camping:[2]

(a) Character building
Rugged outdoor activities were seen as a means of developing courage, friendship, perseverance, trust and initiative. In times past the Christian faith and ethics were more broadly accepted in society and the distinctions between religious and secular were not nearly so marked. Thus the Christian influence in the camping movement can be seen in the YMCA and the Boy Scout movement as much as in official 'church' programs.

Commitment to character-building was very serious. One of the pioneers of the camping movement in America, H.W. Gibson, discusses in his book *Boyology* (1916) numerous aspects of character, including the need to correct 'a tendency to mouth-breathing among boys' and to teach the value of washing 'in such a way as to create in them a hankering for a bath'![1]

(b) Finding God in the outdoors

Christian theology speaks of God as the Creator of the world, whose power and divine nature are observable in the things he has made. In practice, this has encouraged an emphasis on the mystical element whereby 'getting close to God' is sometimes pursued in silence and in natural surroundings.

Outdoor settings for worship, as well as the plain enjoyment of nature, have been common elements in Christian camping.

(c) Christian education

Churches have seen camping as a useful extension of their Christian education programs by providing time and a congenial environment for two-way communication and feedback, developing understanding of individual needs and teaching in the context of lifestyle.

(d) Evangelism

If it is the case that faith is caught rather than taught, camping makes sense as a priority for the church. Many people can trace the disarming of their scepticism and prejudices about Christianity to an experience of Christian camping.

(e) Group building

An appealing feature of camping of any kind has been its potential for developing bonds between people. In our society the experience of group living is a valuable one. The shift towards family camping is likely to increase.

Questioning basic assumptions

All these facets of Christian camping continue to provide motivation for organized camping by the church — including denominations, local parishes and Christian organizations orientated towards youth, welfare and education. However, the same questions raised in Chapter 1 apply to Christian programs as well.

Take the 'problem of success'. The growth of Christian camping in various forms is explicable in terms of one common and rather attractive feature: 'it works'. Give people good experiences in the out-of-doors and they will like it. Camps have an impressive record for evangelism. And most of the time the verdict of the participants in the local church weekend youth camp is that 'everyone had a great time, and we'll have another one next year'.

The difficulty is that everyone having a great time tells us very little if we are to investigate the value of a camping experience in terms of Christian ministry. For some, a 'great time' may even be had at the expense of other people. Even for adults, a good weekend may well include relaxation and family interaction, but still fall short of the full-orbed possibilities of Christian camping.

Because the enjoyment factor is usually high, the key questions rarely get asked. The bulk of published literature on Christian camping fails to come to grips with the crucial question: 'Why Christian *camping*?' Instead writers focus on the secondary question: 'Why *Christian* camping?' This is invariably answered by attempting to demonstrate that camping has a proven track record in teaching and evangelism, or whatever. But they fail to come to terms with the phenomenon of camping as such: What is it about camping which makes it an appropriate form of Christian ministry?

Camping is not part of the unchanging truth of Christianity. It is a culturally-related method of ministry and as such must constantly be evaluated in the light of the gospel, by which our whole world of ethics, values and relationships must be judged. The process of questioning the very basis of the church's involvement in camping is thus of the utmost importance. Even when the result is simply re-affirmation of the existing basis of working, the process of arriving at that conclusion renews our conviction and boosts our commitment, creativity and perseverance. It sharpens our understanding and reminds us of the need to pass on those basic principles in leadership training.

In this chapter we examine the theological and social implications of the temporary community concept for Christian camping.

The church as community

The connections between camping and the church are not in any way surprising, since the concept of the church as community is a quite fundamental feature of the biblical picture. The church is regarded as a spiritual community, the local expression being Christian communities in which people belong to each other. Failure to live in practical fellowship is failure to fulfil or live up to the true nature of the church.

The major biblical metaphors clearly embody this idea: the church is the people of God; it is a building of which Christ is the cornerstone; it is the body of Christ to which all belong; it is an organic unity in which Christians are functionally necessary to one another. The local church is a gathering of people in which unity and practical love are distinguishing characteristics.

In *Living in Christian Community* Art Gish speaks of 'the church as community', locating his concern for community in 'what it means to be the church'. Yet he goes further:

> The basis of the book really is the question of what it means to live out our lives in complete commitment of everything to Jesus and his kingdom and live a life of love to our sisters and brothers.[3]

In other words Gish sees a fundamental, necessary link between the idea of discipleship and membership of the church. But the church is not merely a spiritual, 'invisible' entity. Paul, he says, saw the local church communities as being the church. Gish's vision for the church is rooted in his practical, living experience of Christian community. In this he has solid biblical foundation. Donald Guthrie says in his substantial *New Testament Theology*:

> The importance of the community idea in the New Testament cannot be overstressed. Although salvation is applied individually. . . there is no sense in which the NT conceives of lone believers. The repeated emphasis on groups of believers shows the basic character of the idea of the church.[4]

There are three particular points at which this basic view of the church touches on our treatment of the temporary community: its local expression, its concern with relationships and its contemporary importance in Western society. We look briefly at each point.

1. The local church
The 'personal manifesto' of Art Gish is concerned with flesh-and-blood local communities, based on a deep involvement with one another and affecting possessions, property, worship, authority structures, politics, service — the lot. It involves 'living together':

> The true church is very much a human community. . . The body of Christ, the people of God, must be visible — our faith must take on social form . . . we participate in the universal church through deep involvement in a local church community.[5]

Again he has solid support. Guthrie says of the developing church:

It is not surprising that the initial idea of the church was of local communities of believers meeting together in one place. The extended idea of a universal church which linked these local groups into one entity or body took time to develop, but is well attested in the NT period. It was a logical extension of the local community idea, for if individual members were knit together locally, the same principle would link together communities which were formed on the same basis.[6]

The local church, then, is the focal point of Christian community. This suggests that we should examine the function of camping as a catalyst of community in relation to the local church. We explore this further in Chapter 17.

2. Community and relationships

Being a corporate idea, the idea of community sometimes seems impersonal. One can be a member of 'the community' with very little interaction with others. One can send the rates by letter, drop one's vote in the ballot box, even shop at the supermarket with the barest minimum of conversation or interaction with other people.

Even the church has been infected by the disease of isolationism. In *Cinderella with Amnesia*, Michael Griffiths speaks of 'the extreme individualism and failure to understand the doctrine of the church that results from our neglect of the Bible's emphasis upon the corporate aspects of salvation.' He goes on:

There is even that monstrosity, the drive-in church, which . . . is surely a total denial of what the church is all about. You can go and worship without even getting out of your car. You don't have to meet anybody! Ugh! Yes, the whole concept of a drive-in church is positively nauseating. But the tragedy is that some church members sitting in pews may be as much walled-in by their reserve as they would be by car windows.[7]

The building of true community must proceed by the building of relationships. David Watson devotes a chapter of his book *Discipleship* to ways of creating community, focussing on the key factors of realism, openness and honesty:

We are to take off our masks. We are to be real to one another. . . Christianity is all about relationships: our relationship with God and our relationship with others.

He goes on:

One of the best ways of checking our own discipleship is by being genuine and open with others. It may be painful, but always it will be fruitful.[8]

Michael Griffiths refers to the pain as well:

The congregationally maladjusted Christian must be coaxed out of his cowardice and pathological reserve and encouraged more and more to enjoy normal human relationships with his fellow Christians.[9]

We have laid some stress on the temporary community as a place where relationships develop. In living together and sharing meals, activities, duties and times of relaxation there is not just a growth in knowledge and understanding of one another, but of appreciation and trust. Because the temporary community can provide an environment where this occurs, it can do much for the local church.

3. Contemporary relevance of the church as community
The concept of the church as community is bitingly relevant to an individualistic and technological society. We have already asserted the communal nature of the human being.[10]

George Carey says:

If, as we believe, human beings need the nourishment of a loving, caring society to enjoy full human lives, the development of industrial society into a dominating impersonal colossus threatens this growth. The individual no longer feels he counts in society; he feels instinctively that it is totally indifferent to who he is and what he does. Little wonder that modern man is puzzled by his existence, which is reflected in his feelings of personal insignificance, alienation and meaninglessness.[11]

Carey goes on to analyse modern man's response to these three issues at some length, and then proceeds to the question of the relevance of the church in all this:

If the Christian church is, as Christians claim, the community in which true freedom, growth and fulfilment become possible, it is obvious that its life and mission are of the greatest relevance to the disintegrated world in which we live.[12]

Carey sees the church as having an unparalleled importance in the modern world as a creator of community, 'a community of meaning'. A growing bulk of literature is now addressing itself to the question of how the church can take that challenge seriously.[13]

In concluding an in-depth study of community in the teachings of Paul, Robert Banks outlines the enormous significance of Paul's idea of community and concludes:

> The principles underlying [Paul's views] continue to attract the attention of those actively, even desperately, seeking community. His understanding of what constitutes community raises serious questions both for established ecclesiastical structures which claim a historical link with Paul and the counter-culture groups which ardently promise 'community' to those who join them ... the principles underlying Paul's idea of community remain as revolutionary and challenging in the twentieth century as they did in the first.[14]

We are apt to forget that the church is fundamentally not so much an association of like-minded people as a 'summoned-out' group.[15] Phrases like 'the body of Christ' and 'the people of God' imply this and the teaching of the whole Bible emphasizes it.

This truth is quite central to our purpose in the temporary community. A camp, by its very nature, is something which is consciously planned, structured and conducted. The temptation to disregard the foundational importance of God's Spirit in 'making it work' is therefore great. We need to be conscious that:

> True community is not something that can be created by human effort or by an act of the will as believed by many utopian thinkers ... community cannot be forced ... community can exist only as a continuing gift of the Spirit.[16]

We might be able to run a groovy church service or organize a camp program, but that's a different thing from discovering what God can do in community.

The church and the temporary community

We have before us then evidence of a strong general perception of the importance of the community dimension of the church in theology and in society. At the same time we have obvious reason not to trivialize community or exaggerate the importance of 'the temporary community' as a practical way in which the life and mission of the church can be expressed. Indeed, the temporary community is by definition a short-lived phenomenon, sometimes a mere couple of days. It would be absurd to suggest that Christian camping is a structure for community in the church in an ongoing way.

Nevertheless, the temporary community is without doubt a powerful catalyst to the building of relationships. It provides high points of experience for individuals and for groups of Christians. What we need to do is to be realistic and thoughtful about how we make use of it.

How does the church as community relate to camping theory? This question launches us immediately into some important issues:

* If placing a new disciple into a community of faith is an essential part of evangelism, is evangelistic camping valid if it does not relate to a local church?

* If Christian education is essentially the ongoing task of a faith-community, is it possible to effectively engage in it through broadly-based inter-church camping programs?

* Is the temporary community relevant if it is not related to an ongoing community? Could it be counter-productive?

In the past most organized Christian camping has been carried out by large organizations or by private agencies. There are some obvious reasons for this. For example, few local congregations have had the resources of personnel and facilities required to mount camping programs in the organized camping tradition. That tradition has been based on camping styles which have:

(a) required trained activity leadership
(b) been highly organized
(c) required considerable facilities
(d) majored on children and youth and
(e) dealt with fairly large numbers.

On the other hand, non-organized camping (for want of a better term) has been a private affair for enthusiasts, even for the odd enthusiastic family. Either way, camping has not been seen as a function of the local church. It has not, on the whole, been recognized as having anything to contribute to the local Christian community as such.

Individualistic theology/corporate emphasis
The development of camping in the church has been dictated more by traditional camping styles than by a consistent philosophy. This is probably why there is something of a contradiction in the past between an emphasis on group camping (often on a large scale) and an individualistic theology.

Camping theory has reflected this contradiction. An example is *Camping for Christian Youth*,[17] first published in 1968. This book barely pays even lip-service to the communal dimension of camping. It focusses almost exclusively on the camper as an individual and, in one of the rare references to the local church, reflects the organizational structure of much traditional camping. It lists thirty-two specific objectives for an 'evangelical' camp (the term is given a narrow connotation rejected by many evangelicals). Of these, only two have any real reference to the Christian community, reflecting the loosest possible connection between the camp experience and the local church.

Quite different is the emphasis in *Camping Together as Christians*.[18] Here campers are seen as having an experience in Christian community where 'Christian principles are not just discussed — they are also lived and evaluated'. Fellowship is real because 'the members of the small group, constantly living together... come to know one another with a depth of feeling seldom experienced elsewhere within the church'. The book reflects the tradition of denominational camping for a narrow age-group (junior high school).

In 1975, an important article[19] described trends in church camping in America. The trends included a focus on the small group for programming as well as evangelism, smaller camps and more local church camping. The article did not associate these trends with developments in Christian camping philosophy so much as with more pragmatic factors. For example, the trend toward more local church camping was 'often to the dismay of Conference/district camp leaders'.

In 1979, Werner Graendorf[20] emphasized the connection between Christian camping and church ministry. Despite some hints about a direct local church/camp connection, however, the emphasis is denominational. Furthermore, an individualistic theology is again evident. Speaking of a primary concern for individuals, Graendorf says that 'discipleship is by its nature an individual relationship'.[21] To be fair, the context is a concern not to lose the individual in the program or numbers. But the total emphasis is on the camper (singular), rather than the group.

Local church or large organization?
In Australia it has been common practice for the local youth group or Inter-School Christian Fellowship group to have a weekend

camp. Usually these camps are held at fixed sites reasonably close to the 'home base'. The camps generally have elements of study and worship, while the recreational activities are mostly unsophisticated, requiring little equipment or expertise.

The major emphasis of these camps is on fun and fellowship, with some formal studies of the Christian faith thrown in. In a low-key way they have sought to build up the group and reinforce the teaching program of the local church. Sometimes the camps include a definite evangelistic emphasis.

As the emphasis has moved to the local parish, local group camping has increased, while denominational programs have tended to be wound down. But the best-developed programs are still operated by denominations or other large-scale organizations. The question remains whether this balance is really satisfactory. Again, let us answer this in terms of the five traditional bases of Christian camping.

(a) Character building

Character building is not an exclusively Christian function. It can probably be best developed in longer, more challenging adventure programs — the kind of programs which larger camping organizations, with their resources of expertise, equipment and experience, are able to supply.

(b) Finding God in the outdoors

This is a function which can be catered for in the local camp situation as well as the organizational camp. It is still a relevant aim for both.

(c) Group building

It seems to me that this objective is clearly most relevant to the camping program of the local church or Christian youth group. Is there not something artificial about the pursuit of deep experiences of community when there is no real expectation of an ongoing relationship with the other members? This is not to imply that the community emphasis is not valid in the organizational programs. But it does reflect the view that the local church is the obvious place to begin to build community.

Yet Christian community is wider than its local expressions. Camp leaders can surely hope to develop a level of relationships among campers which takes them beyond the brief, billiard-ball type of encounters which characterize life in church and society. The Ensigns speak of camp providing 'a foretaste of Christian community'.[22] This is surely a legitimate aim.

Of course community can be trivialized. The dimensions of true community range from the sharing of possessions to confession of sin, all in the context of a deep covenant relationship. While the temporary community can help to facilitate the growth of trust, love and understanding, it can never fully replicate the ideal of Christian community.

Leaders of organizational programs need to be aware of this. They should not be content with community experiences as ends in themselves. They should prepare campers for the transition to life back home. And they should be very careful not to induce responses in campers which go beyond what is sustainable in the normal home situation.

(d) Christian education
This is primarily a function of a particular faith community, i.e. a local church (see Chapter 17). Nevertheless, because the Christian church is universal, broadly-based denominational and transdenominational camping still has a relevant function in enlarging the vision of local churches, especially small and isolated ones.

(e) Evangelism
Ideally the local church is the evangelistic agency par excellence as it communicates the gospel in the context of Christian service to its own community. It should understand its own social setting, demonstrate the Christian life and draw people in by its warmth and vitality. There should be a natural transition from interested onlooker to fringe participant to committed member.

Nevertheless, the general relationship between church and community is such that Christians often develop their deepest relationships with non-Christians in another context, such as the school or the workplace. Broadly-based camping programs still offer an attractive venue for evangelism beyond the resources of most local churches to provide.

We can describe the relative appropriateness of local church or large organizational camping in this way:

* Our analysis suggests the desirability of a structural involvement of the church in camping, both at the parish level and a wider organizational level. We explore this in Chapters 17 and 18.

* There is evidence that the various major objectives of Christian camping are being shown to be achievable at both levels. Both

structures are 'working' though some objectives are better achieved through one form rather than the other.
* Our analysis provides distinctive perspectives on camping wherever Christians are involved in it. Some of these are explored in Chapter 19.

1 'Under Canvas, Under Stars', supplement to *On Being*, Vol.9, No.4, May 1982
2 This outline first appeared in the author's article, 'Camping and the Church', *VOEA Newsletter*, November 1982
3 Art Gish, *Living in Christian Community*, Albatross Books, p.16
4 Donald Guthrie, *New Testament Theology*, InterVarsity Press, 1981, p.787
5 Gish, op. cit., p.33
6 Guthrie, op. cit., p.788
7 Michael Griffiths, *Cinderella with Amnesia*, InterVarsity Press, 1975, p.83
8 David Watson, *Discipleship*, Hodder and Stoughton, 1981, pp.49-50
9 Griffiths, op. cit., p.84
10 See Chapter 4
11 Carey, op. cit., p.110
12 Ibid., p.129
13 I especially recommend David Watson's *I Believe in the Church*, Hodder and Stoughton, 1978, as a comprehensive yet highly readable book.
14 Robert Banks, *Paul's Idea of Community*, Anzea Publishers, 1979, p.215
15 Griffiths, op. cit., p.14
16 Gish, op. cit., pp.35-36
17 Todd, op. cit., reprinted unchanged in 1980
18 John and Ruth Ensign, *Camping Together as Christians*, John Knox Press, 1958, pp.7-8
19 'Current Trends in Church Camping', *Journal of Christian Camping*, November-December 1975, pp.6-7
20 Graendorf and Mattson, op. cit., Chapter 1
21 Ibid., p.27
22 Ensign, op. cit., p.65

17

Camping and Christian Education:
How can camping strengthen the church?

I WAS LEADING A WORKSHOP on small group leadership. We were dealing with a case study about a small group which really hadn't 'gelled' after their first five or six meetings. One of the participants suggested some informal social activity as a means of breaking down some barriers. This was the trigger for another participant to explain with great enthusiasm what an enormous difference a weekend camp had made to her small group. I couldn't get my tape recorder out quickly enough!

The 'small group movement' is alive and well in the church. It has been rediscovered as a structure for community life.[1] It is important to recognize that this is not a mere fad, though it is undoubtedly a response to our contemporary culture. Australian theologian Robert Banks sees small churches (not small groups) as 'the only way' of experiencing the kind of community which Paul understood the church to be.[2]

Group building
The building up of the local church has clear connections with the idea of the temporary community. It is not surprising that our friend found that a weekend away together had done wonders for her small group. Many others have found this.

Dick Matthews is a friend who is committed to the concept of the church as community. He has been instrumental in developing 'the Family Group' — in most respects a congregation within the local parish of his denomination. He is also committed to camps for the church family, running two or three a year. At Coolamatong one day he shared what he sees as the strengths of family camps:

(a) They give the community 'common roots' — common experiences you can hark back to just between yourselves: 'Remember the day we. . .?'

(b) They provide breadth in the range of activities undertaken: going down the river in kayaks, having a bush dance, making damper — activities people can relate to — even just eating together.

(c) They help people become involved directly in the lives of other families. In any group of people you see around camp three or four families are usually represented. Kids share other dads and mums, enriching everyone's lives. The single parent also gets help.

(d) They help people discover new aspects about other people, seeing them in a variety of situations. The more natural the situation, the more effective the learning. Parents also learn about other families and observe the expectations other parents have of their children: 'Maybe I'm a bit soft on my kids'; 'Perhaps I'm too hard on mine'.

(e) They provide a cheap holiday for families — especially important for families in need.

The Family Group once tried some weekend camps for children of different ages. This experiment produced the following remark:

> You get the same age-group problems. In the family camp, teenagers love looking after the little kids. There's just something about the family setting which is really important. In age-group camps you don't have the same experiences as you do in multi-generational ones.

There are some striking parallels between the spontaneous responses above and some recent analyses of the church. Michael Griffiths, for example, speaks of the spiritual intimacy achievable in the local congregation:

> This phrase 'household of God', and the similar phrase 'household of faith' in Galatians 6:10, are a real picture of the intimacy of the family in its warmth and security. . . Many other New Testament expressions imply the intimacy of the family.[4]

He goes on to describe the practical outworking of this:

> The congregation is the family of God. We are meant to be able to relax, take our shoes off and let our hair down. Yet so often we dress up and feel very stiff and formal in church, and some even feel that it is only proper and reverent for it to be so! We have made 'going to

church' more like a public occasion with pomp and circumstance instead of a family gathering. The family meets to feast and have fun, to relax and to open their hearts to each other.[5]

Robert Banks asserts that the family nature of the church is in danger of being overlooked in church life at present. He is not talking about superficial terminology — 'the church family' — but a fundamental characteristic of the local congregation:

> Paul established and regarded his communities as genuine extended families . . . It is clear that Paul did not intend this in a narrow spiritual sense. Sometimes these relationships replaced those with members' original families which either the gospel message, or social mobility, had severed. In other instances they supplemented these. In either case, a real involvement in each others' lives, based on a far-reaching commitment to one another, was Paul's intention.[6]

Implicit in this is the 'down-to-earth' character of the local church. We belong to the church 'as imaginative, emotional and physical beings, concerned about the creative, psychological and bodily welfare of others':

> There is room for the sublime and apparently trivial, for the occurrence of some profound experience of the reality of God and for the expression of the most everyday concerns. Unless we can draw in, talk about, pray into and work through our most insistent daily concerns, and those of the world in general, then church is less than it should be. Paul's letters are full of allusions to such matters.[7]

David Watson sees the building of Christian communities as a biblical and historical norm, a deliberate strategy 'to express their distinct identity as the family of God'. He goes on to describe how recent is the concept of the nuclear family and urges community as the only real answer to 'the numerous single and divorced members of many churches', as well as single parents, widows and widowers, the mentally ill, the emotionally crippled and 'those who find forming relationships more difficult than most'.[8]

In speaking of camping and the local church, then, we're talking about the way it can accelerate the growth of mutual understanding, concern and mutual enjoyment among people of all ages. A weekend can produce a hundred valuable insights and a new mood among participants, a rekindled desire to effectively love one another.

Much of this happens because of the cumulative effect of a few

days together. In weekly encounters, we have to start all over again
to establish contact each time we meet. It takes time to overcome
natural reserve. The more time we have the more likely it is that
we will 'unwind' and share. The more varied the contexts in which
we meet, the more likely we are to meet new people or make new
discoveries (like the teenager discovering that the minister can
really kick a football).

Time, a different environment, a leisurely pace, a variety of
social stimuli, a round-the-clock situation — these are the benefits
of camping to the local church. This strengthening of the church
community is the basis of the role of camping in Christian
education.

Is Christian camping Christian education?
Orthodox wisdom suggests that camping can play a role in the
Christian education program of the church. But most formulations
of this idea reflect a concept of Christian education which has been
seriously questioned in recent years.

1. Christian camping is more than Christian education
Consider the following argument in which one writer attempts to
define the purpose of Christian camping:

(a) Christian camping is, at root, basic Christian education, a key
aspect of the church's total Christian education program.
(b) We all know camping has spiritual values, which Christians
would want to define biblically.
(c) The basic spiritual and educational purpose of Christian
camping therefore has an ultimate authority in the Bible.
(d) The overall purpose of Christian camping is to use as fully as
possible the camp experience as an opportunity for discipling
individuals towards maturity in Christ.[9]

While some valuable points are made, the overall argument is
invalid, since the conclusion is effectively contained in the first
premise. It is easy enough to establish a Christian education
purpose for camping if you take as your starting point that
camping is part of Christian education.

Besides matters of logic, this approach unfortunately produces
too limited a view of Christian camping. All that we have said
about group building underlines the inadequacy of seeing camping
merely as a means of individual discipling.

It may be claimed that such a definition of camping is deliberately broad. It may be argued that Christian education *means* 'discipling individuals towards maturity in Christ' — broadly speaking, the task of the church. But this is an unhelpful simplification. It tends to obscure important distinctions, such as those between evangelism and nurture, or between loving fellow-believers and serving the world.

2. Christian education is more than education
There has been considerable discussion in the church about the inadequacy of the Christian education model which has dominated our approach to teaching the faith. We have treated Christian education like all other education, with Sunday schools structured like ordinary schools.

Similarly, the tendency to treat camping as an extension of Sunday school-type education has often resulted in a failure to capitalize on the special possibilities of camping for enriching Christian education.

The early camps run by one secondary school included maths lessons, conducted by a teacher who travelled to camp to conduct them. They were taken indoors, just as they were in the classroom, and bore no relation to the activities of the camp. In the same way, Christian camping programs sometimes teach lessons about following God, forgiveness or overcoming temptation, but they too are conducted in a classroom style, with little or no reference to camp situations which might illustrate that teaching — such as following directions, forgiving others or completing an obstacle course.

John H. Westerhoff lit a fuse with the thesis that the traditional understanding of religious education is bankrupt. Westerhoff spoke from his own experience as a Christian education consultant. His analysis of the failure of the traditional Sunday school program to keep its pupils in the church is not unique. It is certainly reflected in the demise of the Sunday school in Australia, a trend which has been well documented.[10]

We will not attempt to outline Westerhoff's position here. Sufficient to summarize two basic propositions:
* Faith, not religion, must become the concern of Christian education. (By 'religion' is meant 'institutions, creeds, documents, artifacts and the like', whereas 'faith is deeply personal, dynamic, ultimate'.)[11]

* If our children are to have faith, we need to make sure that the
church becomes a significant community of faith.[12]

This gives us a rather different perspective on the relationship
between camping and Christian education. Nevertheless I suspect
that Christian leaders have often *intuitively* accepted that this is
how faith is communicated. It is another thing, of course, to
thoughtfully adopt such a position, and to carry it through in
practice.

Christian camping's contribution to Christian education
We must now ask what the temporary community may have to
contribute to the process of Christian education.

1. Nearness
This is a term drawn from *Faith Shaping* by Stephen Jones, an
account of how faith can be nurtured in youth. 'Nearness' is said
to be a means of advocating faith to youth:

> Faithful activities must be near to youth. There must be a closeness to
> the faithful community.
> The faith is near when Christian adults live their faith in natural ways
> before the young person. The faith is near when the young person
> feels that he or she is a close part of the church. The faith is near when
> the young person is allowed deep relationships with adult Christian
> models.[13]

While clearly the temporary community promotes such nurture,
Jones maintains that 'nothing brings the faith nearer than the way
in which the parents prize their own faith'. Despite this word of
caution against exaggerated claims, camping has a proven record
for bringing young people and adults together in friendship and
understanding.

2. Memorable experiences
This is another feature which Jones convincingly proposes as an
essential ingredient in the faith-journey of young people.

> Most adolescents are actively involved in the task of making sense of
> their experience (of understanding their memory) . . . If young persons
> have no important memories of the faith, of the church, of an
> experience of God, of worship, or of spiritual feelings, they will find
> themselves in a faith vacuum as adults . . . With children and youth we
> need intentionally to provide memorable experiences.[14]

Camping is one of the ways in which memorable experiences can be provided. This has been a feature of Coolamatong we have always prized. Kids who associate Christianity with good memories are going to be more receptive to another Christian experience. Good memories help sustain us through not-so-good times and also provide 'hooks' on to which we can attach specific teaching.

3. Interaction

In living together in the camp situation, teachers and learners interact with each other in a way which makes the structures of Sunday school and Bible class seem rather academic. As far back as 1905 the great American Methodist leader of the Sunday school movement, John Vincent, claimed that:

> It is possible to make too much of method, of recent educational theory, of curricula, teaching and intellectual training

and predicted that:

> In the future the Sunday school will be less like a school and more like a home. Its program will focus on conversation and the interaction of people rather than the academic study of the Bible or theology. The Sunday school will be a place where friends deeply concerned about Christian faith will gather to share life together.[15]

It is Westerhoff's sad conclusion that modern models of Christian education deny the prophetic importance of such a view and that the concept of the teacher pouring knowledge into the passive student is wrong. He believes we need a new way of thinking about educational method. 'Shared experience, story-telling, celebration, action and reflection' should become the tools for the mutual communication and sustaining of faith.[16]

This sort of thinking may challenge a narrow view of Christian education, but it has been part and parcel of Christian camping practice for a long time. Lloyd Mattson illustrates the value of camping in the context of the family:

> Let me add a final value to be found in family camping. Both the family and Dad benefit when he discovers that he does not have to be the best in every way. It takes a big man to risk failure when he can avoid it, and camping inevitably brings risk.

A boy spoke up one evening as we were discussing parent-son relationships. 'If just once my Dad would admit he was wrong, maybe we could get along', he said. The bitterness was evident. Pity the father who must always be right! Camping offers parents an opportunity to become vulnerable, to join the children in an uncertain world.[17]

4. Teaching opportunities

There is a tendency for those of us who gain new and exciting insights to implement them with more zeal than they deserve. We tend to throw the baby out with the bathwater. It is important to assert, therefore, that the teaching of the faith is still an important function of the church. In the Old Testament there is a strong emphasis both on telling the stories of God's dealings with his people and on teaching God's requirements for a right relationship with him (see for example Deuteronomy chapter 11).

Teaching was not all 'chalk and talk' then either. It was a part of life:

> Remember these commands and cherish them. Tie them on your arms and wear them on your foreheads as a reminder. Teach them to your children. Talk about them when you are at home and when you are away, when you are resting and when you are working. Write them on the doorposts of your houses and on your gates.[18]

In the New Testament, teaching is again emphasized as a function of the church. Indeed, although the qualifications of church leaders are overwhelmingly concerned with character, one skill stands out: the ability to teach.[19]

Unfortunately, we are sometimes stuck with a narrow vision of how we can teach effectively. Camping provides a useful context for teaching. Camping provides:
* An atmosphere conducive to informal teaching. Campers are often far more relaxed, open, attentive and interested in listening and discussing informally than when in a formal setting.
* Time for reflection, absorbing of input and feedback.
* Continuity between study, worship, eating and activities. There is not such a conscious break between living and learning!
* Opportunities to make teaching relevant to individuals. Time spent with people, gaining understanding of one another, facilitates effective communication. In a highly compart-mentalized society where we tend to reside, work, relax

and worship in different places, our experience of the church is isolated, and there is often little opportunity for a Bible class teacher, for example, to get to know his class.

* Teaching by demonstration. Because camping is a twenty-four hour living situation, the teachers are seen 'in the round' by the learners. Furthermore, the way people relate to each other in camp life will show how real the doctrine of reconciliation (for example), really is to them. The whole life of the camp tends to authenticate (or contradict!) the message.

* Intensity and variety. The camping situation lends itself to intensive teaching in creative ways. So much can be done in a week or a weekend. The preliminary work of establishing contact, then linking teaching which occurred a week ago with what is occurring now, is largely eliminated. Camping provides many settings not available at home for effectively conveying the teaching of the Bible, so much of which has an outdoor setting.

1 Howard A. Snyder, *The Problem of Wineskins*, InterVarsity Press, 1976, p.17
2 In 'Small is Beautiful: The relevance of Paul's idea of community for the local church today', Zadok paper, Canberra 1982
3 Response from a participant, recorded by Dick Matthews
4 Griffiths, op. cit., p.85
5 Ibid, p.86
6 Zadok paper, op. cit., p.3
7 Robert Banks, Zadok paper, op. cit., p.3
8 David Watson, *I Believe in the Church*, Hodder and Stoughton, 1978, p.84
9 Graendorf and Mattson, op. cit., pp.19-25. This is the starting point for other authors as well (e.g. Ensign and Todd).
10 See Stan Stewart, *The Church's Ministry with Children Report*, Australian Council of Churches Commission on Education, 1976
11 John H. Westerhoff III, *Will Our Children Have Faith?* Dove Communications, 1976, p.22
12 Ibid., p.54
13 Stephen D. Jones, *Faith Shaping*, Judson Press, 1980, p.30
14 Ibid., pp.36, 37 and 40
15 Quoted in Westerhoff, op. cit., p.82
16 Ibid., p.88
17 Lloyd Mattson, *Family Camping*, Moody Press, 1973, p.20
18 Deuteronomy 6:4-9
19 See for example John Stott, *One People*, Falcon 1969, p.45 or Colin Brown in *Ministry in the Seventies* (Porterhouse ed.), Falcon, 1970, p.17

18
Camping and Christian Outreach:
What are the benefits?

MY FIRST CONTACT WITH CHURCH CAMPING was as an eleven-year-old, at a camp run by the boys' society of my denomination. I remember only two things: the enjoyment of showing my skills with an axe on the woodpile, and a mixture of fear and exhilaration about a game of 'flag-raiding' in the bush. My next camping experience was more of the same, the outstanding memory being the discomfort of constipation!

I went to a Scripture Union camp in my fifteenth year. The school captain, whom I adulated, had invited me and I liked the idea of tennis and the ocean beach. The court was made of cracked asphalt, but the beach was great. This was an important week of my life: a major turning point. Here I was, from a regular church family, trying to 'turn over a new leaf' — an almost daily necessity at times. I'd even tried praying and reading the Bible myself quite often.

Yet, when Christianity was explained at camp, I heard it as if I had never heard it before. My perception of life as the pursuit of a clear conscience through dutiful attendance to rules and doctrines was demolished. The striver after goodness became the receiver of a gift. I was launched on the Christian life with an unaffected enthusiasm and conviction which easily withstood the occasional good-natured rubbishing of wary peers!

I soon became aware that these camps appealed equally to my friends. Those who wouldn't go to church were glad to come to camps. What was more, they responded positively to Christianity in this context. It wasn't stuffy and remote, but it was believed and embodied by people who had brains and football skills — and who had time for campers.

Here the games on the beach were fiercely contested by leaders, some of whom were accomplished athletes and sportsmen. Yet the spirit in which they were played was quite unlike normal competition. These leaders were out to win, but didn't mind losing. They'd sooner throw the ball to the camper with five thumbs, just to include him, than throw a winning goal and leave him out.

It is not surprising that camping programs such as these still provide a 'bridge' between the church and the community-at-large. We will return shortly to analyze this further and to examine the way in which the Christian faith can be communicated through camping. But first, a look at the ways in which Christian camping interacts with the community in general.

Christian camping's contribution to the community-at-large
1. Access to camping experiences
A number of large broadly based Christian organizations have a heavy involvement in holiday camp programs. There has been a traditional emphasis on children and teenagers, but family camping is increasingly important. There is a wide range of site-based and mobile programs and, although they serve their own constituents, such Christian camps also attract a large number of campers from a broad community base.

These programs are widely advertised in schools, libraries and elsewhere, giving the general community access to camping experiences. Such programs also act as a social mixer as they are often patronized by campers from diverse social backgrounds. They include a seemingly limitless range of activities from arts, music and technology to surfing, rafting and igloo-building. Many leaders have achieved a high degree of excellence and experience, while the programs provide others with their early experiences of small group leadership.

Alongside the larger programs are a number of other types of Christian camping based mainly on a developed campsite, but including travel camping as well. Some of these are privately (as opposed to organizationally) owned, with voluntary leadership and boards of management. Some major on providing weekend camping programs throughout the year and are patronized by a variety of community organizations as well as churches.

Another important facet of access to camping is the provision of camping opportunities for economically and socially disadvantaged people. Most organizations receive referrals from social welfare agencies and many children and families are thus able to be placed in camps. Fees may be subsidized by a sponsoring welfare agency or by the particular camping organization.

The 'community camps' of St Paul's Discovery Centre are *primarily* for such people. The campers come from referrals made by social workers, welfare officers, church workers or concerned friends who have observed the need for a child, teenager or family to have a break from their normal environment.

These referrals cover a wide variety of situations, camps often including all ages from babies to 'oldies'. Typical referrals include:

* single parent families who rarely, if ever, have holidays
* children from families whose parents are sick or otherwise unable to cope
* children or teenagers who are in institutional care
* teenagers who are unemployed or who have temporary accommodation problems
* handicapped children (e.g. deaf or intellectually handicapped) who are normally treated institutionally, but who need to mix with a wider range of people.

As organized camping grows in sophistication and community expectations rise, so camps tend to become more expensive. This poses a real challenge to all involved, as to how to maintain access to camping for those who can least afford it.

2. Quality of camping

Apart from providing access to camping, Christian camping has an important contribution to make to the quality of camping in the community. In particular, this is reflected in the leadership training function and the development of a full-orbed camping philosophy. A significant feature of most Christian camping programs is the extent to which they rely on voluntary leadership.

This reflects a well-established and continuing emphasis on the centrality of the leader-camper relationship. Many programs have a ratio of one leader to three or four campers. This reflects an emphasis on program-building and relationship-building around the small group, where one leader relates throughout camp to a group of five to six campers. When other leaders (director, cooks, activity leaders etc.) are added, the overall ratio is even lower.

One program, aimed specifically at people with special needs, aims to achieve an adult/child ratio of 1:1. The rationale is simple:

This may appear to be a very low ratio, but only before camp! A large number of leaders allows for 'on the job training' of inexperienced leaders. It also allows individual leaders to spend time with individual campers: doing things together, talking and listening. Thus leaders are able to establish valuable friendships with children and adults.

3. Site hiring

The demand for sites for school camping has meant that church and other Christian camp properties have been sought after in term time, not just at weekends and holidays. This has been a welcome source of income for many owners. At the same time the growth of the commercial camp has provided competition for sites and facilities.

While the provision of good, clean facilities to schools for a fair reward is seen as a legitimate use of campsites, the interface between school camping and Christian camping raises several questions. For example, should site-owners upgrade their educational facilities to compete effectively in the market? Can holiday camp programs survive the level of competition for the camping dollar? Does the income from site hiring benefit the holiday camper proportionately in terms of either reduced fees or improved facilities?

There is continuing scope for a better understanding of the respective rights of camp operators and hirers. Clearly, there is a need for church properties to be used by schools, for example, as well as weekend groups. A few schools have created distrust through their abuse of campsites and unco-operative manner. On the other hand, a few campsite operators have brought disrepute on others with equal injustice by providing poor or unfriendly service, or by taking advantage of a camp to thrust their Christian beliefs onto school groups.

The benefits of organizational camping to the church

In these ways Christian camping can contribute to the community. But the church can also benefit from that more broadly based organizational involvement, despite the advantages of the local church camping as outlined in the last chapter.

First, large-scale camping enables the church to maintain *a standard of expertise*. The larger organizations have the scope to tackle exciting frontiers, offer quality training and provide facilities which are beyond the means of the local church. Without this level of expertise and engagement, church camping would gradually become a pale, conference-like reflection of camping its best. Competition in the market place is a healthy catalyst to quality.

Second, broad programs provide *the visible, recognizable evidence* of what a Christian perspective can contribute to camping and learning amongst Christian camping enthusiasts.

Third, they provide one of *the relevant, common meeting grounds* for people inside and outside the church. Organized camping is able to provide the exciting challenges and quality camping experiences which can attract children, youth and families. At the same time it promotes understanding of the Christian faith. Since that faith is more often misunderstood than thoughtfully rejected, this is an important function.

Evangelism through camping

The word 'evangelism' has many connotations. For some people it means soap-box preaching or being buttonholed by an intense, beady-eyed little person and assaulted with Bible verses. For others it means crusades or door-knocking religious fanatics. Most ideas of evangelism revolve around some method or other.

Our starting point here is the meaning of evangelism. The Lausanne Covenant[2] identifies four major elements of evangelism, which have important implications for camping. The rest of this chapter is structured around these four elements:

(a) A personal context

'Our Christian presence in the world is indispensable to evangelism, and so is that kind of dialogue whose purpose is to listen sensitively in order to understand.'

The community setting of camp provides an excellent context for evangelism.

(b) A teaching function

'To evangelize is to spread the good news.'

The good news is quite specific. It is about the historical person Jesus, especially his death and resurrection and the meaning of those events. Evangelism includes the communication of facts and their meaning. It cannot be assumed that the validity or the meaning of the message will be self-evident: evangelism and teaching are inseparable.

(c) A personal response

Evangelism itself is the proclamation of the historical, biblical Christ as Saviour and Lord, with a view to persuading people to come to him personally, and so be reconciled to God.'

If camping is an excellent context for evangelism — and that includes 'persuasion' — we must look carefully at the question of evangelism with integrity. Manipulation or any form of persuasion which disregards the personal autonomy of the camper, has no place in evangelism.

(d) A costly commitment
'In issuing the gospel invitation we have no liberty to conceal the cost of discipleship. Jesus still calls all who would follow him to deny themselves, take up their cross and identify themselves with his new community. Responsible evangelism doesn't stop with counting converts.' We now turn to a consideration of these four key major elements in evangelism through camping.

The temporary community as a context for evangelism

I spoke to a minister and his wife, about to retire from a church in a remote part of outback Australia. Ministry with the young people had been a struggle. The kids were shy of the church and geographically scattered. George and Hazel found that camping was a means of 'getting nearer' to the children. The key phrase was 'spending time with them': fishing, hiking, games and so on. The kids learnt as they lived with them: 'when you live together things rub off'.

On the other hand, religious instruction time in that outback school was mostly spent trying to get the kids to behave themselves. The way the camping setting helped George and Hazel get along with kids is a reminder of the central feature of God's relationship with mankind — the incarnation.

In Jesus Christ, 'the Word became flesh'. God became visible in Jesus, God's truth enacted and demonstrated in Jesus' life. Similarly Christians are described as 'living letters' written not on stone tablets but on human hearts. Clearly Christians are expected to live out the truth, so illuminating it for others and drawing attention to God. Failure to do so brings the gospel into disrepute.

Thus the life of the Christian community should demonstrate and authenticate the words in which the gospel is expressed. But it is not only a performance, on stage, where the audience are mere spectators. It is a costly involvement in the world, with people. It involves relationships because the church is 'salt' as well as 'light' and has a duty of compassion to the 'outsider' — hence the story of the Good Samaritan.

The gospel therefore 'takes on flesh' in the lives of Christians. This was our starting point: the way in which my own observation of Christianity in parents and others over many years was *crystallized* by the experience of the Christian camp community.

The Coolamatong school camping experience bears this out. Here there is nothing resembling the 'preaching of the gospel' — no tracts, no sermons, no appeals. There is a shared life and a simple invitation to consider the Christian option as a viable possibility. Yet one sixteen-year-old wrote back to say that she had started reading the Bible, discussed some questions with the parish priest and joined a welfare society within the church. She wrote, 'If it hadn't been for you all opening my eyes to Christianity, I would never have taken that first step, reading the Bible... Thank you.'

Another seventeen-year-old student wrote:

Religion has played no significant role in my life until now. I've considered various theories and beliefs, but never very deeply. Churches I've been in and any contact I've had with the Christian religion has only ever displayed to me hypocrisy and archaic ideas which were of no use to any present problem.

At Coolamatong, without smothering us with religion, you showed me a different aspect of something I'd completely written off. Although I may not accept everything you promote or stand for, I'm willing to learn, to see if I justly rejected everything — which I probably didn't. Your attitude, behaviour and genuine belief is inspiring. You don't just talk ; you're doing something that's real and worthwhile. Maybe God can help me find myself — enable me to become the person I want to be.

Camping builds bridges — bridges of understanding and bridges of personal relationship. We are living in a time and in a society where Christianity is supposed by many people to be irrelevant. Camping can change that situation. An Indian Christian said:

People are no longer converted to a doctrine. They can only be attracted to a way of life which they can see as a practical alternative to the values and assumptions of our competitive, alienated, materialistic society.[3]

This challenge can only be met as people see Christian community in action. Many writers are emphasizing the theology of the church as community as the key to effective evangelism.[4] We must not trivialize this by exaggerating the importance of camping.

At best Christian camping is short-lived, an incomplete expression of Christian community. Nevertheless for some people it is the only first-hand expression of Christian community they are likely to experience. Even for many Christians it can provide a level of community which is not achieved in their own congregation.

We may summarize in this way:

* Doctrine takes on flesh in the lives of leaders and campers. The camper can observe the lives of believers and judge whether their faith is true or not.

* Enjoyment of and involvement in camp increases receptivity to new ideas and teaching.

* Relationships can develop in a climate of trust, where campers are freed to be honest in assessing their own lives and share their uncertainties without fear of judgement.

* Understanding is increased as people get to know each other as individuals with specific personal gifts and needs. This is a two-way thing. The non-Christian sees the Christian 'in the round' — not as someone who 'goes to church', but in all kinds of everyday situations, mood and dress. The Christian similarly relates to the non-Christian not as an object of evangelism, but as a person.

Evangelism and teaching in camp

Sometimes evangelism and teaching are regarded as separate functions. The proclamation of the gospel becomes a fixed, narrow, repetitive, even simplistic process. But evangelism which does not include teaching is inadequate. One cannot assume that even the basic terminology of God, Jesus, sin or salvation is understood at all. For many kids 'Jesus' is just an exclamation and 'sin' equals 'sex'.

Perhaps it was never any different, except when the gospel was preached to first-century Jews who already understood the biblical context and terminology. But even then considerable teaching was required to give Jewish converts an adequate grasp of the difference between their traditional religion and faith in Jesus. Paul's argument in his Letter to the Galatians is evidence of that.

This is not to say that there is no place for a simple explanation of, say, how to become a Christian. Given sufficient background, a simple statement may suffice. But for modern-day disciples of Jesus, basic information and evidence must be gathered as the basis for belief:

> No person is evangelized until becoming a Christian seems to him or her a genuine option, and when rejection of this option means setting one's self against powerful evidence.[5]

By teaching, we do not mean 'chalk and talk'. That is simply one model of teaching. We mean that we have to find effective ways to explain and to demonstrate, to answer questions and to give examples. It is not a question of teaching *or* evangelism, teaching *or* demonstrating. Both go together:

> Ideally [evangelism] includes the presence in one's neighbourhood of an obedient believing congregation, so that the unbeliever knows his choice is not only between Christ and false Gods but also between distinguishable societies with which he may identify.[6]

There are two opposite reactions here. One is to be so keen to develop warm, friendly relationships that the 'crunch' issues of the gospel — its unique claims, demands and implications — are never presented. The other is to so concentrate on Bible studies, formal talks and other 'schooling' techniques that campers find the Christian faith theoretical and irrelevant. In some quarters, there seems to be an unwritten assumption that you can bore campers with Christian teaching so long as you excite them with activities. Effective Christian teaching should be both biblical and relevant to the needs of campers, presented in the context of the total camp program.

Seeking responses with integrity
We noted earlier that the process of effective evangelism involves an element of persuasion. This is not disturbing in itself. Parents, teachers and health workers, for example, are all involved in persuasion every day. But the leaders of Christian camps need to answer two specific questions:

(a) Is what they present a true, undistorted account of the truth? Distortion can occur through a defective understanding of the truth, or through a conscious choice to omit some of it. This is a question of content.

(b) Does their approach to persuasion overwhelm or bypass the camper's normal, rational decision-making process? This is a question of method.

To get their content right, all leaders must do their homework.

That is a straightforward matter. However the question of method needs special consideration in the camping context. In Chapter 2 we referred to the effect of a 'different environment' on the thinking of the camper.

The camping situation is usually different from the camper's normal life in a number of ways. In a Christian camp there is often such a sense of warmth, acceptance and enjoyment that the pressures and influences of ordinary life seem far away. Children may want to make responses simply to please leaders. Their emotions are easily aroused.

Our concern here goes beyond merely defending evangelistic camping. There is a fundamental concern for the sacredness of the individual person. This is the sort of concern expressed by Swiss psychotherapist Paul Tournier, himself a Christian:

> Respect for the person includes respect for the right of self-determination, since it is precisely the free and responsible commitment of the self which creates the person . . . We must say all that we have to say with complete frankness, but in such a spirit that the person to whom we say it feels that we are doing so only in order to help him to choose his line of action in full awareness of the issues at stake, and that we are prepared to trust his choice even if it is not the one we should make ourselves.[7]

Jesus himself invited people to follow him, but there is not a trace of compulsion or manipulation in his relationships with anyone. It is preposterous for anyone to justify a technique of persuasion which bypasses a person's rational process on the grounds that he or she knows what is best for the person. Jesus' understanding of people and of the issues at stake in following him was incomparable. Surely he knew what was best for people, yet he actually dissuaded people from following him too readily, without fully considering the implications.[8]

Is there a contradiction here? We have been saying on one hand that camping is a great context for evangelism. Yet we are also saying that the camp situation, because it is sometimes remote from everyday life, carries dangers as well. How can we take advantage of camping for evangelism without 'taking advantage' of campers?

(a) We will respect the integrity of the individual camper. We will concentrate on dialogue, relationships and authentic example, taking time to develop a genuine understanding of each camper as a person. The evangelist in a rally or meeting has only a short time and a verbal method to persuade his hearers. The camp leader has time to listen, clarify and apply.

(b) We will recognize that conversion is supremely something that God does; it is not mere decision. We will be content with a limited response. One camper wrote this unsolicited remark in the Coolamatong visitors' book: 'Even though I don't believe in God, it was good'. At another camp a boy wrote on an evaluation sheet: 'Before camp there was no God. Now there may be!'

These remarks may indicate only an embryonic response to God, but they are necessary stages in the process towards a convinced, personal faith. For kids from Christian homes, these stages occur imperceptibly, very early in life. For others they are significant developments which of necessity occur much later. It's not our business to determine when a person is ready to make a deep, whole-hearted commitment to Christ.

(c) We will recognize the limitations of the temporary community in Chapter 5. These are very relevant here. In particular we should rigorously relate our evangelism to life back home, where the Christian's life has to be lived out. We have to take seriously our responsibility for nurturing young Christians in their faith, seeing them built in to the on-going life of a local church.

(d) We will not appeal to the emotions as a basis for decision. Becoming a Christian and being a Christian is a function of the will, not of the emotions. Although emotions are involved (perhaps in the form of an overwhelming sense of gratitude and indebtedness to God) a conviction in the mind is the only adequate basis for a sustained commitment of the will. In particular, night-time is a bad time to invite a response to the gospel, precisely because it is an easier time to 'give in'. Campers are not just tired, but less able to weigh up consequences and to make true judgements. The cold hard light of day is preferable for life-changing commitments:

> Though commitment may generate an arousal of emotions, it is primarily a decision affecting future action. It is as matter-of-fact in intention as a resolve to clean one's teeth after every meal. We must make that clear.[9]

(e) By our unjudging relationships as well as in words, we will acknowledge that people may hold with sincerity and integrity views contrary to ours. This is an important corrective in an environment where there may be a temptation to declare oneself 'persuaded' as a means to acceptance in the group.

The implications of commitment
We have no liberty to conceal the cost of discipleship. Perhaps the best safeguard against misusing the camp environment for evangelism is the declaration of the cost of discipleship. It has been said that entrance into the kingdom of God is free, but the annual subscription is all you've got. Commenting on Jesus' words about self-denial as a pre-requisite of discipleship (Luke 9:23ff, Luke 14:26,33), British theologian James Packer has said:

> In common honesty, we must not conceal the fact that free forgiveness in one sense will cost everything; or else our evangelizing becomes a sort of confidence trick.[10]

If we are to evangelize with integrity in the temporary community, we must:
(a) Spell out the implications of discipleship
This includes changes of behaviour and attitudes, ranging from what we read and think about to the large questions of our vocation and our social responsibility in the world. It also includes our relationship to the Christian community and the need to be a contributing member in a local church in some form or another.
(b) Take seriously the need to see the new Christian through to incorporation into a local Christian community
Some may already be part of such a group through the involvement of their own family, or even by a loose attachment to a church youth group. This is where local church camping has the advantage. Evangelism actually occurs in the context of a group in which the new Christian feels at home and is known.

In the larger organizational camp, however, it often takes some planning and organization to follow up a camper who has become a Christian, especially if the person is not related to a particular church. Several factors should be considered. The starting point is the leader-camper relationship. In a leaders' team meeting there should be agreement on which leader is actually going to take responsibility for continuing contact with the camper. The leader who has the closest relationship with a particular camper may be the obvious person, whether or not he has been that camper's group leader.

We have already noted that not every camper's needs for continuing contact will be the same. Some may be actively involved in a local church, or members of a supportive family. They may need no continuing contact with any particular camp leader. Others may have come to camp with a Christian friend, who would be the obvious person to keep in touch. Others again may not know any other Christians and have no idea where to start in finding a Christian group to belong to.

Once it is agreed what the 'follow up' needs are, practical questions take over. Letters, birthday cards and phone calls are a good start. In the case of young people, parents may be a bit uncertain about what is going on. A personal visit to them would be in order. It will help the leader to understand the parents' reactions, and to see the young person in his or her home setting. Such visits should build trust between camper, leader and parent, and help the leader to decide on appropriate ways of helping the camper.

So much of a new Christian's growth in understanding is going to depend on getting a grasp of the Bible. The camper can be encouraged to read the Bible regularly. This and other related matters of Christian discipleship can become a point of regular contact with the leader. Camp Mini-Yo-We in Ontario, Canada, services a group of denominational churches. It publishes its own Bible-reading resources for young campers to take home and runs regular regional get-togethers. At these there is a program of fun and teaching, which brings together the associations and memories of camp and reinforces the implications of commitment.

Additional camping experiences are sometimes urged as a means of 'follow up'. I would want to support that, but do so guardedly. I know that many young people get an annual 'shot-in-the-arm' from camps. This is useful, especially if there is a progression to more challenging activities and experiences as the years go on. But there is a danger that camping people become content with that annual boost as a way of growing mature Christian people. Maturity must be worked at and faith worked out: in the home, the workplace, the local community and the local church.

1 St Paul's Discovery Centre Leaders' Manual, p.7
2 Contained in *Let the Earth Hear His Voice*, Worldwide Publications, Minneapolis, 1975, p.4

3 Quoted by David Watson, *I Believe in Evangelism*, Hodder and Stoughton, 1976, p.105
4 e.g. Watson and Snyder, ibid., and Peter Savage, 'The Church and Evangelism' in *The New Face of Evangelicalism*, 1976, Chapter 6
5 Carl F.H. Henry in 'The Purpose of God', *The New Face of Evangelicalism*, p.31
6 Ibid., p.31
7 Tournier, op. cit., pp.207-208
8 See for example Luke 14:25-33
9 Brian V. Hill, *Evangelistic Camping*, Frontier Youth Services, WA, p.3
10 J.I. Packer, *Evangelism and the Sovereignty of God*, InterVarsity Press, 1961, p.73

19

Leadership on Christian Camps:
What are the practical challenges?

CHRISTIAN CAMPS SHOULD BE MORE than just methods of Christian education or evangelism. In fact any camp run by Christians in a Christian way should be different. By the criteria outlined in this book, a good camp run by a law-abiding atheist should be similar in many respects to a good Christian camp.[1] But leadership on a Christian camp raises some special challenges of a quite practical nature. What are these challenges, and how should leaders respond to them?

Counselling

It is interesting that in the camping tradition the term 'counselling' has often been almost synonymous with small group leadership — certainly in the North American context. This is not because the leader is seen in any sense as a professional counsellor. Nor is camp counselling an amateur practice of psychology. What it does mean is that the camp leader is broadly a 'helper'. He or she is in the people-helping business.

Counselling has also come to have a particular, narrow use in an evangelistic context, but that is not what we are talking about here either. By 'counselling' we mean simply the communication between a helper and a person who is being helped. Dr Robert Duvahl says that camp counselling (by which he means camp leadership) has similar features to three other human relationship fields — parenting, leadership and clinical counselling:

> All involve both a person in a structured helping role . . . and a person being helped.[2]

This suggests our first main emphasis. Counselling is a natural, everyday process and the more naturally it is approached the better. We are not talking about communication which follows a predetermined course.

But if counselling is such a natural process, how can a camp leader improve as a counsellor? Duvahl draws attention to studies in the three fields of parenting, leadership and clinical counselling. These studies point to two common features of communication in successful counselling situations. They show that the effective counsellor is one who can do two things:[3]

(a) Communicate warmth, respect, empathy and genuineness

The counsellor who can do this will be one who is natural and relaxed. He will be a listener as well as a talker. He will be interested in the camper and not self-centred. He need not be old and wise, helpful though wisdom and experience are. He will be approachable, not censorious or superior.

(b) Confront problems, be specific and deal with present
   behaviour and situations

Although the communication doesn't follow a predetermined course, this does not imply that the counsellor has nothing to say or advice to give. The counsellor will help the camper identify problem areas and then face up to them. He will help the counsellee to assume responsibility for his problems. It is not a matter of imposing solutions, but it does clearly go beyond mere listening or empathy.

The convinced Christian believes that God is willing and able to help all who come to him for help. But we can clearly see, even from Jesus' example, that helping people is more than just applying proof-texts from the Bible like band-aids. We say 'even from Jesus' example' because one would think that if anyone was ever in a position to short-circuit the counselling process, he was. He certainly knew the scriptures — and used them tellingly. This is surely the foremost asset of the Christian counsellor: to be able to 'correctly teach the message of truth', the message which is useful for 'rebuking error, correcting faults, and giving instruction for right living'.[4]

Yet Jesus' encounter with the woman at the well (John 4) shows him to be both a teacher and a counsellor. We see in this incident, first and foremost, a person of understanding, who knew how to relate to this woman and how to impart the truth to her. Leon Morris connects this encounter with that with Nicodemus (John 3) emphasizing the incomparable ability of Jesus to understand, relate and impart.

> Nicodemus was an eminent representative of orthodox Judaism. Now John records an interview Jesus had with one who stood for a class which was wholeheartedly despised by orthodox Judaism. The rivalries and hatreds which were meat and drink to the Jews of his day mattered not at all to our Lord. His was a ministry for all men. In the former incident Jesus spoke of the importance of the new birth. Here his theme is the living water which he came to bring to men. The terminology is different, but the basic message is the same.[5]

Here is relevant teaching applied to two people from totally different backgrounds and with quite different sets of needs. Here is counselling as well. The skill, understanding and sensitivity which Jesus was able to bring to the woman at the well is brought out superbly in this quotation:

> Jesus came to the fountain as a hunter. . . He threw a grain before one pigeon that He might catch the whole flock. At the beginning of the conversation He did not make Himself known to her — but first she caught sight of a thirsty man, then a Jew, then a Rabbi, afterwards a prophet, last of all the Messiah. She tried to get the better of the thirsty man, she showed her dislike of the Jew, she heckled the rabbi, she was swept off her feet by the prophet and she adored the Christ.[6]

It goes without saying that, unlike Jesus, we do not have all the answers or his perfect wisdom and understanding. It is important for the camp leader not to go beyond his own knowledge, but to be ready to admit his limitations. A few little clues would be in order to conclude this fleeting look at counselling:
* Just listening may be a real help. Knowing answers and giving direction are not everything. In some cases there may be no answer that is not already known to the person who needs help.
* Communication skills can be learned. For example, one can learn to distinguish between responses which produce trust, warmth and empathy and those which do not. Seeing other good counsellors in action is one good way to learn. Role-playing, plus evaluation, is another.
* Be aware of the temptation to subsequently relate to the camper in terms of his problem, rather than to the person himself with all his 'positives'.
* Don't be content with slick answers. Trite cliches and quotes can actually be damaging if they fail to take the person seriously, or

simply create expectations or burdens of responsibility which cannot be realized or borne.
* If people ask you for a straight answer, and you really do know it, give it to them — with chapter and verse if you like! But don't make their decision for them.

Dealing with difficult campers
Every camp which welcomes all who want to come has its share of campers who are difficult to handle. Apart from insights of psychology and experience, are there any Christian principles which could provide a starting point for the Christian camp leader? Three key words can help: acceptance, understanding and reconciliation.

1. Acceptance
The Bible sees each person as God's good creation, each uniquely known by him, and created for his pleasure.

The incarnation of Jesus is the profoundest possible expression of God's love for persons and a unique expression of our significance. This significance is derived from our nature as God's creation — not from any other advantage such as intelligence, physical prowess or good looks with which we may have been endowed.

This alone should deeply affect our determination to treat each camper with care and respect. It is vital not to reject the camper, even if we reject certain behaviour. How can the camp leader make this work in practice?
* Meditate on the significance of each person in God's sight. Practise thinking of individual campers as people created and loved by your own heavenly Father.
* Look for strong points. Get to know the positive aspects of the difficult campers and recognize the things they can contribute. Work on the assumption that each one can become a contributor. Don't 'write people off'. Resist the temptation to stereotype people. Look beneath the surface.

2. Understanding
As well as having the most exalted view of human beings, the Bible also recognizes failure. The root cause of our problems is our rejection of God, which leads to the breakdown of human relationships. Sin is self-centredness and therefore the attempt to

live in community has a very profound force working against it.
Some practical implications are obvious:
* Recognize your *own* sinfulness. This helps to avoid the
  scandalized reaction to difficult behaviour. The leader who is
  finding a camper troublesome may be part of the problem.
* Avoid hasty reactions. They tend to reflect our own annoyance
  or wounded pride. Considered responses are usually better than
  heated ones. Most situations can 'cool off' over a short period
  and allow us time to ask questions.
* Don't accept things at face value too easily. Spend time trying
  to relate to and understand difficult campers. The more obvious
  or violent rebel may be 'set up' by another camper, shy and
  clever enough to be 'innocently' looking on when trouble occurs.
* Share insights among leaders. Some will have knowledge and
  insights into particular campers which others don't have.
* Try to avoid isolating the difficult camper altogether. Isolation
  creates a real feeling of rejection and sense of injustice, thus
  creating one problem in the course of solving another.

3. Reconciliation

We pointed earlier to the failure of society to live at peace. The
evidence for this assertion is unassailable. And we noted Bertrand
Russell's despairing conclusion that love was both the only possible
answer, yet beyond our reach.

This would have to be our own conclusion: the uniqueness and
magnificence of mankind on the one hand and the reality of failure
on the other — *but* for the doctrine of reconciliation. What
mankind couldn't do, Jesus did do. Through his life, death and
resurrection, he reconciled us to God, now giving us power to live
in obedience to God and to love God and our neighbour.

What are the implications of this for camp leaders?
* Don't avoid difficulties. Difficulties and problems can be
  expected. It is not a sign of failure that they arise. The important
  thing is how we resolve them. Reconciliation is not achieved by
  ignoring problems, hoping that they will go away.
  Reconciliation was a product of Jesus' commitment to truth and
  justice, as well as to love.
* Don't be content with just smoothing over problems.
  In *Faith at the Blackboard*, Brian Hill speaks of reconciliatory
  discipline in the classroom. The same principle applies to
  camping:

The effective [leader] will not permit disruptive behaviour in the name of a romantic philosophy of freedom. But neither will he deem it sufficient merely to subdue those who offend. Rather, he will seek the opportunity to bring them to terms with themselves and with the external forces that goad them.[7]

* Focus on reconciliation in teaching. Reconciliation affects issues as broad as ecological survival and world peace, as well as social harmony and everyday happiness. It should often be a focus of teaching and activity. Some consider that conflict should be welcomed rather than avoided in camp, providing an opportunity to work things through. Studies, structured activities and everyday life provide opportunities to focus on this issue — an issue of human survival, as well as a matter affecting 'quality of life'.

   Teaching opportunities in the real-life camp situation have already been stressed. In dealing with difficult campers we have the chance to learn, teach and demonstrate to *all campers* — difficult or otherwise — the central Christian *responsibility* of reconciliation, and the power of the gospel to break down hostility between races, sexes, groups and individuals.

Relying on God

A distinctive feature of Christian camping ought to be a practical focus on getting help from God. The idea of loving one's neighbour is not merely a suggestion or an ideal; it is a command. The Christian believes that God has made it possible to obey his commands by giving us the Holy Spirit. Love is a gift from God. Joy and peace, patience and self-control are his gifts also.

This is such a basic feature of Christian living that it almost seems unnecessary to draw attention to it. Yet there is a real temptation to suppose that because group camping experiences are normally enjoyable, everything will 'go OK'.

We need help from God even at the enjoyment level. In Chapter 2 we drew attention to the fact that the elements in 'good experiences' are often intangible. We can't even guarantee our ability to reproduce them. We spoke of the best sort of camp atmosphere as that which emerged 'unselfconsciously'. We referred to the elusiveness of special experiences when we consciously pursue them. We are touching here on the central Christian notion of grace. Grace is God's undeserved favour, given by God to us as a free gift. It is not earned and by definition cannot be.

* We need to pray together as leaders. 'God *does* reward those who seek him'. He does 'give grace to the humble'. We need to focus our attention on God. This means making time to pray — as a team of leaders or as a total community.
* We need to leave the work of 'converting' the individual to the Holy Spirit.
* Time should be made for people to be by themselves. Constant communal activity can be a hindrance to our personal relationship with God.

   Dietrich Bonhoffer wrote, 'Let him who cannot be alone beware of community.'[8] Community can be an escape from the need to develop an individual relationship with God. We must not rely on the community to satisfy those needs which can only be met as we come before God as individuals.
* Make time for individual prayer. I'm not necessarily arguing for the traditional 'quiet time' in camp. In fact, there are problems with it. For example, no one blows a whistle at home for 'quiet time'. The individual has to compete there with rattles in the kitchen or interruptions from other members of the family. But it *is* important for leaders to find time to pray and for all campers to be encouraged to at least spend some time in quietness — without distractions — and seek God. Many will have to be given practical clues on how to do this.

A Christian model of leadership

We have already stressed the importance of good leadership, considering issues of authority and discipline as well as organization. We have stressed some qualities of leadership (such as humility), which do not readily fit some images of the up-front charismatic dynamic leader. But Jesus explicitly taught a model of leadership which ran counter to the general view of leadership in the world.

> You know that in the world, the recognized rulers lord it over their subjects, and their great men feel the weight of authority. That is not the way with you; among you, whoever wants to be great must be your servant, and whoever wants to be first must be the willing slave of all.[9]

When there is not quite enough fruit-cake to go around, or when volunteers are required for extra cook's dishes, this model of leadership is put to the test. Clearly, it is a model which Jesus' whole life exemplified. Jesus went straight on to say, 'For the Son of Man did not come to be served but to serve and to give his life as a ransom for many'.

Jesus also gave a special object lesson about this concept of service when he took a towel and washed his disciples' feet, an act which was socially extraordinary, yet performed as an example for his disciples.[10] It was something like a managing director cleaning the staff washrooms.

It is important for the Christian leader therefore to be secure in his role, recognizing that his authority doesn't rest in a name-tag or a title, but in the fact that God has given him a job to do. Of course, servant leadership does not consist in being passive or capitulating to the demands of others. Its essence is that the leader is acting in the interest of others, not his own.

In one circumstance this may mean, in fact, 'doing the dirty work' oneself. In another it may mean taking time to pray, or to talk to someone, while others do the dirty work. At one time it will mean insisting on something for the well-being of the community; on another it will mean 'giving in' on a point — for the same reason.

A reference-point for values

We do not need to reiterate the need for rules and standards in the temporary community. Indeed, when it comes to Christian camping, this issue is often relatively straightforward. Large issues concerning values will probably not even arise in the local church family camp — although differences may well emerge in what different parents let their children 'get away with'.

But leaders in evangelistic camps and in youth camps in general face the question of what standards to insist on. The question really is: What are Christian values in this matter and should we insist on people conforming to them? These questions have been partially dealt with in Chapter 10, but the following considerations are particularly important in the Christian camp:

* There are *biblical* values which cannot be ignored. I have argued elsewhere that sex outside marriage is one such value; co-ed sleeping arrangements in youth camps would be a contradiction of the need to uphold that principle.[11]
* Some values in the church are *cultural* rather than biblical. They may be worthwhile, but they do not have the same importance.

234/Leadership on Christian Camps

Things in this category should not be allowed to become the basis of a breakdown in relationships with campers.

* Leadership should have a *positive* approach to rules and standards. The Christian camp is an opportunity for people to observe and experience the powerful transformation from imprisonment to freedom which the Spirit brings about. The idea that Christianity takes the fun out of everything is an absolute travesty of the truth, yet it is a prevalent attitude.

It is perhaps not surprising that a religion which sees sex as an act of deep significance and moral implications is seen as restrictive. After all, the media powerfully and relentlessly present sex as having no such deep personal significance or even joy, but simply as the animal satisfaction of a biological urge. The consumption of alcohol and the acquisition of more and more possessions — especially the ownership of a good car — are consistently portrayed as means of gaining freedom and satisfaction.

In such a society as we live in, it is often seen as 'wowserish' and negative to draw attention to the destructive social consequences of such a hedonistic morality. Young people living under this sort of pressure need to see and experience positive, affirming, male-female relationships, characterized by real joy, caring love and mutual respect. They need help in understanding both the goodness of sex and its God-given function in secure and committed relationships. They need guidance on how to enjoy each other without exploiting one another. They also need people who can enjoy life wholeheartedly, helping them intelligently and uncensoriously to see through the illusory freedom of popular hedonism.

We as Christians can be thankful to have a real reference-point for values, not just in the commandments and the Sermon on the Mount, but in countless examples in the Bible, through history and in our own day. Our aim should be to provide an attractive, enjoyable, positive alternative lifestyle, with as few negatives, rules and purely cultural restrictions as possible. As I have said in another place:

A Christian camp has enormous potential to demonstrate that life in the Spirit is not only possible, but more enriching and satisfying than the hedonistic lifestyle and the pursuit of pleasure or self-aggrandizement at the expense of others. Is it not now the case that high-minded non-Christians are often more forthright advocates of the Christian principle of looking after the body (be it through diet, adequate exercise or non-smoking) than Christians are prepared to be? To take the gospel seriously is to believe in the possibility that a community of Christians can be a 'demonstration unit of the kingdom of God'. We must continue to learn how to scrutinize our Christian culture and work out what in it is truly biblical and what is simply cultural. But let's show, as well as talk about, a 'more excellent way' with joy and a total lack of self-righteousness.[12]

Relevant teaching

Unfortunately there has often been a polarization of views on what constitutes relevant teaching.[13] Some appear to feel that the best way to communicate relevantly to young people today is to plod through Romans verse by verse, following this up with talks at night on 'the way to salvation' and a devotional in tent groups before lights out. Others appear almost to have opted out of verbal or literary communication altogether. A brief devotion for five minutes at some point of the day is all the formal 'teaching' that takes place. The rest is left to personal conversation, and the experience of the camp program.

I see nothing wrong *in principle* with either approach. But I do believe it is a rare group of campers for whom either of these approaches would be the ideal. We should be in the business of making the most of our opportunities to communicate spiritual truth in what is really a desperate world. An effective teaching program should satisfy three criteria:

(a) Appropriate method

Discussions, film-strips, films, dramas, role-plays, private research on set questions, talks by leaders, open forums, values clarification exercises, simulation games, singing, human sculptures, meals, special activities, direct Bible study, preaching, one-to-one conversation (structured or casual), word studies, issue studies and, perhaps above all, story-telling all can be used to get the message across.

We should recognize the value of the well-told story. It has a universal appeal; Jesus used it a great deal and the Bible is more a story-book than a text-book on doctrine. The important point is to choose a variety of appropriate methods — appropriate to the subject and interesting to the campers.

Digby Hannah speaks from experience in this challenging statement:

Teenagers whose home lives are disturbed rarely find school to be a happy place. So it is small wonder that there is a strong reaction of antipathy when we subject groups of teenagers to talks, questionings, discussion groups, academic exercises, written work and the like. But what methods of raising questions or communicating information remain? Dramatic presentations seem to be quite effective, especially when they are grounded in familiar events surrounding the lives of the kids.

We have also been surprised at a teenager's willingness to pray. Praying, after all, is only talking to a person who is always there and who always cares. Praying can be an immediate response to what has happened and to how we are feeling. Praying is telling God our feelings, thanking, asking and saying sorry. Much teaching is implicit in the act of prayer: that God is there, that he hears, he is able, he cares and so on. Much teaching can arise as a direct result of praying in a particular circumstance. Has God heard? How do we know? What does he want us to do? How can we hear him?[14]

On the other hand, other teenagers and adults may thrive on talks, questionings, discussion groups and the like. Children who do well at school love written work. Nevertheless, this is still a challenging idea. In any case, where there is a mixture of backgrounds and interests, we should at least employ a variety of methods, perhaps majoring on the dramatic and active rather than the literary and passive.

(b) Biblical content

There is, of course, an overlap here with method. It may even be thought that biblical content only comes from doing direct Bible study. We talk about giving students 'hands-on' experience in outdoor education: patting animals, sifting dirt through their fingers... We also need to give people 'hands-on' contact with the Bible.

They need to hold it in their hands and read it for themselves. A good way to do this is to give campers their own copy of a portion of the *Good News Bible* — say one of the Gospels. The most 'unlikely' campers will really get engrossed and read it for themselves.

But direct Bible study is not the only measure of biblical input. Biblical concepts can be conveyed by many methods, drama being a very obvious one. The point is that Christianity is recognizably a 'revealed religion'. The emperor Diocletian, said H.G. Wells, recognized this in destroying books and writings in his persecution of Christians. If we are talking about relevant teaching of

Christianity, then it must be teaching which is communicating a
biblical faith. There is a tendency for 'method' to take over, and
become an end in itself. The use of values clarification techniques
on their own is a classic example. But even discussion groups can
do the same. Brian Hill writes:

> It is educationally preferable to draw adolescents and adults into
> discussion groups dealing with the problems of modern living, as an
> alternative to confining them in parallel pews to be passive listeners.
> But if, at some point, there is not a controlled input of biblical data
> which is viewed as central rather than supplemental to the discussion,
> then the gospel may not have been communicated but supplanted by
> private opinion.[15]

(c) Relevance to the camper
First, the teaching needs to be 'earthed' in real-life situations and
applied to the situations in which campers are finding themselves.
We should ask ourselves: what might be the implications of this
teaching for these campers in the next week? Teaching that is not
soon applied is quickly forgotten, or never really absorbed at all.

Second, the teaching needs to be suited to the age and previous
experience of the campers. We cannot assume that campers from
outside the church will understand what we mean by even basic
terms like 'Jesus', or have any idea how to look up Philippians
chapter 3. Not even the great stories of Samson, Daniel in the
lions' den or David and Goliath are known to most young people
today.

A good example of a thoughtful approach to relevant content
again comes from Digby Hannah:

> The children whom we see at St Paul's are familiar with the terms
> 'God' and 'Jesus Christ' only in the context of the abusive language
> which unfortunately surrounds them when they are not in camp.
> Small wonder that a nine-year-old boy stared at me in genuine
> amazement when, in answer to one of his questions, I assured him
> that it was God who first made all the animals — in fact the whole
> world!
> With such theological awareness as a starting point, it is necessary
> to be careful not to make too many assumptions when embarking on
> a teaching program for children.[16]

He goes on to outline the main propositions which underlie the
Christian education program at St Paul's. They are:

* God made the world and everything in it.
* Everything that God has made is good.
* He is still in charge of everything.
* God made people special — they can choose to love him or ignore him.
* God is a person. He is like a perfect father.
* God helped us to get to know him by becoming a man: Jesus.
* Jesus showed us how God wants us to live.
* Some people loved Jesus and followed him.
* Some people hated Jesus and killed him.
* Jesus rose from the dead and is alive.
* We can talk to Jesus (or God) — he always hears us and is always with us.
* If we decide to follow Jesus it will mean caring for others as he did.
* Jesus is like a perfect friend, who knows everything about us and still loves us.

Having said all this, we must take care not to allow the search for relevant content to dictate content altogether. I remember hearing a nun rebuking a girl for saying nasty things about her mother. This girl had been badly let down and abused, yet the nun was saying, 'You have to remember that your mother has got problems too'. This woman's unquestionable love and care for the girl did not stop her confronting the girl with truth.

This is the challenge of teaching relevantly, yet teaching faithfully: relevant to the camper, faithful to the truth and effective in method. It would be a useful exercise to study the list of propositions above in the light of this question: Is this an adequate summary of the Christian teaching which would be appropriate to the needs of children at camps in which I am involved?

Adventure
The church and the world need adventurers for God, people who will take risks and live strongly. In our affluent society, it is easy to sit back and be entertained. The influence of television alone has had an enormous impact on the way we entertain ourselves. Within one generation we in Australia, New Zealand and the UK

have changed from active involvement to passive observation in the way we use our spare time.

> The need for adventure has never been greater. Young people especially need large doses of adventure in order to change, discover and grow. If they aren't sufficiently challenged by real life adventures, they will seek and find other fictitious adventures of significantly less value.[17]

So writes Tim Hansell, leader of a mountaineering and wilderness experience school. Hansell's thesis is that real wilderness adventure is a uniquely suitable opportunity not merely for entertaining but for 'training servant leaders to meet the desperate needs of the world around us'.

For Hansell, the wilderness is an environment where learning 'is at its steepest curve', an unknown environment providing challenge as well as excitement, 'a non-neutral learning environment which demands change and fosters community, trust and interdependence'.[18]

How many Christian camping programs have that kind of cutting edge? Living strongly for Christ is more than singing choruses and saying grace at meals. It has to do with being courageous enough to trust God in difficulties. It means learning self-control and persistence in the face of temptations and fatigue. It means developing an enlarged vision for God's goodness and an eager confidence in his purposes.

There is scope for much more adventure camping in Christian circles today. But even base camps can resist the temptation to be content with the comforts and entertainments of the camp-site itself. The simple experience of sleeping under the stars, or even in a little tent, is exciting and challenging for most people now. And these pleasures are always rewarding and enriching, even for the experienced light-weight camper.

But the challenge to be adventurous goes beyond the physical dimension. The rewards of overcoming physical, or any other big challenges, go beyond the exhilaration of the moment. At best, they include the gaining of confidence and poise which results from the knowledge that one has achieved a difficult goal or learnt something important.

Perhaps H.G. Wells captured a dimension of the Christian life which we comfortable believers sometimes miss, when he wrote concerning the challenge of Christ:

For to take him seriously was to enter upon a strange and alarming life, to abandon habits, to control instincts and impulses, to essay an incredible happiness.[19]

Christian camping should be distinguished above all by the way in which it provides, through Christian community, a way to get closer to him.

1 Ignoring the question as to whether any *consistent* atheist could ever run a good camp according to the criteria of this book.
2 Robert Drovdahl, 'Communication, Key to Counselling', in *Journal of Christian Camping*, May-June 1982, p.8
3 Drovdahl's headings, my summary of what Drovdahl calls 'facilitative communication' and 'action-oriented communication'
4 2 Timothy 2:15 and 3:16
5 L.L. Morris, *The Gospel according to John*, Eerdmans, 1971, p.254
6 Ibid., p.254 footnote
7 Brian Hill, *Faith at the Blackboard*, Eerdmans, 1982, p.125
8 Dietrich Bonhoeffer, *Life Together*, SCM, 1972, p.57
9 Mark 10:42-44
10 See John 13:13-15
11 *The Camping Book*, pp.17-19
12 *Challenges to Camping*, p.10
13 See my own 'The Gospel Challenges Camping' in *Challenges to Camping*
14 Supplement to *On Being*, op. cit., p.34
15 Brian V. Hill (ed.), *A Charge to Keep*, 1971, p.3
16 Supplement to *On Being*, op. cit., p.34
17 Tim Hansell, 'Holy Sweat', *Journal of Christian Camping*, May-June 1982, p.10
18 Ibid., pp.11-12
19 H.G. Wells, *A Short History of the World*, Pelican, 1962, p.157

Appendix A:
Defining Camping

In Chapter 3 we looked at the question: What is camping really? We found that definitions always seemed debatable. There are three groups for whom a clear definition is necessary:

(a) Government authorities

In Victoria, Australia, it used to be the case that when government health authorities looked for regulations applicable to permanent campsites, they applied the Boarding House Regulations.[1] Some definition of camping might have been helpful here as a basis for a more realistic appraisal!

Then again, supposing a government were persuaded to allocate some funds for organized camping — someone would have to decide who was in fact eligible for funds. A caravan owners' club? Schools? A scientific expedition to the Antarctic? Traditional holiday camp organisers?

The question of what we understand by organized camping affects those who administer the public purse.

(b) The camping fraternity

Arguments sometimes rage between proponents of different camping styles about what camping really is. 'Call that camping do you?' we say as our mate sits in his aluminium chair, cooking frozen hamburgers from his portable refrigerator on his gas barbecue.

This may be said as a joke, but sometimes feelings of antagonism and distrust are concealed or aroused by this sort of comparison. The ongoing dialogue about what 'true camping' is requires some clear reference points.

(c) The community at large

There is a sense in which we all know what camping means. That is not because we have read a dictionary definition necessarily, but because we have all heard the word and applied it to a variety of activities.

It is important for the future of camping in our society that the word be attached to activities which represent the best in camping. Words can be devalued or made so broad in definition that they lose all meaning. What people mean by 'camping' is determined by what the word is commonly attached to. The more precise we are about what we want the word to mean, the better.

Attempts at definition

When we are talking about dictionary definitions, we are talking about what the word denotes: defining characteristics which must be present if we are to use the word correctly.

This is not as straightforward as it seems. That is partly why dictionary definitions often don't say much at all. Take the definition of a table, for example. Shape, size, colour and the number of legs are all variables. But can you have a table without legs? Does a table have to have a flat top? In other words, what characteristics denote, or are absolutely necessary to, the idea of a table?

Various elements of camping are argued as being definitive in this way. They include the attributes we have already looked at: camping's outdoor emphasis, community nature and educational purpose.

Here is a classic example of the way in which such arguments proceed:

> The sine qua non [literally 'without which not'] of the organized camp is an outdoor setting and experiences that are indigenous to living in the out-of-doors. This is the basic, indispensable characteristic of camping.[2]

Precisely what is meant by this is not clear, though the general intent is obvious. But just how much outdoor setting and outdoor living is required? What are the limitations of this requirement?

Can a person be said to be camping, for example, when he is living in a caravan and simply walking to the beach each day? Is living in a tent a sufficient criterion? What about living in a cabin at a campsite or a cabin at a beach resort? Could we live in a well-equipped lodge in a 'camping ground' and still call ourselves campers? Do we have to cook outside?

This is not mere quibbling. Dimock, just quoted, goes on to say:

It is common knowledge that some 'camps' have failed to utilize the outdoor setting for camping purposes and are therefore considered unworthy of the name they carry.[3]

In other words you can't call yourself a camp unless you are providing experiences that are 'indigenous to living in the out-of-doors'. This is a very tall order indeed if it implies an aboriginal sort of existence. If, however, it means indigenous to outdoor living in our Western affluent white culture, it is only a moderately uncomfortable requirement!

Now I'm all for a more thorough-going use of the outdoor environment. Camping is an outdoor pursuit. I'm happy to agree it is even a basic characteristic of virtually all camping. But this does not entitle us to say it is indispensable unless and until we can precisely define the minimal outdoor ingredients.

What of the other two alternatives? Do they hold the real key to what camping really is? The educational purpose of camping is certainly important, more important than much current camping in this country would suggest. But I don't believe it is essential.[4]

What about the community nature of organized camping then? Is that the one feature which must be present if an activity is to qualify for the title of a 'camping' activity? Elsewhere[5] I have made such a claim in much the same way as Dimock does for the outdoor setting. My general point was that living together twenty-four hours a day was a definitive characteristic, making the term 'day camping' self-contradictory.

Yet would *one* 24-hour period at a campsite qualify as a camp? Could we not conceive of a city camp where the campers slept at home overnight, but were together from breakfast until supper every day? Would the fact that they slept at home disqualify the activity from the name of camping, even if the children were wholly involved in outdoor cooking and outdoor activities?

This is where definitions are inadequate. I would maintain that a 48-hour living-together experience in an outdoor environment was a camp. I'd also happily argue that an eight-hour visit to a campsite was not. But where does one draw the line?

It is tempting to overcome the problem by simply choosing to define camping in a certain way. But as we have seen this may create hostility when you come to apply the definition (to allocate funds, win an argument or whatever) — and it does little to enlarge our understanding very much either.

From definition to description

Is the process of defining camping simply futile then? It depends on what we are looking for. We must look not for a final definition to end all disputes, but for agreement as to what emphasis we want to convey. To put it another way, we need to move beyond the *denotation* of the word 'camping' (dictionary definition) to the *connotation* (the images that come to mind when people hear the word).

Consider the difference between characteristics which merely define a thing and those which describe it. The dictionary says a dog is 'a quadruped of many breeds', but this does not convey the slightest idea of what a dog really is.

We would need to add more descriptive characteristics: a dog is smaller than a cow but bigger than a frog, it barks when it is disturbed and generally eats meat. This sort of information really helps to communicate the meaning of 'dog' to the ordinary person.

In this way we can convey a mental picture by using relevant descriptive phrases. But words communicate even more. They communicate feelings and emotions. To a dog lover, 'dog' means a warm, loyal, affectionate animal. To someone else it may mean a pest which knocks over garbage bins and bites postmen's legs.

One can imagine an argument between two such people about what a dog really is. The first might say: 'It's just an animal anyway'. The other would retort: 'It's not! A dog is a real friend — and intelligent at that!' The protagonists may be talking about what a dog *is* — but it's not a question of definition at all, or even just description. It is an argument about what sort of words can be *worthily* applied to a dog.

Similarly, a bushwalker, fond of solitary tramping in the mountains, may scoff at the sophisticated site-based program: 'Real camping takes us back to nature — to self-reliance, simplicity, independence and the natural environment'. The campsite director may retort: 'Real camping is a socializing thing — if we don't learn to live together and co-operate, there'll be no natural environment left to enjoy anyway'.

Here, the protagonists are not really arguing about whether the others are camping at all. What they are arguing about is what are the best values of camping — the true spirit of camping.

This is the course we took in Chapter 3. We decided to leave aside the matter of mere definition and look at an 'inherited understanding' of the term camping. We asked not 'What does the dictionary say?' but 'How is camping conceived by its thoughtful exponents?' In Chapter 4 we began to give to the term 'organized camping' an emphasis, a particular flavour.

Our remaining question then is what we want 'camping' to convey. Let us answer that question in terms of the three groups for whom the matter of definition is of obvious importance:

(a) Government authorities

Take the problem of how the standard of facilities at a permanent campsite should be regulated. The problem here is to define camping in a way which does justice to the *spirit* of camping. What are the expectations of the community and the intentions of camping organizers? The washing facilities required in a hospital are one thing. The same standards of ablution would be ludicrous in a camping situation where people were consciously, deliberately choosing a style of living that was basic and close to nature.

In an over-zealous community requiring motel-type accommodation for campsites, it would not be surprising to find camps eventually advertising, as a key attraction, 'This campsite does not conform to the health regulations!' It is obviously essential to safeguard health, but at the same time we must preserve that important dimension of the camping experience which implies simplicity of lifestyle.

(b) The camping fraternity

It is obvious that the whole process of giving 'the right emphasis' to the concept of camping in an urban society is important. Whether or not Dimock was justified in describing the outdoor context as the *sine qua non* of camping, he was certainly justified in drawing attention to its importance in a fully-fledged camping program. It is a matter of judgement for all of us as to where our own emphasis should lie.

But failure to make these judgements will result in confusion. In a basic text on camping administration, one contributor talks about 'the twenty-four-hour living experience' and 'group living' as two of four major camping distinctives. Yet another contributor to the same volume refers to day-camping as a form of 'non-resident camping'.[6] These are contradictory notions.

An Australian recreation consultant argued that, despite the fact that the term 'day-camping' has been legitimized in North America,[7] a camping experience must have a residential component to distinguish it from an ongoing day activity program.[8] This echoes the concern that the term camping has been 'de-valued' by being applied to non-residential activities. The same legitimate concern is being expressed when people argue the merits or demerits of various forms of camping. It is important that a healthy dialogue is maintained within the camping fraternity to develop a shared and improved understanding of what camping, at its best, ought to be.

(c) The community at large
This is the question of what 'camping' means to the person in the street. When a child comes home from school with a notice about a Grade Five camp, what images are evoked in the parent? Perhaps dad has been in army camps. Perhaps mother read in the paper recently about a youth camp scandal. L.B. Sharp, a pioneer of outdoor education, has written:

> The public's opinion of camping is built on what it knows of individual camps and the public's opinion of any given camp is affected by its favourable or unfavourable opinion of camping as a whole. What is the thing camping has to 'sell'? What reasonable expectations should the public have? How are they created? . . .
> Until the public has a reasonably clear and accurate idea of what camping is and what it has to offer, little will be done to provide camping experiences for the ninety-five per cent of children who do not now have them. An essential starting-point is common agreement among camping leaders as to what is meant by camping.[9]

Much of what passes for camping today is a poor reflection of what camping is at its best. We must continue to seek better and more relevant emphases — not so that we can make the institution viable, but so that we can bring the best camping experiences possible to people who really need them.

Appendix I
1 At the time of writing it still is. I write in hope!
2 Dimock, op. cit., p.29
3 I would not like to be accused of having ignored a logical peculiarity. In Dimock's argument that 'camps which have failed to use the outdoor setting *for camping purposes* (italics mine) do not deserve to be called camps', the phrase in italics is redundant. In the context, 'camping purposes' *means* 'use of the outdoor setting'. I mention this only as a matter of insufferable personal pride. It doesn't affect my thesis or his.
4 That is unless we define education so broadly that it covers everything necessary for the continuation of human civilization — in which case it doesn't help at all. Certainly I would reject the notion that camping must be intentionally educational, though again the more it is the better.

5 *The Camping Book*, p.9
6 Dimock, op. cit., pp.21-41. The term 'day camping' is sometimes applied to a single day visit to a campsite. Alternatively it is used to refer to a holiday activity programme on several consecutive days on outdoor locations.
7 See Armand Ball Jnr in *Victorian Camping Conference 1982 Proceedings*, Melbourne 1983, p.4
8 Penelope Fogarty, responding to Armand Ball, *Victorian Camping Conference 1982 Proceedings*, p.37
9 L.B. Sharp in Dimock, op. cit., pp.216-217

Appendix B:
The Management Structure
of Coolamatong

1. Ownership

Coolamatong is owned by Scripture Union of Victoria, an autonomous member body of a national and international Christian organization with branches in about eighty-five countries around the world. Scripture Union is a volunteer, interdenominational body which aims to communicate Christianity to the contemporary world. In particular, it aims to help bridge some of the gaps between organized Christianity and the person in the street.

As well as camping and schools work, its diverse activities in Australia include outreach youth work, evangelism among children and young people, Christian education, leadership training, family enrichment, Bible-reading promotion and Christian publishing.

2. Functions

Coolamatong has a dual role. First, it provides a camping base for a substantial part of Scripture Union's large and diverse holiday camping program. These are the camps which are planned, prepared and conducted with voluntary camp directors and leaders during school holidays.

Second, the resident staff at Coolamatong provide a year-round school camping program. As a staff-intensive program, this is something of an exception in the activities of this voluntary organization. But it is consistent with Scripture Union's long-standing and innovative involvement in educational programs, particularly in secondary schools.

3. Management structure

(a) A state *council* is the final policy-making body, the chairman of the Coolamatong management committee being a member of that council.

(b) The Coolamatong *management committee* is responsible for the maintenance and development of the site, facilities and program directions, as well as the financial management. This committee consists of a voluntary chairman, volunteers and paid staff.

(c) Day-to-day maintenance, program and management are in the hands of the Coolamatong director and the other resident *staff*.

(d) *Volunteer workers* still play an important part in the maintenance of the site and equipment, and the planning of holiday programs.

4. Finance

Although the great majority of income is derived directly from camp fees, additional income (about 13%) is in the form of regular donation support for staff salaries. As well, depending on seasons, a small contribution (1-2%) comes from the farming activities. With additional help from donations towards Scripture Union's camp sponsorship fund, these other sources allow Coolamatong fees to stay more than competitive, despite the high level of staff input and standard of facilities.

Appendix C:
Some Guidelines to Health
and Safety

No comprehensive introduction to organized camping would be complete without reference to the large and important subject of safety. The health and physical survival of the camper is perhaps the most fundamental expression of caring. Even though we do not have the scope to deal with the topic exhaustively, here are the basic elements of camp safety which conscientious leaders should be aware of:

1. Scope
It is a mistake, when planning for camper health and safety, to think only in terms of accidents or illness. It is obvious that we need to prevent accidents which may cause loss of life and limb. But there are more common and deceptive threats to camper health and safety. Here are two examples:

(a) Sunburn
Sunburn just happens without the camper even realizing it. Severe cases and even common overdoses can cause considerable pain and discomfort, spoiling a whole camp. Prevention is essential, requiring vigilance on the part of leaders to remind people of the danger, encourage appropriate clothing, set an example of sensible prevention and carry proper first aid equipment.

(b) Overtiredness
Overtiredness can reduce the camper's ability to cope with physical stress. Indeed, it is one of the common contributors to exposure, which can be fatal. It can impair people's judgement in situations which require alertness and a high degree of self-control. Clearly, the quality of the camping experience is directly related to conscientious and sensible attention to matters of health and safety.

2. Hazards

(a) Weather

A knowledge of local weather patterns, monitoring of weather forecasts and the advice of locals are essential where activities such as water-sports and light-weight expeditions are concerned.

The biggest difficulty about weather is that it is rarely predictable. It demands maturity and discipline on the part of leaders to cancel or postpone planned adventures because of a bad forecast, particularly when the weather appears to be perfect beforehand.

The dangers range from heat exhaustion and sunstroke, on one hand, to exposure on the other. Rain is an obvious threat, if not prepared for. Storms can blow up huge waves, tear tents to shreds or break branches from trees.

(b) Other natural hazards

Urbanized people need to learn about many hazards which are part of the natural world. Shade is attractive in summer, yet it is dangerous to pitch tents under certain trees because of the possibility of dead branches falling, even on a calm, windless day. A swim on a summer's day is attractive, but unknown currents, snags, submerged rocks or unexpectedly chilly water can turn fun into disaster.

Bushfires, poisonous snakes and spiders, barnacles on a post in the water, crumbling rock on a mountain side, sword-grass — all these natural phenomena are hazards which can mar a camp for individuals or the whole group.

(c) Food service

Food should be attractive, nutritious and of sufficient quantity to satisfy. Food preparation areas should be clean, all food being checked for freshness. It is vital to get cooked meat and other hot foods cooled and into refrigeration quickly if they are not being eaten hot. People handling food must have clean hands, and any leader or camper with 'the gastro' should not prepare or serve food.

One camp director used to promise 'raging dysentery' for all if hands were not washed at the toilet! Communal living does present real hazards, but there should be very few instances of widespread ill-health in camps if simple hygiene is properly observed in relation to meals — including very hot water for washing up.

(d) Fooling around

Experience suggests that many more accidents occur to campers through spontaneous and high-spirited antics than through camp activities which have a planned element of danger. Campers will safely ride horses, climb obstacles, ski on water and find their way through the bush with compass, only to stub their toes running to the shower, twist their ankles chasing someone around a corner, or break their teeth running into obstacles in the dark.

(e) Campsite equipment
Campsite owners, staff and users should periodically check for hazards around the campsite — tent pegs and ropes where people will trip over them, barbed wire, badly lit traffic areas, inflammable liquids, poisons and equipment left lying around. The location and proper setting up of campfires outside, and urns for tea and coffee-making inside, are equally important.

(f) Organized activities
There are many dangers inherent in the activities we take for granted. In Canada, where horseriding is a far more prominent part of the culture than in Australia, camp leaders appear to be far more casual about horse safety than in Australia. On the other hand, the Canadians are far more scrupulous and vigilant about swimming than those of us for whom swimming may be an everyday pastime.

The lesson is that we need to be vigilant in recognizing activities where dangers can arise from inexperience or carelessness, not just those activities which are inherently risky. Leaders should certainly be familiar with the accepted codes, as well as government regulations, covering the conduct of many outdoor pursuits.

3. Leadership
Prevention of accidents and the protection of campers' health is the responsibility of all leaders, not just of the camp medical officer. The requirements of leadership can be summed up in this way:

(a) Preparation
This involves identification of various potential dangers and then adequate planning either to eliminate these dangers or to deal with accidents which may occur or problems that arise. Emergency plans should be prepared well in advance and be known to all leaders.

(b) Instruction
Campers must be adequately instructed in what the dangers are, what to wear for each activity and how to do it safely.

(c) Skills
Leaders must have the necessary skills to conduct activities safely.
(d) Attitude
Leaders must have a no-nonsense attitude when there are perceived hazards in any facet of camp. Sheer fun is great and has a real place, but never at the expense of safety.
(e) Supervision
Camp leadership carries with it important moral and legal responsibilities. There is no substitute for supervision in either 'free time' or organized activities. Camp organizers need to recognize that there must be a sufficient ratio of leaders to campers to enable them to maintain adequate supervision of campers at all times.

4. First aid
Leadership recruitment must include people with first aid knowledge. Adequate supplies of first aid equipment should be available at the base camp and on expeditions.

5. Legal liability
Our society is becoming increasingly aware of the possibility of successfully suing for damages in the case of claimed negligence by teachers and other authorities. Camp leaders have a legal responsibility, a 'duty of care', for campers.

The exact nature and extent of that responsibility is sometimes difficult to define, but it is a real one, as many successful court actions have shown. Camp directors and organizations should become more aware of their legal obligations and instruct leaders in them. A good starting point would be *Camping, Leadership, Insurance and the Law*, published by the Department of Youth, Sport and Recreation (State Government of Victoria, 1982).

Index

abuse of camping	8, 26
authority	91-92, 105ff, 127
behaviour	59, 111ff, 124, 128, 134
— anti-social	32, 118, 127
— standards	34, 36, 60, 107, 126-127
bullying	45, 57, 111
conflict	33-34, 45, 54, 68, 92, 113, 148, 152
cultural differences	113, 123
decision-making	64-65, 77, 113, 154
difficult campers	107-108, 229-231
director	71, 75-76, 80-81, 103-104, 111, 118-119
disadvantaged groups	24, 121-122, 147, 213-214
discipline	60, 108ff, 124, 128
evaluation	
— criteria	30-31, 89, 97
— of behaviour	117
— process	73-74
families	24-25, 63, 83, 88, 133, 144, 146ff
family camps	25, 63, 146ff, 203-204
groups, small	62-63, 77, 82, 213-214
in loco parentis	58, 131
leadership	20, 42, 66-68, 91-104, 111, 252-253
— Christian	232-233
— roles	98-102
— style	58, 113ff
— training	93, 103-104, 214
legal responsibility	92, 107, 111, 133, 253
meals	35-36, 62-63, 89, 90, 151, 184

objectives	43, 58, 71-73, 76-77, 80, 83-84, 92-93, 107-108, 110, 168, 174
organizations	71-73, 82, 104, 111, 122, 126-127, 133, 147
— Christian	213, 215-216
outdoor education	49, 137ff
parents	53, 87-88, 107, 119, 126-127, 131-132, 144-145
punishment	109, 113, 117, 118-119
reflection	39, 86, 90
rules	60, 105, 108ff, 128, 130, 134, 143, 183, 234
safety	60, 92, 127-128, 250-253
school camping	23-24, 45ff, 53, 60, 126-127, 132, 138-145, 215
— at Coolamatong	164ff, 218
Scripture Union	161ff, 248-249
smoking	114, 127, 128-129, 130
socialization	53-55, 63, 131-132, 143
team concept	96-97
technological society	25, 39
theory of camping	20-21, 27-39, 47, 73, 103
timetable	89-90
urbanization	25, 141
values	60, 107-108, 121ff, 233
— clarification	131-132, 135, 235, 237
— teaching	33-36, 134-136
weekend camps	77, 213, 215